Thomas Pynchon

THOMAS PYNCHON

Modern Critical Views

Henry Adams
Edward Albee
A. R. Ammons
Matthew Arnold
John Ashbery
W. H. Auden
Jane Austen
James Baldwin
Charles Baudelaire
Samuel Beckett
Saul Bellow
The Bible
Elizabeth Bishop
William Blake
Jorge Luis Borges
Elizabeth Bowen
Bertolt Brecht
The Brontës
Robert Browning
Anthony Burgess
George Gordon, Lord
  Byron
Thomas Carlyle
Lewis Carroll
Willa Cather
Cervantes
Geoffrey Chaucer
Kate Chopin
Samuel Taylor Coleridge
Joseph Conrad
Contemporary Poets
Hart Crane
Stephen Crane
Dante
Charles Dickens
Emily Dickinson
John Donne & the Seven-
  teenth-Century Meta-
  physical Poets
Elizabethan Dramatists
Theodore Dreiser
John Dryden
George Eliot
T. S. Eliot
Ralph Ellison
Ralph Waldo Emerson
William Faulkner
Henry Fielding
F. Scott Fitzgerald
Gustave Flaubert
E. M. Forster
Sigmund Freud
Robert Frost

Robert Graves
Graham Greene
Thomas Hardy
Nathaniel Hawthorne
William Hazlitt
Seamus Heaney
Ernest Hemingway
Geoffrey Hill
Friedrich Hölderlin
Homer
Gerard Manley Hopkins
William Dean Howells
Zora Neale Hurston
Henry James
Samuel Johnson and
  James Boswell
Ben Jonson
James Joyce
Franz Kafka
John Keats
Rudyard Kipling
D. H. Lawrence
John Le Carré
Ursula K. Le Guin
Doris Lessing
Sinclair Lewis
Robert Lowell
Norman Mailer
Bernard Malamud
Thomas Mann
Christopher Marlowe
Carson McCullers
Herman Melville
James Merrill
Arthur Miller
John Milton
Eugenio Montale
Marianne Moore
Iris Murdoch
Vladimir Nabokov
Joyce Carol Oates
Sean O'Casey
Flannery O'Connor
Eugene O'Neill
George Orwell
Cynthia Ozick
Walter Pater
Walker Percy
Harold Pinter
Plato
Edgar Allan Poe
Poets of Sensibility & the
  Sublime

Alexander Pope
Katherine Ann Porter
Ezra Pound
Pre-Raphaelite Poets
Marcel Proust
Thomas Pynchon
Arthur Rimbaud
Theodore Roethke
Philip Roth
John Ruskin
J. D. Salinger
Gershom Scholem
William Shakespeare
  (3 vols.)
  Histories & Poems
  Comedies
  Tragedies
George Bernard Shaw
Mary Wollstonecraft
  Shelley
Percy Bysshe Shelley
Edmund Spenser
Gertrude Stein
John Steinbeck
Laurence Sterne
Wallace Stevens
Tom Stoppard
Jonathan Swift
Alfred, Lord Tennyson
William Makepeace
  Thackeray
Henry David Thoreau
Leo Tolstoi
Anthony Trollope
Mark Twain
John Updike
Gore Vidal
Virgil
Robert Penn Warren
Evelyn Waugh
Eudora Welty
Nathanael West
Edith Wharton
Walt Whitman
Oscar Wilde
Tennessee Williams
William Carlos Williams
Thomas Wolfe
Virginia Woolf
William Wordsworth
Richard Wright
William Butler Yeats

These and other titles in preparation

Modern Critical Views

THOMAS PYNCHON

Edited and with an introduction by

Harold Bloom

Sterling Professor of the Humanities
Yale University

CHELSEA HOUSE PUBLISHERS ◇ 1986
New York ◇ New Haven ◇ Philadelphia

Library of Congress Cataloging-in-Publication Data
Main entry under title:
Thomas Pynchon.

(Modern critical views)
Bibliography: p.
Includes index.
Summary: A collection of critical essays on Pynchon
and his works. Also includes a chronology of events in
the author's life.
1. Pynchon, Thomas — Criticism and interpretation.
[1. Pynchon, Thomas — Criticism and interpretation.
2. American literature — History and criticism]
I. Bloom, Harold. II. Series.
PS3566.Y55Z94   1986   813'.54   86-8266
ISBN 0-87754-715-7 (alk. paper)

Contents

Editor's Note   vii

Introduction   1
Harold Bloom

The Use of Codes in *The Crying of Lot 49*   11
Frank Kermode

Pynchon's Gravity   15
Edward Mendelson

Gravity's Rainbow: Science as Metaphor   23
Alan J. Friedman and Manfred Puetz

What Is Thomas Pynchon Telling Us?   37
Josephine Hendin

The Importance of Thomas Pynchon   47
Richard Poirier

Risking the Moment   59
George Levine

Pre-Apocalyptic Atavism: Thomas Pynchon's Early Fiction   79
Catharine R. Stimpson

Profaned and Stenciled Texts: In Search of Pynchon's *V.*   93
Melvyn New

Thomas Pynchon and the Language of Allegory   111
Maureen Quilligan

The New Jeremiad: *Gravity's Rainbow*   139
Marcus Smith and Khachig Tololyan

Order in Thomas Pynchon's "Entropy"   157
David Seed

The Crying of Lot 49   175
    Tony Tanner

Recognizing Reality, Realizing Responsibility   191
    Craig Hansen Werner

Merrill and Pynchon: Our Apocalyptic Scribes   203
    Charles Berger

Chronology   217

Contributors   219

Bibliography   221

Acknowledgments   223

Index   225

Editor's Note

This volume gathers together what I consider to be the best criticism so far ventured upon the fiction of Thomas Pynchon, arranged in the chronological order of its original publication. I am grateful to Peter Childers, David Bloom, and Susan Laity for their aid in editing this book.

The editor's introduction is devoted to "The Story of Byron the Bulb" from *Gravity's Rainbow*. Byron's story is closely read here as a gateway both to Pynchon's Kabbalism and to his authentic nihilism, his refusal of the transcendental aspects of his own Gnostic vision.

Frank Kermode's exegesis of *The Crying of Lot 49*, in which that novella is used to illustrate the limits of Barthesian Structuralism, commences the chronological sequence of criticism, which continues with Edward Mendelson's passionate review of *Gravity's Rainbow*. Alan J. Friedman and Manfred Puetz also address themselves to *Gravity's Rainbow* in an attempt to define "the thermodynamics of life" as the vast novel's central metaphor.

A vision of Pynchon as "the American Goya" is presented by Josephine Hendin, who sums up both *V.* and *Gravity's Rainbow* as spiritual self-portraits of the author and even ventures the hypothesis that Byron the Bulb is a surrogate for Pynchon. A very different perspective, that of the distinguished critic Richard Poirier, results in our being enveloped in Pynchon's own multiple perspectives, all of which partake of one another. To Poirier, "Pynchon is a great novelist of betrayal," and the true contemporary heir of Hawthorne, Emerson, and Melville, and so another seer "of cultural inundation, of being swamped, swept up, counted in before you could count yourself out."

George Levine offers yet another perspective, a suggestion that Pynchon's work disorients us, risks every moment, and for the sake of the ideal (if it is that) named by Pynchon as "sado-anarchism." Part of Levine's strength comes in his agile movement between all three of Pynchon's major fictions, which are thus read as an implicit and rather drastic unity. In an essay on the early stories, Catharine R. Stimpson meditates upon the problematic place of women in Pynchon's work, seeing it as akin to what always renders women equivocal actors in apocalyptic imaginings. Melvyn New, examining *V.*, concludes that Pynchon allows only two functions for the literary artist: to prefigure apocalypse or to lie. A somewhat more varied sense of literary function is sketched in Maureen Quilligan's account of allegorical language in Pynchon, with her acute realization that the reader is compelled to be the allegorist: "Whether Slothrop's last moments are to be dismissed as true transcendence or a kind of Mucho-Maas dematerialization is something, however, which the text forces us to decide on our own."

A very specific allegorical reading of *Gravity's Rainbow* as an American jeremiad is attempted by Marcus Smith and Khachig Tololyan, who find in the novel an ultimate demonstration of how Puritan tradition never abandons the American literary imagination. The early story "Entropy" is analyzed by David Seed as a kind of inverted allegory of order, an analysis worked out also by Tony Tanner in his examination of the opposition between thermo-dynamic entropy and entropy in information theory, an opposition he defines as central to *The Crying of Lot 49*.

The entropy of love, its tendency to collapse back into solipsism, is the emphasis of Craig Hansen Werner's discussion of *Gravity's Rainbow*. Charles Berger, contrasting James Merrill's *The Changing Light at Sandover* and *Gravity's Rainbow*, ends our book of apocalyptic musings upon the apocalyptic Pynchon by finding hints of survival in both Merrill and Pynchon. Such a discovery returns us full circle to the editor's introduction, with its broodings on the failures of the Counterforce in Pynchon and on the madness of poor Byron the Bulb, while it reminds us nevertheless that there is a Counterforce, and that Byron the Bulb's illumination remains indomitable, though to his own eternal frustration.

Introduction

I

We all carry about with us our personal catalog of the experiences that matter most—our own versions of what they used to call the Sublime. So far as aesthetic experience in twentieth-century America is concerned, I myself have a short list for the American Sublime: the war that concludes the Marx Brothers' *Duck Soup*; Faulkner's *As I Lay Dying*; Wallace Stevens's "The Auroras of Autumn"; nearly all of Hart Crane; Charlie Parker playing "Parker's Mood" and "I Remember You"; Bud Powell performing "Un Poco Loco"; Nathanael West's *Miss Lonelyhearts*; and most recently, the story of Byron the light bulb in Pynchon's *Gravity's Rainbow*.

I am not suggesting that there is not much more of the Sublime in *Gravity's Rainbow* than the not quite eight pages that make up the story of Byron the Bulb. Pynchon is the greatest master of the negative Sublime at least since Faulkner and West, and if nothing besides Byron the Bulb in *Gravity's Rainbow* seems to me quite as perfect as all of *The Crying of Lot 49*, that may be because no one could hope to write the first authentic post-Holocaust novel, and achieve a total vision without fearful cost. Yet the story of Byron the Bulb, for me, touches one of the limits of art, and I want to read it very closely here, so as to suggest what is most vital and least problematic about Pynchon's achievement as a writer, indeed as the crucial American writer of prose fiction at the present time. We are now, in my judgment, in the Age of John Ashbery and of Thomas Pynchon, which is not to suggest any inadequacy in such marvelous works as James Merrill's *The Changing Light at Sandover* or Philip Roth's *Zuckerman Bound* but only to indicate one critic's conviction as to what now constitutes the Spirit of the Age.

For Pynchon, ours is the age of plastics and paranoia, dominated by the System. No one is going to dispute such a conviction; reading the *New York Times* first thing every morning is sufficient to convince one that not even Pynchon's imagination can match journalistic irreality. What is more startling about Pynchon is that he has found ways of representing the impulse to defy the System, even though both the impulse and its representations always are defeated. In the Zone (which is our cosmos as the Gnostics saw it, the *kenoma* or Great Emptiness) the force of the System, of They (whom the Gnostics called the Archons), is in some sense irresistible, as all overdetermination must be irresistible. Yet there is a Counterforce, hardly distinguished in its efficacy, but it never does (or can) give up. Unfortunately, its hero is the extraordinarily ordinary Tyrone Slothrop, who is a perpetual disaster, and whose ultimate fate, being "scattered" (rather in the biblical sense), is accomplished by Pynchon with dismaying literalness. And yet—Slothrop, who has not inspired much affection even in Pynchon's best critics, remains more hero than antihero, despite the critics, and despite Pynchon himself.

There are more than four hundred named characters in *Gravity's Rainbow*, and perhaps twenty of these have something we might want to call personality, but only Tyrone Slothrop (however negatively) could be judged a self-representation (however involuntary) on the author's part. Slothrop is a Kabbalistic version of Pynchon himself, rather in the way that Scythrop the poet in Thomas Love Peacock's *Nightmare Abbey* is intentionally a loving satire upon Peacock's friend the poet Shelley, but Kabbalistically is a representation of Peacock himself. I am not interested in adding *Nightmare Abbey* to the maddening catalog of "sources" for *Gravity's Rainbow* (though Slothrop's very name probably alludes to Scythrop's, with the image of a giant sloth replacing the acuity of the Shelleyan scythe). What does concern me is the Kabbalistic winding path that is Pynchon's authentic and Gnostic image for the route through the *kelippot* or evil husks that the light must take if it is to survive in the ultimate breaking of the vessels, the Holocaust brought about by the System at its most evil, yet hardly at its most prevalent.

The not unimpressive polemic of Norman Mailer—that Fascism always lurks where plastic dominates—is in Pynchon not a polemic but a total vision. Mailer, for all his legitimate status as Representative Man, lacks invention except in *Ancient Evenings*, and there he cannot discipline his inventiveness. Pynchon surpasses every American writer since Faulkner at invention, which Dr. Samuel Johnson, greatest of Western literary critics, rightly considered to be the essence of poetry or fiction. What can be judged Pynchon's greatest talent is his vast control, a preternatural ability to order so immense an exuberance at invention. Pynchon's supreme aesthetic quality is what Hazlitt called *gusto*, or what Blake intended in his Infernal proverb: "Exuberance is Beauty."

Sadly, that is precisely what the Counterforce lacks: gusto. Slothrop never gives up; always defeated, he goes on, bloody and bowed, but has to yield to entropy, to a dread scattering. Yet he lacks all exuberance; he is the American as conditioned reflex, colorless and hapless.

Nothing holds or could hold *Gravity's Rainbow* together—except Slothrop. When he is finally scattered, the book stops, and the apocalyptic rocket blasts off. Still, Slothrop is more than a Derridean dissemination, if only because he does enable Pynchon to gather together seven hundred and sixty pages. Nor is *Gravity's Rainbow* what is now called "a text." It is a novel, with a beginning, an end, and a monstrous conglomerate of middles. This could not be if the *schlemiel* Slothrop were wholly antipathetic. Instead, he does enlist something crucial in the elitest reader, a something that is scattered when the hero, poor Plasticman or Rocketman, is apocalyptically scattered.

Pynchon, as Richard Poirier has best seen and said, is a weird blend of the esoteric and insanely learned with the popular or the supposedly popular. Or, to follow Pynchon's own lead, he is a Kabbalistic writer, esoteric not only in his theosophical allusiveness (like Yeats) but actually in his deeper patterns (like Malcolm Lowry in *Under the Volcano*). A Kabbalistic novel is something beyond an oxymoron not because the Kabbalah does not tell stories (it does) but because its stories are all exegetical, however wild and mythical. That does give a useful clue for reading Pynchon, who always seems not so much to be telling his bewildering, labyrinthine story as writing a wistful commentary upon it as a story already twice-told, though it hasn't been, and truly can't be told at all.

II

That returns us to Byron the Bulb, whose story can't be told because poor Byron the indomitable really is immortal. He can never burn out, which at least is an annoyance for the whole paranoid System, and at most is an embarassment for them. They cannot compel Byron to submit to the law of entropy, or the death drive, and yet they can deny him any context in which his immortality will at last be anything but a provocation to his own madness. A living reminder that the System can never quite win, poor Byron the Bulb becomes a death-in-life reminder that the System also can never quite lose. Byron, unlike Slothrop, cannot be scattered, but his high consciousness represents the dark fate of the Gnosis in Pynchon's vision. For all its negativity, Gnosticism remains a mode of transcendental belief. Pynchon's is a Gnosis without transcendence. There is a Counterforce, but there is no fathering and mothering abyss to which it can return.

And yet the light bulb is named Byron, and is a source of light and cannot burn out. Why Byron? Well, he could hardly be Goethe the Bulb or Wordsworth the Bulb or even Joyce the Bulb. There must be the insouciance of personal myth in his name. Probably he could have been Oscar the Bulb, after the author of *The Importance of Being Earnest* or of that marvelous fairy tale "The Remarkable Rocket." Or perhaps he might have been Groucho the Bulb. But Byron the Bulb is best, and not merely for ironic purposes. Humiliated but immortal, this Byron, too, might proclaim:

> But there is that within me which shall tire
> Torture and Time, and breathe when I expire;
> Something unearthly, which they deem not of,
> Like the remembered tone of a mute lyre.

Byron the Bulb is essentially Childe Harold in the Zone:

> He would not yield dominion of his mind
> To spirits against whom his own rebell'd.

Like Childe Harold, Byron the Bulb is condemned to the fate of all High-Romantic Prometheans:

> there is a fire
> And motion of the soul which will not dwell
> In its own narrow being, but aspire
> Beyond the fitting medium of desire;
> And, but once kindled, quenchless evermore,
> Preys upon high adventure, nor can tire
> Of aught but rest; a fever at the core,
> Fatal to him who bears, to all who ever bore.

There are, alas, no high adventures for Byron the Bulb. We see him first in the Bulb Baby Heaven, maintained by the System or Company as part of its business of fostering demiurgic illusions:

> One way or another, these Bulb folks are in the business of providing the appearance of power, power against the night, without the reality.

From the start, Byron is an anomaly, attempting to recruit the other Baby Bulbs in his great crusade against the Company. His is already a voice in the Zone, since he is as old as time.

> Trouble with Byron's he's an old, old soul, trapped inside the glass prison of a Baby Bulb.

Like the noble Lord Byron plotting to lead the Greeks in their Revolution against the Turks, Byron the Bulb has his High-Romantic vision:

> When M-Day finally does roll around, you can bet Byron's elated. He has passed the time hatching some really insane grandiose

plans—he's gonna organize all the Bulbs, see, get him a power base in Berlin, he's already hep to the Strobing Tactic, all you do is develop the knack (Yogic, almost) of shutting off and on at a rate close to the human brain's alpha rhythm, and you can actually trigger an *epileptic fit!* True. Byron has had a vision against the rafters of his ward, of 20 million Bulbs, all over Europe, at a given synchronizing pulse arranged by one of his many agents in the Grid, all these Bulbs beginning to strobe *together*, humans thrashing around the 20 million rooms like fish on the beaches of Perfect Energy—Attention, humans, this has been a warning to you. Next time, a few of us will *explode*. Ha-ha. Yes we'll unleash our *Kamikaze squads!* You've heard of the Kirghiz Light? well that's the ass end of a firefly compared to what we're gonna—oh, you haven't heard of the—oh, well, too bad. Cause a few Bulbs, say a million, a mere 5% of our number, are more than willing to flame out in one grand burst instead of patiently waiting out their design hours. . . . So Byron dreams of his Guerrilla Strike Force, gonna get Herbert Hoover, Stanley Baldwin, all of them, right in the face with one coordinated blast.

The rhetoric of bravado here is tempered and defeated by a rhetoric of desperation. A rude awakening awaits Byron, because the System has in place already its branch, "Phoebus," the international light-bulb cartel, headquartered of course in Switzerland. Phoebus, god of light and of pestilence "determines the operational lives of all the bulbs in the world," and yet does not as yet know that Byron, rebel against the cartel's repression, is immortal. As an immortal, bearer of the Gnostic Spark or *pneuma*, Byron must acquire knowledge, initially the sadness of the knowledge of love:

One by one, over the months, the other bulbs burn out, and are gone. The first few of these hit Byron hard. He's still a new arrival, still hasn't accepted his immortality. But on through the burning hours he starts to learn about the transience of others: learns that loving them while they're here becomes easier, and also more intense—to love as if each design-hour will be the last. Byron soon enough becomes a Permanent Old-Timer. Others can recognize his immortality on sight, but it's never discussed except in a general way, when folklore comes flickering in from other parts of the Grid, tales of the Immortals, one in a kabbalist's study in Lyons who's supposed to know magic, another in Norway outside a warehouse facing arctic whiteness with a stoicism more southerly bulbs begin

strobing faintly just at the thought of. If other Immortals *are* out
there, they remain silent. But it is a silence with much, perhaps,
everything, in it.

A silence that may have everything in it is a Gnostic concept, but falls
away into the silence of impotence on the part of the other bulbs when the
System eventually sends its agent to unscrew Byron:

> At 800 hours—another routine precaution—a Berlin agent is sent
> out to the opium den to transfer Byron. She is wearing asbestos-
> lined kid gloves and seven-inch spike heels, no not so she can fit
> in with the crowd, but so that she can reach that sconce to unscrew
> Byron. The other bulbs watch, in barely subdued terror. The word
> goes out along the Grid. At something close to the speed of light,
> every bulb, Azos looking down the empty black Bakelite streets,
> Nitralampen and Wotan Gs at night soccer matches, Just-Wolframs,
> Monowatts and Siriuses, every bulb in Europe knows what's
> happened. They are silent with impotence, with surrender in the
> face of struggles they thought were all myth. *We can't help*, this
> common thought humming through pastures of sleeping sheep,
> down Autobahns and to the bitter ends of coaling piers in the North,
> *there's never been anything we could do.* . . . Anyone shows us the
> meanest hope of transcending and the Committee on Incandescent
> Anomalies comes in and takes him away. Some do protest, maybe,
> here and there, but it's only information, glow-modulated, harmless,
> nothing close to the explosions in the faces of the powerful that
> Byron once envisioned, back there in his Baby ward, in his
> innocence.

Romantics are Incandescent Anomalies, a phrase wholly appropriate to
John Ashbery's belated self-illuminations also, defeated epiphanies that always
ask the question: Was it information? The information that Pynchon gives
us has Byron taken to a "control point," where he burns on until the committee
on Incandescent Anomalies sends a hit man after him. Like the noble Lord
Byron, who was more than half in love with easeful death before he went
off to die in Greece, Byron the Bulb is now content to be recycled also, but
he is bound upon his own wheel of fire, and so must continue as a now
involuntary prophet and hero:

> But here something odd happens. Yes, damned odd. The plan is
> to smash up Byron and send him back right there in the shop to
> cullet and batch—salvage the tungsten, of course—and let him

be reincarnated in the glassblower's next project (a balloon setting out on a journey from the top of a white skyscraper). This wouldn't be too bad a deal for Byron—he knows as well as Phoebus does how many hours he has on him. Here in the shop he's watched enough glass being melted back into the structureless pool from which all glass forms spring and re-spring, and wouldn't mind going through it himself. But he is trapped on the Karmic wheel. The glowing orange batch is a taunt, a cruelty. There's no escape for Byron, he's doomed to an infinite regress of sockets and bulb-snatchers. In zips young Hansel Geschwindig, a Weimar street urchin—twirls Byron out of the ceiling into a careful pocket and Gessssschhhh*win*dig! out the door again. Darkness invades the dreams of the glassblower. Of all the unpleasantries his dreams grab in out of the night air, an extinguished light is the worst. Light, in his dreams, was always hope: the basic, mortal hope. As the contacts break helically away, hope turns to darkness, and the glassblower wakes sharply tonight crying, "Who? *Who?*"

Byron the Bulb's Promethean fire is now a taunt and a cruelty. A mad comedy, "an infinite regress of sockets and bulb snatchers," will be the poor Bulb's destiny, a repetition-compulsion akin to the entropic flight and scattering of the heroic *schlemiel* Slothrop. The stone-faced search parties of the Phoebus combine move out into the streets of Berlin. But Byron is off upon his unwilling travels: Berlin to Hamburg to Helgoland to Nürnberg, until (after many narrow escapes):

> He is scavenged next day (the field now deathempty, columned, pale, streaked with long mudpuddles, morning clouds lengthening behind the gilded swastika and wreath) by a poor Jewish ragpicker, and taken on, on into another 15 years of preservation against chance and against Phoebus. He will be screwed into mother (*Mutter*) after mother, as the female threads of German light-bulb sockets are known, for some reason that escapes everybody.

Can we surmise the reason? The cartel gives up, and decides to declare Byron legally burned out, a declaration that deceives nobody.

> Through his years of survival, all these various rescues of Byron happen as if by accident. Whenever he can, he tries to instruct any bulbs nearby in the evil nature of Phoebus, and in the need for solidarity against the cartel. He has come to see how Bulb must move beyond its role as conveyor of light-energy alone. Phoebus

has restricted Bulb to this one identity. "But there are other fre-
quencies, above and below the visible band. Bulb can give heat.
Bulb can provide energy for plants to grow, illegal plants, inside
closets, for example. Bulb can penetrate the sleeping eye, and operate
among the dreams of men." Some bulbs listened attentively—
others thought of ways to fink to Phoebus. Some of the older
anti-Byronists were able to fool with their parameters in systematic
ways that would show up on the ebonite meters under the Swiss
mountain: there were even a few self-immolations, hoping to
draw the hit men down.

This darkness of vain treachery helps to flesh out the reason for Byron's
survival. Call it the necessity of myth, or of gossip aging productively into
myth. Not that Phoebus loses any part of its profit; rather, it establishes a
subtler and more intricate international cartel pattern:

Byron, as he burns on, sees more and more of this pattern. He
learns how to make contact with other kinds of electric appli-
ances, in homes, in factories and out in the streets. Each has something to tell him. The pattern gathers in his soul (*Seele*, as the core
of the earlier carbon filament was known in Germany), and the
grander and clearer it grows, the more desperate Byron gets. Someday he will know everything, and still be as impotent as before.
His youthful dreams of organizing all the bulbs in the world seem
impossible now—the Grid is wide open, all messages can be over-
heard, and there are more than enough traitors out on the line.
Prophets traditionally don't last long—they are either killed outright,
or given an accident serious enough to make them stop and think,
and most often they do pull back. But on Byron has been visited
an even better fate. He is condemned to go on forever, knowing
the truth and powerless to change anything. No longer will he seek
to get off the wheel. His anger and frustration will grow without
limit, and he will find himself, poor perverse bulb, enjoying it.

This seems to me the saddest paragraph in all of Pynchon; at least, it hurts
me the most. In it is Pynchon's despair of his own Gnostic Kabbalah, since
Byron the Bulb does achieve the Gnosis, complete knowledge, but purchases
that knowledge by impotence, the loss of power. Byron can neither be martyred,
nor betray his own prophetic vocation. What remains is madness: limitless
rage and frustration, which at last he learns to enjoy.

That ends the story of Byron the Bulb, and ends something in Pynchon also. What is left, whether in *Gravity's Rainbow*—or in the immense work-in-progress, a historical novel depicting the coming-on of the American Civil War and reported to have the title *The Mason-Dixon Line*—is the studying of new modalities of post-Apocalyptic silence. Pynchon seems now to be where his precursor Emerson prophesied the American visionary must be:

> There may be two or three or four steps, according to the genius
> of each, but for every seeing soul there are two absorbing facts,—
> *I and the Abyss.*

If at best, the *I* is an immortal but hapless light bulb and the *Abyss*, our Gnostic foremother and forefather, is the socket into which that poor *I* of a bulb is screwed, then the two absorbing facts themselves have ceased to absorb.

FRANK   KERMODE

The Use of Codes
in The Crying of Lot 49

Perhaps some readers may have been induced, by the foregoing [discussion of Barthes's *lisible* and *scriptible*], to think of a more familiar book—one that contrives, without explicit advertisement, to raise the question of suspended meaning and ask questions which cannot be answered by an appeal to some incontrovertible, unproblematic structure. In *The Crying of Lot 49*, Pynchon's Oedipa, as her name implies, is also confronted with riddles and with the obligation to discover an order. The origin of these riddles is in doubt; it may be the nature of the human world, viewable as waste or as system; it may be a man called Inverarity, who in turn may be either untruth or *dans le vrai*. The book is crammed with disappointed promises of significance, with ambiguous invitations to paradigmatic construction, and this is precisely Oedipa's problem. Is there a structure *au fond*, or only deceptive galaxies of signifiers? Like California itself, the text offers a choice: plenitude or vacuity. Is there a hidden plot concerning an almost Manichaean conflict, which makes sense, whether evil or benign, of the randomness of the world?

Consider the opening: we find Oedipa returning from a Tupperware party; I understand that on these occasions goods are sold outside the normal commercial system. She stands in her living room before a blank television set (communication system without message) and considers the randomness she projects on the world: thoughts about God, a Mexican hotel, dawn at Cornell, a tune from Bartok, a Vivaldi concerto for kazoo. Soon we hear about the coded voices of Inverarity, the culinary jumble of a Southern California supermarket, her husband's life as a used-car salesman, systematizing,

From *Approaches to Poetics.* © 1973 by Columbia University Press. Originally entitled "The Use of the Codes."

giving meaning to, the trash in old cars, Now he works on a pop radio station, the communication system—without content—of another culture. Later
he will start *listening* to Muzak, another type of the empty system. In a world
where the psychiatrists provide material for paranoid fantasies, and lawyers
are locked in imaginary rivalries with Perry Mason, everybody is tending toward his own dissident universe of meaning; Oedipa is Rapunzel, her own
reality let down like hair from her head. Minority cultures, bricolaged from
pop, old movies, astrology, coexist in a world whose significances, if any,
relate to no conceivable armature.

But Oedipa has "all manner of revelations," and a shadowy armature seems
to be taking shape. Is she still in her head, or is the great plot real? If so, is
it malign? To discover it may be the same thing as inventing it. What Peter
Berger and Thomas Luckmann call "the social construction of reality" proceeds
because there are phenomena we cannot simply wish away; death is one, but
there are others. The construction is what our social situation permits—say,
the national limits, the limits of California, ultimately the limits of dissident
groups and our protestant selves. As we plot against reality we comply with
or deviate from the institutionalized plots; a great deviation is called a sect
if shared, paranoia if not. There is always a way of coding the material, even
that which on other views is simply waste. Having instituted a system one
keeps it intact either by legitimating extraneous material or, if that is too
difficult, or the threat too great, by nihilating it.

Making sense of other somewhat arbitrary symbolic universes, understanding their construction, is an activity familiar to all critics. Certainly it
involves choices, a limitation of pluralities. The activity of the critic, thus
understood, is nomic. It seeks order, and is analogous to the social construction of reality. What Oedipa is doing is very like reading a book. Of course
books can be read in very strange ways—a man once undertook to demonstrate infallibly to me that *Wuthering Heights* was an interlinear gloss on
Genesis. How could this be disproved? He had hit on a code, and legitimated
all the signs. Oedipa is afraid she may be like that man, or that she is drifting
into paranoia, the normal hermeneutic activity in disease, and Pynchon's
great subject.

She has contact with many sects: in advanced societies, such as Southern
California, "socially segregated subuniverses of meaning," as Berger and
Luckmann observe in *The Social Construction of Reality*, tend to multiply. When
she sees a way of linking them together Oedipa is conscious of other terrors
than paranoia. She dreads the anomic, the world collapsed into filth and
randomness; but she also dreads an evil order. Pynchon invents the Schurvhamite
sect, who abandoned a very mechanical double predestinarianism ("nothing

ever happens by accident") for the consolations of single predestination to damnation. Yet even on her wild San Francisco night Oedipa doesn't unambiguously believe in the patterns to which the evidence is apparently pointing. For instance, she dismisses the evidence of the children's rhymes. The entire structure is *à la fois posé et déçu*. We do not learn whether the dove, harmonizer of tongues, which would make all these meaning-systems mutually intelligible, descended with the auctioneer's hammer; *au fond*, the plot remains suspended.

What concerns us is precisely the existence of what seem to be systems that could transmit meanings, as in the account of San Narciso, the town which looks like a printed circuit, "an intent to communicate. There'd seemed no limit to what the printed circuit could have told her (if she had tried to find out); so, in her first minute of San Narciso, a revelation trembled, just past the threshold of meaning." The revelation would be of the kind that explains the whole of history, the present condition of America, Inverarity, Wharfinger's play, and so on; it would explain how waste has meaning, just as, couched as an acronym, WASTE forms a sentence ("We await sad Tristero's empire"). But Oedipa is poised on the slash between meaning and unmeaning, as she is between smog and sun; interminably confronted with meaningless binary choices—artificial light in sunlight, the statue of the hooker/nymph, which is both still and windblown—and by repetitions of the San Narciso situation: windows and bottles emptily reflecting the sun, messageless. The need of a revelation, the sense that such systems exist to transmit sense, drives us to find meaning in them, for we feel "as if, on some other frequency . . . words were being spoken." This is the sense in which Professor Mendelson is right in emphasizing the pentecostal themes in the book; fifty may follow forty-nine, and if it were called we should all become competently polyglot, able to hear the words we think are being spoken but cannot quite hear.

This is why Oedipa continues her game of strip-Botticelli with the world. Her trial run with Metzger—merely on the plot of an old movie—sensitized her for a revelation; just as the flight of the rogue aerosol foreshadows a world which, though unpredictable, is determinate. And so she continues to spot the clues, though never sure where they are, in her head or out there. The text only says it is "as if . . . there were a revelation in progress all round her." Options remain naggingly open, as when the naval action of Peter Pinguid, that ancestor of Inverarity, is described: "off the coast of what is now Carmel-by-the-Sea, or what is now Pismo Beach, around noon or possibly towards dusk, the two ships sighted each other. One of them may have fired; if it did the other responded." This niggling dubiety is Oedipa's, and the text's.

The messages sent by the illicit system are normally without content; this could be true of the novel. The clues pile up. *The Courier's Tragedy* (played

in a theater located between a traffic-analysis firm and a wildcat transistor outfit, circulation and communication) relates not only to the supposed history
of Tristero but to incest, tongueless attempts to pray, an anti-Paraclete. The
bones of the dead are turned into ink, a means of empty communication (or
into wine and cigarettes, which belong to other systems). Ralph Driblette has
heard a message in the system of the play; so could Oedipa, if she gave herself
to it. Everything can be legitimated, systematized. But there are only clues,
"never," we are told, "the central truth itself, for if that should blaze out it
would destroy its own message irreversibly." If the systems are to work, and
the book to work as a system, it will be because the reader can do what Oedipa
could not when confronted with Maxwell's demon: make the piston move,
reverse the entropy of communication as that device reverses physical entropy.
But if you make the eyes of this novel move, or if you believe in the original
plot on which it depends, you risk a kind of madness, which is the ultimate
human cost of holding everything together in a single design. The systems are
there to be filled: children's rhymes, the "coded years of uselessness" in the
mattresses of the poor, the societies of queers and failed suicides, all to be handled
if you want a central truth, a word to reconcile your time with eternity. Nobody
helps; Oedipa's friends drop away. The more she encodes the trash of America
the more critical her isolation becomes. She is like the poor of whom she has
heard, camping among telephone wires; she walks as if inside a digital computer,
among either-ors, waiting for the system to contain a message. Either there
is a Tristero, or she is "orbiting in the ecstasy of a true paranoia."

  We can't, of course, be told which, and we question the novel as Oedipa
does the Tristero plot. That plot is pointed to as the object of some possible
annunciation; but the power is in the pointing, not in any guarantee. One
could talk for hours about this remarkable work, but at the bottom of all one
said would be the truth that it imitates the texts of the world, and also imitates
their problematical quality. If one coded *Lot 49*, its radical equivocations
would be instantly evident—the cultural code, for example, is as little the inert
congeries proposed by Barthes as the hermeneutic code is a progress to *dévoile-
ment*. Its separation from its exterior and its totality are precisely what it is
about. It is an invitation to the speaking animal to consider what he makes
of the world into which he introduces his communication systems; and it asks
him to read a text, to reread it, to produce it if that is a better word. In its
totality it poses the choice: *plein/vide*, as it so often does in its texture. To
seek an answer is to be disappointed, *déçu*. Deception is the discovery of
the novel, not of its critics.

EDWARD MENDELSON

Pynchon's Gravity

In Thomas Pynchon's first novel, *V.*, everyone and everything declines toward inanimate passivity. The emblem of this pandemic decline, its hypostasis, is the woman V., whose history is reconstructed by one Herbert Stencil, who is perhaps her son. The life of V. is a series of coincidences and connections, all relating to the world's progress toward entropy and the inanimate. When Stencil recognizes some of these coincidences he speculates that he has "never encountered history at all, but something far more appalling"—the possibility of design in the universe. Pynchon's second novel, *The Crying of Lot 49*, records its heroine's discovery of a clandestine postal system whose existence comes to represent the possibility of transcendence, of "another mode of meaning behind the obvious." Yet both novels, while offering the possibility of significance and order beyond human measure and understanding, also allow the possibility that the transcendence and design that they postulate are merely illusions, or the result of deliberate conspiracies to confuse and control. Each of Pynchon's novels, including his latest and most extraordinary, lets itself be read as a paranoiac vision, yet in each book paranoia is only a vehicle that bears a larger significance. Despite their surface iteration of the paranoiac mode, none of Pynchon's novels is concerned with the self. *Gravity's Rainbow* asserts that paranoia is in fact "nothing less than the onset, the leading edge, of the discovery that *everything is connected*, everything in the Creation." Pynchon's subject, throughout his work, is not self-obsession but the connectedness and coherence of the minute particulars of the world—a rare concern in modern fiction, and one that demands of an author exceptional resources of intelligence and compassion.

From *Yale Review* 62, no. 4 (Summer 1973). © 1973 by Yale University.

The amount of intellectual and emotional ground covered in Pynchon's novels is so enormous that, on first reading, each one appears insurmountably difficult — *Gravity's Rainbow* has already been described as "indescribable" — yet each book connects each element in its vast network to a common thematic center. Once these centers are recognized much of the difficulty vanishes. *Gravity's Rainbow* is Pynchon's most extraordinary example of breadth and compression. While the main action of the book is set in London and occupied Europe, covering a gestative nine months in 1944 and 1945, the narrative also extends back to colonial Massachusetts and seventeenth-century Mauritius (and glances at tenth-century Germany and at Abraham and Isaac), includes scenes in Southwest Africa and the Kirghiz, extends forward to the next war, and includes characters ranging from sailors and dope peddlers to scientist-polymaths and the ghost of a cabinet minister — and an immortal light bulb for good measure. The book is an immense synthesis of modern literature and modern science — it is equally adept with Rilke and organic chemistry — and it interprets brilliantly both modern history and the processes of historical thought. It is also an exceptionally funny and terrifying novel.

In *The Crying of Lot 49* Pynchon wrote of the "high magic to low puns" — the means by which connections and relationships that appear only arbitrary can become comic indications of the real and inexpressible coherence of the world. Pynchon's own variety of low puns — he produces such Rube Goldberg contraptions as the law firm of Salitieri, Poore, Nash, De Brutus and Short — seem as arbitrary and muscle-bound as, on a first reading, does the book itself. How, one wonders while staggering through the last few hundred pages, can he keep it going so long? Yet on a second reading the book's economy and coherence become dazzlingly clear. The first reading induces astonishment, tedium, hilarity, disgust, terror, and bewilderment. A second reading provides the kinds of recognitions that are available only in the most accomplished works of high art.

Gravity's Rainbow, despite its occasional genuflections to Borges, is an "impure" novel, passionately concerned with the way we live now. But because it is a book about the nature and consequence of origins it takes place not in the present but at the end of the Second World War. The book's totem is the V2 rocket, which until the very end of the book appears either before its flight, in the process of design and construction, or at the dead end of its trajectory, in the wreckage it has visited on London. Only as the book closes — and a more terrifying and skillful conclusion to a novel has rarely been written — is the rocket seen in flight. It "rises on a promise, a prophecy, of Escape," yet when its engine shuts off, its "ascent will be betrayed to Gravity." The first moments of the flight determine its entire course. The shape of the parabolic arch of the rocket's trajectory—gravity's rainbow—is fixed by its brief first moments of origination and possibility. Pynchon's novel of the modern condition dwells on the initial moments of ascent, when the important alternatives were considered, when the means of control were set in operation, when the direction we were to follow was chosen once and for all. The Potsdam conference occurs near the middle of the novel. Yet this is not a despairing book: it is instead a deeply moral one. Pynchon knows that it is only the inanimate rocket that is fully and irrevocably determined—the rocket and anything or anyone else that yields to the systems of control, who refuses to make the continuous effort demanded by freedom. As in Pynchon's earlier books the possibilities for freedom, responsibility, and love are rare and difficult, yet the possibilities are real. *Gravity's Rainbow* is a tragic, not a pessimistic, novel. It is perhaps the most extensive and profound synthesis yet written of the ways in which the contemporary world lives with and accepts the obstacles to freedom, yet with all its knowledge of the obstacles and barriers it insists on the necessity and possibility of freedom.

Each of Pynchon's books glosses a single historical theory, a single historical intelligence. *V.* exfoliates from the chapter on "The Dynamo and the Virgin" in *The Education of Henry Adams*. The woman V., the Virgin who becomes the Dynamo, embodies the transfer of allegiance from the power that resides in the human and the living to the power of the inanimate machine. *The Crying of Lot 49* dramatizes Mircea Eliade's discussion of "hierophany," the manifestation of the sacred. The thesis illustrated continuously in *Gravity's Rainbow* is Max Weber's account of the "routinization of charisma." The V2 rocket, one character reports, "really did possess a Max Weber charisma . . . some joyful—and *deeply* irrational—force the State bureaucracy could never routinize, against which it could not prevail." For Weber charisma in its pure form exists only in the process of originating. It cannot remain stable but yields to economic and psychological pressure to become traditionalized or rationalized, to develop an attendant bureaucracy. *Gravity's Rainbow* culminates in a social history of the rocket's rationalization into systems and ideologies, its transformation into the traditions of sacred texts and holy centers. "Heretics [also] there will be: Gnostics who have been taken in a rush of wind and fire to the chambers of the Rocket-throne . . . Kabbalists who study the Rocket as Torah . . . Manichaeans who see two Rockets, good and evil." But the systems spawned by the rocket are only the most recent, the most appalling of the novel's bureaucracies. Cartels, interlocking governments, even the bureaucracies of the dead, all find their place in the book.

Most of these bureaucracies take special interest in the book's central character, Lieutenant Tyrone Slothrop of the U.S. Army, stationed in London.

As an infant Slothrop had been used by one Laszlo Jamf as the subject of a Pavlovian experiment—its exact nature is never revealed—and Slothrop's activities have been kept under surveillance ever since by American, German, and English cartels. A few months after the V2 rockets begin to fall on London, British Intelligence discovers that a map kept by Slothrop of his sex life— either real or fantasized—corresponds point by point to a map of V2 impact sites. The stars on Slothrop's map appear two or three days before a corresponding rocket lands on the point indicated. The relation between Slothrop and the rocket is mysterious to everyone, and Slothrop himself is unaware of it, but whatever it is, it lies outside the familiar and comfortable parameters of cause and effect. Slothrop's case is assigned to a psychological warfare office, a decidedly strange collection of Pavlovians, spiritualists, Skinnerites, Ouspenskians and cranks and maniacs of every kind. To the Pavlovians and the behaviorists, intent on demonstrating "the stone determinacy of everything, of every soul," intent also on allowing "precious little room for any hope at all," the extraordinary communication, control, connection, or relationship between Slothrop and the rocket is an object of terror and bewilderment. Slothrop's primary observer, the Pavlovian Dr. Edward Pointsman ("the man who throws the switches") insists that "*We must never lose control. The thought of him lost in the world of men, after the war, fills me with a deep dread I cannot extinguish.*" Slothrop takes on a charismatic power he never understands, and the bureaucracies fear and despise him for it.

At first Slothrop has no idea that he is the center of such frantic activity. But when he discovers that he is the object of an elaborate conspiracy he manages to escape into occupied Germany, into the chaos Pynchon calls simply "the Zone." Outside the Zone is the world intertwined by the impersonal networks of international politics and industry, joined together through the connections between Shell, Harvard, IG Farben, ICI, and just about every other possible coconspirator. Inside the Zone is an analogous network of black marketeers and dope peddlers with "connections," *Verbindungsmänner*, of their own. Earlier, under the eyes of Pointsman's agents, Slothrop had learned about an unusual—and eventually charismatic—version of the V2, a mysterious example numbered 00000 which contained a unique and unidentified apparatus. A major component of that apparatus was made of a plastic devised by the man who had once experimented on Slothrop, Laszlo Jamf. As Slothrop tries to learn more about the 00000, and moves through hundreds of pages of other adventures, he begins to develop different varieties of charisma. At one point he dresses in the costume of a Wagnerian tenor (there is an implied debate throughout the book between enthusiasts of Rossini and Wagner) complete with a pointed helmet reminiscent of the nose of the rocket. He immediately finds himself referred to as Rocketman and is expected by the rather strange crew he is with at this moment to have the charismatic powers of any respectable comic-book hero: "No job is too tough for Rocketman." Later Slothrop adopts a different sort of charisma when, at a festival in a North German town, he is asked to take the part of the town's legendary deliverer and hero: a pig, with appropriate costume.

But Slothrop's escape into freedom is insufficient to earn him anything more than a temporary, assumed charisma. Eventually he is defeated. With all the bureaucracies around the Zone out to capture him, a group of his old colleagues organize a plan to find him and save him, a "We-System" in opposition to all the malevolent "They-Systems" that are after Slothrop. This Counterforce fails at its first goal—Slothrop disappears irrevocably into the chaos of the Zone—but it apparently rationalizes itself into other purposes. Slothrop himself is betrayed, his original importance denied: " 'We were never that concerned with Slothrop *qua* Slothrop.' " The events of Slothrop's history, the origin of his special relation with the rocket, are explained away by psychiatry: " 'There never was a Dr. Jamf,' opines [a] world-renowned analyst . . . 'Jamf was only a fiction, to help [Slothrop] explain what he felt so terribly.' " Slothrop himself, separated from the bureaucracies that both victimized him and provided him with a context and a history, begins to disintegrate, to scatter. A character in the book postulates a law: "Personal density is directly proportional to temporal bandwidth," that is, "the more you dwell in the past and in the future . . . the more solid your persona." Deprived through his own escape and his own freedom from an originating past or a future to which he could be responsible, Slothrop is gradually reduced to his final emblem: the Fool in the Tarot deck, the only card without a number, lacking a place in the systems of the world.

The Counterforce fails, but so do some of the agents of the They-System it opposes. The only character whose life after 1945 is described in the book itself (some appear "later" in history in Pynchon's earlier books, and *V.* describes the early life of some of the characters as well) is Pointsman: "he's an ex-scientist now . . . he'll be left only with Cause and Effect, and the rest of his sterile armamentarium." Pynchon's account of Pointsman's decline is, in effect, a celebration of a world in which the knowledge achieved by a behaviorist is not worth knowing.

This bald summary ignores at least four-fifths of *Gravity's Rainbow*, but for the moment it will have to do. The book contains about five other important plots, all closely interconnected, and each the length and density of most ordinary novels. There are at least three hundred characters in the book as a whole—readers are advised to keep an index of first appearances—and

Pynchon justifies the book's length, and its insistent vision of coherence, by the elaborately developed relationships he establishes among this enormous population. A persistent theme in the book is Preterition, the Calvinist doctrine that, after choosing the elect, God passed over all the rest. Every page of this novel is informed by sympathy with the preterite of the earth—the powerless, all those excluded from knowledge of the "terrible structure behind the appearances of diversity and enterprise." None of the characters is left out of the book's large structure, none is subject to the author's preterition. (The rocket's trajectory is perhaps a visible representation of the act of passing over, of preterition.)

Pynchon's use of the techniques and assumptions of film have been discussed elsewhere in some detail, but it is worth mentioning that Pynchon is consistently ingenious where the opportunities for fashionable cliché are so numerous and varied. One or two examples out of a score of possibilities must suffice. Pynchon traces the germ of cinema to Leibniz's invention of the calculus, in which motion in time and space is divided into an infinite number of motionless "frames." The calculus is also, of course, the means of calculating the trajectory of the rocket. Where the calculus uses an infinite number of frames to counterfeit motion, and film uses twenty-four every second, Captain Blicero of the SS, the novel's central embodiment of evil, extends this technique "past images on film, to human lives." Blicero permits an engineer under his command, whom Blicero needs for the eventual modification of the unique rocket 00000, to visit his daughter for only a few weeks out of every year. The engineer, aware that the frames of a film only give the illusion of continuous motion, is never certain that he is visiting the same girl. (The daughter is herself the "product" of a film: she had been conceived after her father was sexually aroused by a film in which another daughter was also conceived. Yes, I know this sounds complicated; it is even more elaborate in the book.) At the farthest end of this scale is one character's reference to the consciousness of rock: "We're talking frames per century." Pynchon occasionally refers to the book itself in terms of old movies, and the continuous present tense in which it is written attempts to imitate the sequential immediacy of film. All this culminates in a final passage of stunning virtuosity and power: "we" are sitting in an old theatre, the film has just broken, and we are facing an empty screen. In another moment a much greater catastrophe will occur, but in the fraction of a second that remains we are invited to sing a hymn written by Slothrop's Puritan ancestor. The hymn not only gathers the book's major themes into eight lines, but also concludes the novel with an intimation of a more distant ending: the end of history, the Parousia.

The end of the book does not solve all its mysteries. By the last page, hundreds of relationships have been established or revealed, the connectedness of the world has been asserted, but many issues raised in the book have deliberately been left unresolved. For Pynchon a knowledge of relationships does not lead immediately to a knowledge of obligations—as it does, for example, in Dickens, at the end of whose novels every character has learned exactly whom he must love and whom he must reject. When Pynchon's characters become aware of patterns and relations, choices become available to them, but their decision remains their own. By the end of *The Crying of Lot 49* the heroine has become almost saturated by her knowledge of coincidence and cohesiveness, but this knowledge only leaves her with the "binary choice" of either the One of transcendent meaning or the Zero of chaos and paranoia. In *Gravity's Rainbow* the choices available at the end of the book involve not only belief, but action. In the final chapters one group of rocket engineers in the Zone has built a second example of Captain Blicero's special V2, an example numbered 00001, but to complete this rocket and fire it off involves a serious ethical decision. The apparatus that went into the 00000 (since Pynchon does not describe the apparatus until the end of the book I shall honor his secrecy) cannot be repeated in the 00001 without making a decision of extraordinary difficulty. Yet Pynchon does not say how the problem is resolved, does not reveal which alternative is chosen. This is only the most striking example among many.

When a book is proclaimed a masterpiece within days of its publication it is usually a sign that the book has merely confirmed the reviewers' theories and prejudices. But *Gravity's Rainbow*, which by now has received every conceivable adjective of praise, is far too complex and disturbing, and demands far too extreme an adjustment in its readers' conception of the scope of the novel, to give much comfort to anyone. Few books in this century have achieved the range and depth of this one, and even fewer have held so large a vision of the world in a structure so skillfully and elaborately conceived. This is certainly the most important novel to be published in English in the past thirty years, and it bears all the lineaments of greatness.

A L A N   J.   F R I E D M A N   A N D

M A N F R E D   P U E T Z

Gravity's Rainbow:
Science as Metaphor

Thomas Pynchon is an author in search of a metaphor, a fictional scheme
to ask and answer the question of what prevails in the physical and in the
spiritual universe—order or disorder, distinction or chaos, pattern or the
existential blur? Most obviously in his earlier works, Pynchon experiments
with metaphors from modern physics in his fictional investigations. The key
metaphor of "Entropy," an early short story, is explicit: the disintegration of
human society and the intellectual world is like the "heat death" of the physical
universe predicted by thermodynamics. Nature, according to the second law
of thermodynamics, must reach a state of maximum entropy (disorder) and
minimum available energy. All change will cease. In *V.*, Pynchon's first novel,
metaphors from thermodynamics are again present but reduced in scope. We
still have the increasingly disordered universe, but there is also mystery, a hint
of a way to order. Herbert Stencil, one of the main characters of *V.*, fights
back by sorting through the chaos in hope of finding some pattern to cling
to. *The Crying of Lot 49* retains both the search for order and the all-pervasive
entropy image. The two patterns merge in brilliant analogy, as the searcher-
for-order becomes a duplicate of "Maxwell's demon," a hypothetical invention
created by the real nineteenth-century physicist Clerk Maxwell, who designed
the concept specifically to challenge the second law of thermodynamics.

In *Gravity's Rainbow* Pynchon has found another universally applicable
metaphor, giving what is probably the final answer to his questions. The

From *Contemporary Literature* 15, no. 3 (1974). © 1974 by the Board of Regents of the University of Wisconsin System. Originally entitled "Science as Metaphor: Thomas Pynchon and
Gravity's Rainbow."

metaphor again originates in modern science, which so clearly plays an important part in the novel. Equations of calculus decorate the pages, and from the quantum mechanical behavior of elementary particles to the Friedmann geometry of the curved universe, we are teased with facts about chemistry, physics, mathematics, and cosmology. Even the microscopic Maxwell's demon reappears, both in explicit references and as a minor character peering out at us between the scenes: "From way down the hall, a tiny head appears around a corner, a tiny hand comes out and gives Slothrop the tiny finger." The central image from science, which Pynchon develops into a striking parable of all existence, is nothing less than the thermodynamics of life itself. While the general tendency of physical processes is towards increasing disorder, twentieth-century biophysics has realized that life violates this pattern. We grow from a few molecular cells, increasing in complexity and order, adding atoms from potato fields, the ocean depths, and the earth itself: "new molecules assembled from the debris of the given. . . ." Of course, entropy will take over eventually, individuals will decay, die, and return to a disorganized scattering of atoms, "in a long gradient of rot, leaching, assimilation with the earth." Yet life continues to go against the general flow, even after the individual disintegrates. Life is that "conjuror's secret by which—though it is not often Death is told so clearly to fuck off—the living genetic chains prove even labyrinthine enough to preserve some human face down ten or twenty generations. . . ."

In the final analysis, life does not really violate the laws of thermodynamics, since any particular system *can* become more ordered and energetic if it does so at the expense of greater disorder and loss of energy in the rest of the universe. Any living system can increase its order and energy by "removing from the rest of the World these vast quantities of energy to keep its own tiny desperate fraction showing a profit. . . ." The secret of the life process is the trick Pynchon calls "Entropy Management." Entropy management means that order can only be produced along with a compensating amount of disorder, the same widespread chaos that always puzzles Pynchon's characters. Death and decay are the disorder that makes possible the endless variety and renewal of life.

The essential pattern of life, from dust to order to dust, is echoed in the title image of the novel: gravity's rainbow, the parabolic path that gravity imposes on the V2 rocket. Indeed, Pynchon spends so much time on the biography of the rocket just to point out how apt the parallel is. The rocket, too, starts as a disordered scattering of atoms, from iron in the mountains to alcohol latent in potatoes. Man begins to reduce the entropy of those collected atoms, assembling them in one place, arranging them to take on technological life. "Beyond simple steel erection, the Rocket was an entire system *won*, away from the feminine darkness, held against the entropies of lovable but scatter-brained Mother Nature. . . ." The rocket is fired, and carrying out its analogy to life, burns and rises—"You will come to understand that between the two points, in the five minutes, *it* lives an entire life." Eventually its maximum altitude is reached, where gravity, the manifestation of destiny and the laws of physical process, overcomes the vertical momentum. The rocket must bend to the general flow, and it descends to the earth to disintegrate in a final burst of energy and scattering of atoms. Applied technology has recapitulated fundamental science. Both life and the rocket rise from the rubble, burn bright for a while, and then return to the rubble to be rewoven into life again. The moment of life has been made thermodynamically possible by a continuous process of decay and reconstruction: "But every true god must be both organizer and destroyer."

The implicit theme of the transitoriness of life as a necessary adjunct to continuing existence is also stressed by poetic allusions in *Gravity's Rainbow*. Several times Captain Blicero, the German rocket-squadron leader, quotes from the *Duino Elegies* of Rainer Maria Rilke, a work which for him expresses the secret of all existence. "Want the Change," he recalls, "O be inspired by the Flame!" And in another passage we find the words "Once, only once . . ." which are from the opening passage of Rilke's "Ninth Elegy," a passage which reads in full:

> But because being here is much, and because all this
> that's here, so fleeting, seems to require us and strangely
> concerns us. Us the most fleeting of all. Just once,
> everything, only for once. Once and no more. And we,
>   too,
> once. And never again.

In the "Ninth Elegy," Rilke over and over again celebrates transitoriness and transformation as the unavoidable and yet rewarding condition of life. Rilke's praise culminates in the words: "Earth! invisible!/What is your urgent command, if not transformation?" This sentence, in turn, curiously recalls the opening epigraph of *Gravity's Rainbow* in which Wernher von Braun attempts to reason out the underlying continuity of existence: "Nature does not know extinction; all it knows is transformation. Everything science has taught me, and continues to teach me, strengthens my belief in the continuity of our spiritual existence after death." Pynchon's argument, however, is not identical to von Braun's because in the novel we are not shown the transformation from life to supernatural existence after death but a transformation in the long chain that links one instance of material life to another.

The fact that biological life takes the same path as the rocket is repeatedly illustrated in the novel by what could be called the compost-garden image. At least seventeen times we are shown a collection of things (animal, mineral, and vegetable) that have begun the return to complete disorder and loss of differentiation—to maximum entropy. Yet this collection of the dying is also shown as the garden of birth for life:

> Corydon Throsp . . . liked to cultivate pharmaceutical plants up on the roof . . ., most returning, as fragments of peculiar alkaloids, to rooftop earth, along with manure from a trio of prize Wessex Saddleback sows quartered there by Throsp's successor, and dead leaves off many decorative trees transplanted to the roof by later tenants, and the odd unstomachable meal thrown or vomited there by this or that sensitive epicurean—all got scumbled together, eventually, by the knives of the seasons, to an impasto, feet thick, of unbelievable black topsoil in which anything could grow, not the least being bananas.

The repeated compost-garden images hold remarkable parallels to the terms in which the rocket's rise from the rubble is described: "as one by one these old toothpaste tubes are emptied and returned to the War, heaps of dimly fragrant metal, . . . waiting now—it is true return—to be melted for solder, for plate. . . . Yet the continuity, flesh to kindred metals, home to hedgeless sea, has persisted." The bizarre event marking the end of the novel again stresses this parallel between the fate of the rocket and that of human life. Captain Blicero, one of the demonic forces of the novel, ties the youth Gottfried to a specially prepared rocket, the famous production number 00000, and fires both on their final trajectory. *Gravity's Rainbow* ends in a haunting passage describing ascent and descent of this lifeless/living monster which more than symbolically represents the ultimate fusion and symbiosis of rocket and man.

The marvelously improbable occurrence of life is brought to our attention in a variety of other ways, again with images from science. Nature does sometimes produce ordered states that last indefinitely, but they are usually brittle and dead. Crystals represent this extreme state, and they appear no less than thirty-five times in various guises during the course of the novel, from real crystals of snow and cocaine, to "crystalline season" and "crystal terror." Life's surprising increase in order is also emphasized by the notion that a reversal in the normal direction of process (from order to disorder) is analogous to a reversal of time, like a movie run backwards, or the curious way in which our senses perceive the explosion of a supersonic rocket—feeling the blast first, then hearing the noise of the rocket engine. Individual life, too, is a

"thermodynamic surprise," but the reversal of normal process and time characteristic of this surprise can only be temporary, for both a rocket and a man:

> nothing can really stop the Abreaction of the Lord of the Night
> unless the Blitz stops, rockets dismantle, the entire film runs
> backward: faired skin back to sheet steel back to pigs to white
> incandescence to ore, to Earth. But the reality is not reversible.
> Each firebloom, followed by blast then by sound of arrival, is a
> mockery (how can it not be deliberate?) of the reversible process:
> with each one the Lord further legitimizes his State.

Within the framework of this universal movement running its cyclic course
from chaos to complex forms of organization and back to decay, an argument
over the cause and predictability of the overall trajectory takes place. Man
must be around to cause the ordering of the rocket. Who initially arranges
for his order in turn? Is the universal movement of ascent and descent control-
lable at all or is it unpredictable accident? Such problems are actually fought
over in the novel by opposing groups of characters, and the respective positions of the participants are embodied in two main figures of the book:
Pointsman and Roger Mexico. While Pointsman, the Pavlovian, stands for
strict determinism and predictability of material as well as psychic events,
Roger Mexico, the statistician, represents the approaches of randomness gov-
erned by the laws of probability. For both groups Tyrone Slothrop's latent
talent to predict involuntarily the strikes of the rockets is a case in point. Consider
the following situation: "When Slothrop was discovered, late in 1944, by 'The
White Visitation' . . . different people thought they'd discovered different things."
In the evolving passage various interpretations are listed, ranging from Roger
Mexico's assumption that Slothrop's talent must be "a statistical oddity" to
Pointsman's firm conviction that it has to be some form of conditioned reflex.
Both assumptions are based on scientific credos that are worth closer
examination. There is first Pointsman's philosophy of material/mechanical
cause-and-effect:

> Pavlov believed that the ideal, the end we all struggle toward in
> science, is the true mechanical explanation. He was realistic enough
> not to expect it in his lifetime. Or in several lifetimes more. But
> his hope was for a long chain of better and better approximations.
> His faith ultimately lay in a pure physiological basis for the life
> of the psyche. No effect without cause, and a clear train of linkages.

It is obvious that if the Pavlovian assumption is right and everything can be
explained mechanically, it follows that most things and events eventually can

also be manipulated and controlled that way. Thus Pointsman's followers pursue Slothrop as an object of experimentation which can be converted into an operational tool once his specific mechanism is understood. This is also the reason Pointsman is involved with the military, whose interest in human life is primarily an interest in available and practically applicable forces.

But the approaches of predictability and mechanical causality are not confined to psychic processes in *Gravity's Rainbow*, and Pointsman is not their only prophet. The novel abounds with figures whose activities are based on the same deterministic principle. Evidently all the engineers, and in particular the builders of the rocket, have to follow the guiding star of determinism at all times. Katje says of the rocket after it has been launched: "All the rest will happen according to laws of ballistics. The Rocket is helpless in it. Something else has taken over. Something beyond what was designed in." Pökler is "the cause-and-effect man." Laszlo Jamf's scientific experiments rest on similar assumptions. Webley Silvernail has a suspicion that the behaviorists running the conditioned rats in their artificial maze are in turn observed and conditioned by an anonymous power from above. He also assures the animals in his laboratory that they live in a consistently deterministic universe: "I would set you free, if I knew how. But it isn't free out here." One U.S. colonel speculates on the colors of the sunset: "The question is, are they changing *according to something?* Is the sun's everyday spectrum being modulated? Not at random, but systematically, by this unknown debris in the prevailing winds? Is there information for us? Deep questions, and disturbing ones." Even the reader, Pynchon assumes, must be a follower of the calculus of certainty. In a rare authorial intrusion, Pynchon opens a chapter by addressing us with the words: "You will want cause and effect." And as the crowning achievement of certainty two Pavlovians assure each other that, even if they were wrong in Slothrop's case, their principal approach of strict cause-and-effect to the phenomena of this world would in no way be invalidated.

The accompanying themes of linear control and hidden plot are ubiquitous in the novel. "There is a theory going around that the U.S.A. was and still is a gigantic Masonic plot under the ultimate control of the group known as the Illuminati." A whole village in postwar Germany (Mecklenburg) has been taken over by escaped army dogs which have been conditioned to kill everybody except their masters and cannot be deconditioned because their masters are dead or lost. World War II is seen as an event which is not political (and thus traceable to conflicting human interests and decisions) but a hidden consequence of technology which dominates everything: "It means this War was never political at all, the politics were all theatre, all just to keep the people distracted . . . secretly, it was being dictated instead by the needs of technology . . . by a conspiracy between human beings and techniques, by something that needed the energy-burst of war. . . ." What finally emerges is that the Pointsman faction in *Gravity's Rainbow* sees mechanistic determinism as more than just a heuristic principle of investigation. It is, in fact, as somebody puts it, an attempt at writing a comprehensive "secular history." Maybe it is even more than that, a theological exegesis to explain the ordering of life, a universal variation of Mondaugen's "electro-mysticism," with all belief "In the name of the cathode, the anode, and the holy grid."

Opposing the determinists are the statisticians, headed by Roger Mexico, but also including others, from Argentine anarchists to organic chemists. They see life as a freak deviation from the probable, representing the truly random state of nature. They bolster their case by finding more and more random events, and their symbol is the "Poisson distribution"—a well-known bell-shaped curve used in statistics, and yet another rainbow figure:

> But to the likes of employees such as Roger Mexico it is music, not without its majesty, this power series
>
> $$Ne^{-m}\left(1 + m + \frac{m^2}{2!} + \frac{m^3}{3!} + \ldots + \frac{m^{n-1}}{(n-1)!}\right)$$
>
> terms numbered according to rocketfalls per square, the Poisson dispensation ruling not only these annihilations no man can run from, but also cavalry accidents, blood counts, radioactive decay, number of wars per year.

Along with the curve goes another metaphor from modern physics, the Heisenberg Uncertainty Principle, which established a randomness inherent in the nature of matter and physical measurement. Heisenberg's work is mentioned explicitly, but usually it is a metaphor to express the chance nature of life. The African rocket-corps commander Enzian sees existence as a random event in the following manner: "Well, I think we're here, but only in a statistical way. Something like that rock over there is just about 100% certain—it knows it's there, so does everybody else. But our own chances of being right here right now are only a little better than even—the slightest shift in the probabilities and we're gone—schnapp! like that." This paragraph reflects (if hyperbolically) the "wave-mechanical" picture of matter that Heisenberg and others developed.

Among the statisticians, Roger Mexico is the purest. He attaches neither hope nor desire to his view of the universe: "Never had a prophetic dream, never sent or got a telepathic message, never touched the Other World directly. If anything's there it will show in the experimental data won't it, in the numbers . . . but that's as close or clear as he'll ever get." Quite aptly Roger Mexico is called the "Antipointsman." (Incidentally, in the novel Pavlov is said to have been "fascinated with 'ideas of the opposite.'" So is Pynchon, as numerous pairs of opposites besides Pointsman and Mexico testify.)

For other characters, the randomness exemplified by the Poisson distribution of rocket strikes is cause for abandonment of hope and faith. Enzian believes "There was no difference between the behavior of a god and the operations of pure chance." His people, the Herero, see themselves as moving toward total entropy and randomness in extinction, and one of their subgroups, "The Revolutionaries of the Zero," consequently no longer wants to play the game of life and proposes deliberate racial suicide. The Herero identify with the random elements in the rocket's "life," and the rocket's imminent return to maximum entropy symbolizes their own circumstances:

> One reason we grew so close to the Rocket, I think, was this sharp
> awareness of how contingent, like ourselves, the Aggregat 4 could
> be—how at the mercy of small things . . . dust that gets in a timer
> . . . corrosion, a short, a signal grounded out, Brennschluss too
> soon, and what was alive is only an Aggregat again, an Aggregat
> of pieces of dead matter, no longer anything that can move, or
> that has a Destiny with a shape.

For other statisticians, the uncertainty principle means that no possibility can be ruled out, and that there is hope that nature's constant reshuffling will produce desirable new opportunities. Byron the Bulb has been given not only life but by chance even immortality (Byron's story is a brief epitome of the whole novel). Tchitcherine, the Russian officer, sees endless paths and possibilities for himself: "he is a giant supermolecule with so many open bonds available at any given time, and in the drift of things . . . others latch on, and the pharmacology of the Tchitcherine thus modified, its onwardly revealed side-effects, can't necessarily be calculated ahead of time." Tchitcherine's mission, which he assumes to give structure to his whole life, was to find and kill his black half-brother Enzian. When they finally meet near the end of the novel (by chance, of course), they do not recognize each other. Tchitcherine merely begs some cigarettes and raw potatoes, and they separate forever. Pynchon's detached and ironic comment on this total expression of randomness marks the exit of Tchitcherine and Enzian from the novel: "This is magic. Sure—but not necessarily fantasy. Certainly not the first time a man has passed his brother by, at the edge of the evening, often forever, without knowing it."

For the statisticians, in an unpredictable universe there could even be a way out of the entropy cycle. Mexico tells his counterpart Pointsman: "but there's a feeling about that cause-and-effect may have been taken as far as it will go. That for science to carry on at all, it must look for a less narrow, a less . . . sterile set of assumptions. The next great breakthrough may come when we have the courage to junk cause-and-effect entirely, and strike off at some other angle." The rocket promises to become an actual way out: "We'll all use *it*, someday, to leave the earth. To transcend." But the rocket cannot escape physically because "Gravity rules all the way out to the cold sphere. . . ."

Yet the hope of escape by the rocket remains, and Captain Blicero, alias Weissmann (who also appears in *V.*), is the man trying to reach the last enclave of at least partial freedom. In his final vision he sees the rocket as a way to break the vicious circle of what he calls the "cycle of infection and death." This is why Gottfried, who is Blicero's only hope for a continuation of life, is finally coupled to the rocket and blasted off. Pynchon does not specify who is speaking, but Blicero's voice is clearly audible in the final *extasis*: "This ascent will be betrayed to Gravity. But the Rocket engine, the deep cry of combustion that jars the soul, promises escape. The victim, in bondage to falling, rises on a promise, a prophecy, of Escape. . . ." As the novel ends, the rocket descends, and the final words urge us to sing along with William Slothrop's hymn, suggesting that the escape from the parabola of thermodynamics is possible and is far more than Blicero's and Gottfried's personal concern:

> There is a Hand to turn the time
>
> . . . .
>
> Now everybody—

The delineation of Pynchon's central metaphor so far may seem to belong to the realm of the abstract, the theoretically expressed, but not to the detailed events and the artistic fabric of a 760-page novel. This impression, however, is misleading. While outlining the unifying images of his book, Pynchon at the same time manages in almost documentary fashion (which makes plot summary a hopeless endeavor) to catch the radical diversity, complexity, and incoherence of the concrete. At once in pursuit of the stasis of ideas and the dynamics of actual events, he unites both in one wild, authentic, cinematographic happening. The law of physical order and disorder becomes a metaphor for the state of social affairs.

Pynchon is well-equipped to embrace an enormous range of material in these fictional excursions into the thick of concreteness. Like Joyce who wrote most of *Ulysses* more than a thousand miles and ten to seventeen years removed from Dublin and yet managed to make it an exact guide to the city,

Pynchon writes convincingly and with great authenticity about what is far away from him (in fact, about what he *cannot* have experienced). As we know from several sources, Joyce achieved exactness by working, among other things, with *Thom's Directory* (of Ireland, Dublin, etc.) and a mass of up-to-date information from his friends and relatives. Similarly, Pynchon seems to do solid research work before he embarks on his excursions into strange lands; and he usually drops sly hints to his sources. Thus the main source for the historical sketches of *The Crying of Lot 49* was Lothrop Motley's *The Rise of the Dutch Republic* (which he mentions once in another context). And there is more than a suspicion that, for instance, the dictionary of technical German he casually places on Slothrop's desk or Cranz's *Lehrbuch der Ballistik* are some of the sources of the weird familiarity with German rocket jargon Pynchon displays in *Gravity's Rainbow*.

It is worthwhile to take a short deviation to point to the uncanny overall exactness (apart from a few warped details) of Pynchon's picture of England, France, Holland, or Germany during and shortly after World War II. Consider the following collection of examples concerning the German scene which may well stand for the rest of the novel's meticulous apparatus of historical, geographical, political, and scientific technicalities. Pynchon shows that he is familiar with the constantly changing zones that split what are now West Germany's eastern regions between Russian and American troops moving in during the last days of the war. He knows what was going on at that time in small towns such as Halberstadt, Bad Harzburg, Clausthal-Zellerfeld, Hachenburg, Nordhausen, and Bleicheröde though the bedlam of private skirmishes, roaming ex-prisoners, and official as well as semi-official retaliation and mopping-up operations have withstood clarification by historians to this day. Pynchon has detailed knowledge about the activities of figures behind the scene, such as Hugo Stinnes, or political also-rans like Albert Speer and his train of followers. He correctly lists the kind of trees that grow in the area where Slothrop roams (spruce, fir, larch, and pine). He knows that homosexuals in German slang are sometimes referred to as 175s (after a paragraph in the penal code) and he is familiar with bizarre terms of German everyday speech ("Haferschleim"). There are, of course, in the same picture deviations from the factual, but they are usually obvious larks such as the Herero "Schwarzkommandos" (it is historically true, however, that there were ties between Germany and the population of formerly occupied Southwest Africa). Direct mistakes, on the other hand, often boil down to language slips and many of them could even be printer's errors.

It is this scene of detailed authenticity and wide range into which Pynchon packs all he knows about science, art, rocket technology, contemporary history, political, cultural, and economical undercurrents, and, for good measure, assorted ramblings through the fields of film, fashion, and various subcultures. It is also this scene which becomes the background for Slothrop's wild peregrinations, which are all concrete examples, palpable facts, and evidence of a bewildering actuality. Slothrop is the one character of the novel who paradigmatically follows the parabola of life's trajectory, the one character on whom all forces so far mentioned are shown to work. Like a modern Everyman he is less the engineer of his own fate than the eternally engineered. (His name, incidentally, might be an allusion to Thomas Love Peacock's rambunctious, love-starved hero of *Nightmare Abbey*, Scythrop.)

The cause-and-effect buffs of the novel, such as Pointsman, "The White Visitation" and the "PISCES" people, chase him because they want to learn something about the mechanics of his conditioning apparatus. Major Marvy, Tchitcherine, the OSS, and several other Russian, American, and English intelligence groups pursue him for similar reasons. One of these organizations bears his name: "Slothropian Episodic Zone, Weekly Historical Observations (SEZ WHO)." The Argentine anarchists make use of his person for their own ends. The Berlin underground employs him in various functions. In his love life he is the object of manipulations: for Laszlo Jamf, who conditioned infant Tyrone erotically, and for Katje, who starts an affair with him for the sake of observation. Even his unconscious needs are subject to meticulous analysis and manipulation. Dr. Rózsavölgyi specifically develops a "projective test" for Slothrop. He is explicit about his aims and expectations: "We, are in control. He, cannot *help*, himself." Small wonder that Slothrop, the eternal instrument, finally falls into despair: "all in his life of what has looked free or random, is discovered to've been under some Control, all the time, the same as a fixed roulette wheel." The "*great bright hand reaching out of the cloud*" is omnipresent in Slothrop's life.

In this pandemonium of forces pushing, shoving, pursuing, and manipulating, Slothrop inevitably loses track of what exactly is working upon him. Like the rocket, like World War II, like the world-at-large, Slothrop has been sent on his specific trajectory without knowing what launched and later proceeded to propel him. Some of the forces influencing Slothrop are objects of manipulation in other contexts. The engineer Franz Pökler helps to construct the rockets which haunt Slothrop. He, in turn, is the victim of anonymous "Theys": "They are using him—have been, various theys, for ten years." He is seen as "an extension of the Rocket, long before it was ever built." And the engineers working on the rocket "were all equally at the Rocket's mercy." Katje Borgesius is instrumental in a control scheme devised to win guidance over Slothrop. She, in turn, is the helpless tool of Blicero and, later, the Allied

Slothrop hunters. In fact, the whole novel abounds with shuttlecocks of various anonymous or personalized forces. Some of these shuttlecocks of fate remain entirely passive and fatalistic; others seem to be under the illusion that they understand and control. Notable examples, partly reflecting Slothrop's fate, are the uprooted Zone-Hereros, Greta Erdmann, Gottfried, and the whole assortment of characters on board the "Anubis," another "ship of fools."

To be sure, the counterforces of freedom, randomness, self-centered and self-engineered activity are also represented in Slothrop's struggle. Against the ubiquitous facts of conditioning, Slothrop pits his almost inarticulate wish to be let alone, to be free to pursue personal goals. Love seems to become his temporary sanctuary though the conditioning forces have already invaded this paradise (in England his sexual responses are tied to the stimulus of the rocket's approach) and though the abundant repetition of all kinds of sex acts threatens to make them just another mechanical and hence engineered activity. Sexual images such as the rocket itself ("giant penis") or attempts to couple with it or with other machines (compare the "rocket limericks") are frequent motifs in this context. Slothrop's wild ramblings all over Western Europe also show clearly that he is not yet entirely fenced in. In fact, his perennial escape from the crunching thrust of fixation seems to argue that in the fight over control or nonregulation, in the struggle of necessity versus freedom, the latter may well hold the upper hand for good.

Paranoia again looms large in Pynchon's novel—as in all of his works. Only this time it is no longer a suspicion but a necessity. For what else can Slothrop and all the others become but paranoid, when they continuously catch glimpses of plots and thermodynamically defiant structures without ever seeing the whole. Under such circumstances history itself sponsors the foundation of such periodicals as the 1920s German magazine "Paranoid Systems of History." People see tips of many icebergs in *Gravity's Rainbow* and sometimes quite naturally conclude that a conspiracy of icebergs is under way. In Pynchon's own terms, "paranoia, it is nothing less than the onset, the leading edge, of the discovery that *everything is connected*, everything in the Creation, a secondary illumination—not yet blindingly One, but at least connected. . . ."

The proverbs for paranoids and the ever-present references to the anonymous "They" play endlessly on this theme. But in contrast with Pynchon's other novels, this time we are given to understand why paranoia has to be *the* dominant condition of the human mind. The reason is that all we usually see on our wide trajectory of ascent and descent are isolated beginnings, apexes, ends, or various other substructures of the rainbow curve of existence. Are we really to blame for our attempts to imagine the rest or for our attempts to proceed from the awareness of partial control to the suspicion of total control? "The innocence of the creatures," says proverb number two, "is in inverse proportion to the immorality of the Master." Of course, there seem to be other, self-induced cases of paranoia, such as Slothrop's own case: "Paranoids are not paranoids (Proverb 5) because they're paranoid, but because they keep putting themselves, fucking idiots, deliberately into paranoid situations."

But all these cases of paranoia uniformly originate from the situation of life which Pynchon has been describing for us in his central metaphor. This is even valid for the strange phenomenon of antiparanoia which finally counterbalances paranoia just as certainty had its opposite in uncertainty, control in randomness, and ascent in descent. "If there is something comforting—religious, if you want—about paranoia, there is still also anti-paranoia, where nothing is connected to anything, a condition not many of us can bear for long." It is this occurrence of antiparanoia which finally throws a sharp light on what Pynchon himself is doing. Pynchon's gigantic effort in *Gravity's Rainbow* can be seen as the effort of a writer who fully realizes the potentials of paranoid as well as antiparanoid delusions. His answer to the challenge of this dichotomy is the attempt to expose at once the dangers of both by showing that their respective ideals, structured order and entropic chaos, do not stand in final opposition to each other. If there is any single message cutting loud and clear through the infernal din of *Gravity's Rainbow*, it is the message that order and chaos (and hence paranoia and antiparanoia) should not be seen as antagonists of the either/or type but as elements of one and the same universal movement. And without these elements there would be no such movement, no rainbow curve of existence, and no living universe for gravity to reign over.

JOSEPHINE HENDIN

What Is Thomas Pynchon Telling Us?

Thomas Pynchon knows the high cost of living better than anybody except the devil. Pynchon is the evil genius of our time, the man with the quickest eye for what makes this an age of rapacity and sexual hate. He is the American Goya whose dazzling canvases are lit from hell, whose message is: Death Rules.

The dream of this age is the dream of vulnerability conquered. Pynchon's first novel put life together as a diabolic pact in which you could trade your soul for insurance against hell on earth. At twenty-five he dared to say that what his generation required was salvation from death *and* life. His novel *V.* showed the way to eternal experience without anger, pain, or fear. Published in 1963, it was set in 1955 because the Cold War was an unbeatable image for the standoff between Eros and Thanatos in suburban marriages, in New York games of musical blankets, for the deadlock whose linear representation was the symmetrical letter V. Pynchon saw the freeze as an emotional necessity. He wrote about people who knew that love could not diminish suffering because it was love that produced half the anguish there was. He knew what the world wanted was not another Christ but an end to the daily passion play.

Pynchon's symbol for human salvation was not the cross but the partridge in the pear tree: the bird lives off the pears; his droppings fertilize the tree so it can make more pears; the bird makes more droppings. Nature is a Newtonian motion machine powered by crap. Among people, too, salvation is symbiosis. The prime mover shows you how to keep it going without upsetting the bird! Pynchon's Christmas present to his generation was the God who was a birdbrain machine.

From *Harper's* 250, no. 1498 (March 1975). © 1975 by The Minneapolis Star & Tribune Co., Inc.

Technology is commonly blamed as the source of all our woes, our short-circuited relations, our IBMized lives. But many people envy machines. Pynchon loves and hates his messiah machine in *V.*, Benny Profane, a man whose nightmare is that his "clock-heart" and "sponge" brain will be disassembled on the rubble-strewn streets, but whose grace is his ability to be a perpetual-motion man who rolls on too fast to lose his heart or let anyone touch the controls of his mind. The profane Christ is the one who won't get crucified.

Profane's world is no vale of tears. His nativity is one Christmas Eve in the Sailor's Grave Bar, the hip world where every man's a drunken sailor, and women are interchangeable quick lays. Everyone's waiting for Suck Hour, the moment when Chow Down calls the sailors to custom beer taps made of foam rubber in the shape of large breasts. There were seven taps and an average of 250 sailors diving to be given suck by a beer-breast. There's very little nourishment in Pynchon's world. His wise man controls his thirsts. Profane does not really want to turn on anything, even a beer tap. He wants a woman who will not love him but be a really self-contained machine: "Any problems with her you could look up in a maintenance manual. Remove and replace was all." He gets an erection thinking about the sex money can buy while reading the want ads, and notices his erection traces a line in the *Times*. But he waits until it subsides so he can choose the agency where it comes to rest. He wants the least exciting job. He has the peace that passeth understanding.

History produced this human yo-yo. The profane light began with the Victorians' penetration of darkness. Pynchon's favorite explorer, Godolphin, went to Africa to civilize the natives and discovered the cannibal in himself, the need to murder the beauty whose sexual pull made him want to mutilate her. In a spectacular scene he flees to the South Pole and finds, while digging a hole to plant the British flag and reassert his arctic respectability, an African spider monkey all tail, clutch, and cling. The heat of sex is connected with the ice of death. Does one lead to the other because intimacy kills? Realizing he will never escape the destructiveness in himself, the explorer embodies civilization's crucial question: how to keep the monkey off your back?

The history of male striving for control can be written in excrement, as Norman O. Brown implied. Pynchon wrote it in his wacky sewer scenes where evil is the devil you can't flush any further away. Three of *V.*'s characters descend into the urban colon. A Victorian priest preaches in the sewers of New York because he sees people as rats trying to become sanctified. He and his generation could still believe rats had souls. A middle-aged man goes through the sewer looking for clues to his mother, V., because life is possible for him only as the endless romantic quest that keeps him too busy to notice the stench. Young Profane is on the sewer patrol just to earn the money for women and food.

He embraces his meaninglessness as a value. He makes the directionless flow of crap his life.

V. herself is female serenity, the clean, eternal balance of emotional control. She absorbs the force of war, of all male thrusts, as erotic curios, and returns them when as mother she abandons, as protectress she corrupts, as lover she murders, as transvestite priest she damns. She is the destructive, indestructible objet d'art who mutilates her body to adorn it with golden feet and a glass eye. She is always young, always fascinatingly beautiful. One man dreams of her ecstatically as a young machine: "At age 76, skin radiant with the bloom of some new plastic, both eyes glass, but now containing photoelectric cells connected by silver electrodes to optic nerves. . . . Perhaps even a complex system of pressure transducers located in a marvelous vagina of polyethylene, all leading to a single silver cable which fed pleasure voltages direct to the correct register of the digital machine in her skull." She is Profane's woman, the girl who has lost her virginity to the gear shift of her MG, whose great love is her car or its human equivalent, Profane. V. is a self-contained autoerotic machine. V. is the crucial pivot, the profane fulcrum on which you can survive forever. V. is vulnerability conquered.

Life is best as a machine! The degree to which men and women want each other to be ever-ready erotic tools, needing neither tenderness nor love, is one sign of sexual hate. Pynchon is saying that men control their destructiveness through Profane-like passivity and disengagement; that women conquer their vulnerability to men, life, and death by becoming virtual automatons who cannot feel a thing. "Keep cool, but care," someone advises. The only way to contain your destructiveness is to deadlock the two, to be the partridge and pear tree locked in endless, profane life, forever content.

O trees of life, when will your winter come?" asked Rilke. For Pynchon winter came somewhere between V. and Gravity's Rainbow. Pynchon stopped playing the V. game, stopped telling us how to survive. He broke the balance of V., released the deadlock between destructiveness and control, melted the Cold War into an open battle in which the rats surfaced, and violence broke free for a war between life and death. Death won. Pynchon became the devil, the fantasist whose rainbow has its origin in gravity, the spirit of the down. Gravity's Rainbow is death's fantasy that life exists.

World War II is an irresistible image for death's primrose path of heroes and villains who kill each other off. Pynchon's psychopolitical fantasy of war, for all its stunning historical detail, is an apolitical circus in which national differences do not matter, and allies and enemies are more dangerous to themselves than to each other. The combat unit for Pynchon is the whole Age of Aquarius encapsulated in the microcosm PISCES, the Psychological

Intelligence Schemes for Expediting Surrender. In that psychological warfare unit, it is never clear whose surrender is being plotted because everyone is busy devouring each other.

Why is the world so full of hate? How did death beat out life? Pynchon embeds his question in a Western in which the fastest gun in London is Tyrone Slothrop, an American officer who is the ultimate lady-killer. The places where he has gone to bed with his pickups are exactly the spots where the V-2 rockets fall. The psychological warfare unit knows this because Slothrop, who is a member of it, keeps a map, charting with gold stars the places where he has scored. Yes, he is exactly the sort of man who would do this. Roger Mexico, a statistician, charts the bomb sites. His map and Slothrop's are congruent. Is it the bomb that excites Slothrop or sex that draws destructiveness on the girls? Which came first, the bloodsurge or the bloodbath? Will anyone stop the deadliest gun in London?

America's good guys are the engineers who claim to have all the answers. Pynchon makes his points about the quality of emotional life in this culture through their "practical" expertise. Pointsman, a Pavlovian, believes there is a point, a particular switch in the brain, that turns on sex or death. If only he could find the mystery stimulus that controls the switch, he could turn off death and win the Nobel Prize! He could end the war between the sexes! Pointsman salivates as he devises ways of checking out Slothrop's erections through a system of spies, seductresses, and voyeurs, longing like the creep he is to kill Slothrop's one enthusiasm and eventually to castrate him. Slothrop begins to suspect his penis is no longer his own. Paranoia rules as Pointsman's stimuli leave Slothrop less and less able to tell pleasure from pain, dominance from submission. "Paranoia, even Go-ya couldn't draw ya!" sings Pynchon. But Pynchon drew it in this fantasy: we are all dead and have been for years. The devil is tricking us into believing we are alive.

Pointsman's intelligence creates models of human reality as off/on switches that emit the gases of the grave. Pynchon's harshness toward Pointsman is the mark of his total rejection of his own belief in the right tactic, the balance point he explores in *V.* which can prevent human relations from toppling into death. What Pynchon now hates is his own will to find the point outside in space — in spaciness — from which you can move the earth, or keep the life cycle going.

Mathematics increasingly allows for pointlessness, contingency, probability. Pynchon's anti-Pointsman is Roger Mexico, who tells the Pavlovian there is no explanation for the identical graphs for Slothrop's pickups and the bomb sites. "Bombs are not dogs. No link. No memory. No conditioning." Mexico seems to be happy with the discrete, chancy droppings of the bomb.

Gödel's theorem showed the existence of unprovable assumptions in mathematic systems, in effect incorporating chance by institutionalizing it. Mexico is Chance, Inc. He is desperately clinging to meaninglessness to avoid the obvious fact in his life: his intense sexual passion for an unloving woman will be the death of him. Contingency, probability are ways of clouding what Pynchon sees as a fact: sex and death are the same; slaughter is a certainty. As Rilke wrote to a friend, "The future is stationary, dear Herr Kappus, but we are moving in infinite space."

Points and pointlessness, meaning and meaninglessness are opposite sides of the same delusion, diversions into the traps of control or chance and away from the fact that life is uncontrollable. For Pynchon, only physicists give clear unequivocal statements that death has his undisputed hegemony in the universe, that life moves from order to disintegration, from differentiated structures to dispersed, undifferentiated matter, according to the second law of thermodynamics. Pynchon's law of human entropy orchestrates the life of the nation, the couple, the family, the individual into a symphony of death centuries in the unrolling, its pattern inaudible to any one listener because a lifetime unfolds only the most minuscule movement tricked out by the devil as the song of life.

What could look more like life than sex with an irresistible blonde who makes you feel like a leading man? Katje, sent by Pointsman to check out Slothrop's performance, makes him feel like a hero. He suspects she's out for more than she lets on, but he is, too. He hopes she knows the secret that will unlock his humanity and make him feel some emotion. "His face above her unmoved, full of careful technique—is it for her? His desperate hope. . . . She will move him, she will not be mounted by a plastic shell. . . . Her breathing has grown more hoarse, over a threshold into sound. . . . Thinking she might be close to coming he reaches a hand into her hair, tries to still her head, needing to see her face; there is suddenly a struggle, vicious and real—she will not surrender her face—and out of nowhere she does begin to come and so does Slothrop." The hope for a woman who will connect, who will be your connection to life is betrayed by the recognition that the woman is as plastic as you are. What looks like the movements of love is really the dance of death.

Detached sex is depressing, but involved sex is death. Pynchon sees women who are in touch with their feelings as only in touch with evil. Greta Erdmann, an actress whose life is an Expressionist s-m movie, is Pynchon's vision of woman as lover, mother, a "total" woman who demanded to be gangbanged by the entire cast dressed in monster costumes after a filming, whose daughter is fathered by one of these beasts, who commits a series of child-murders, who raises her daughter for S-M incest with her and eventually murders her. Slothrop only dimly realizes in his affair with her that he craves cruelty, too, and is not the good guy he thought he was. She looks into a mirror one day and ecstatically sees the face of the devil. But Slothrop dreams of her as the Earth Mother, the genetrix at the bottom of an industry-poisoned river, her womb breeding all manner of monsters. Who fathered the mutants?

The devil of male industriousness, the polluted orgasms of industry, the male mind that creates structures, forms, controls that kill life, Pynchon's devil is a formalist; his evil is his ability to rape nature with elegance, with all the classiness of Thomas Pynchon's symmetrical alignments. Impersonal, scientific intelligence did Slothrop in; one of its devil geniuses with Kekulé, the pioneer of synthetic chemistry who dreamed of *his* baby, the benzene ring with an X-ray vision that revealed all the hidden structures of life. He dreamed of it as the great serpent that surrounds the world, its tail in its mouth, symbolizing the world as a closed thing, cyclical, eternally returning, inviolate. But he was only looking for the weak link, the vulnerable point where he could strike. His vision began the system that produced the plastic man Slothrop, the system that substituted for the eternal return the movement from death to death transfigured, the development of synthetic polymers whose origin and structure reflect gravity. In human terms this vision is expressed in Nazi "love," the homosexual sadism of Blicero, the German rocket man, toward young Gottfried, who, looking innocently at his "master," hears, "Can you feel in your body how strongly I have infected you with my dying? Fathers are the carriers of the virus of Death, and sons are the infected."

The history of death is the history of parental love. Slothrop is granted a buffoon's revelation of creation when he throws up in a barroom toilet and drops his harmonica into his slop. He dives in after it, only to get heaped with the excrement of others and flushed into a wasteland where he sees the souls of babies waiting to be born. They look like the remains of basket cases from the Great War. You are your parents' droppings, the remains of their discontent! Slothrop emerges from the wasteland without realizing the extent to which he is made of excrement. But Pynchon knows, he knows it all. He tells you how this culture turns life into plastic shit.

In 1925 Rilke wrote that "Dummy life from America" is replacing "the cared-for animate houses, wines, apples" of Europe. Pynchon goes further, claiming that what America was manufacturing best were plastic *people*. Imipolex G, the polymer whose every fiber is capable of erection, is the sexiest cloth there is, the mystery stimulus that conditioned Infant Tyrone's erections. Were they measured against the foolproof factory-tested polymer's? Slothrop's real father sold out his baby boy to a stimulus-response experiment in return for the money to send him to college. Pynchon is telling you that you are geared to excitement by synthetics, cast into your programming too soon to know what is happening, too ignorant to realize that your father's love for your human possibilities was so meager he was willing to plasticize you so that, alive or dead, you would get through Harvard.

Slothrop's love-hate affair with the V-2 rocket is the paradigm of his conditioning, of your conditioning. The rocket outstrips sound; the noise of its coming rises only after it has already exploded. Before you know what has hit you, you are dead. This is Pynchon's most powerful symbol for the subliminal takeover of your mind. Every Infant Tyrone gets blasted by the violence of his parents' war with each other, by their rage toward him, by the anger of the Greta-Mother and the Blicero-Father who divide your physical and mental pain between them.

The American Oedipal situation is the place where you lose your valence, your attraction to everything, your enthusiasm for life. This is the game where the mother who would like to kill, and the father who controls, team up against the son who has to outwit them both. Pynchon believes "Perilous Pop" is the antagonist of every Western, every comic strip. He is "every typical American teenager's own father, trying episode after episode to kill his son. And the kid knows it. Imagine that. So far he's managed to escape his father's daily little death plots—but nobody has said he has to keep escaping." Pop and his gang may not kill you, but they kill everything that makes life worth living. They steal the Radiant Hour from the day, steal life itself. Can anyone get it back?

Pynchon's rescue team is a catalogue of the kinds of people he feels this culture is producing, people bent on contemporary bliss: Myrtle the Miraculous is a wonder woman who hates people but adores the perfection of efficient machines. Marcel, the mechanical chess player, is the ideal male, a robot tactician. Maximilian forsakes these fake humans, gets beyond male and female by allying himself with rhythms, all rhythms up to and including the cosmic. He's a fragmentation freak. Slothrop is the "glozing neuter" who cannot recognize himself as a man or a machine and whose fate is simply to run down ignorantly in the dimness of his vision. None of them finds the Radiant Hour.

The American street is full of people looking for the Great Glow in the gold-star night with a pickup. Pynchon's *Platz* is full of antigravity forces— people popping pills, morning-glory seeds, the "winerush" that rockets upward, making "the woman screaming, the knife in your hand, your head down a toilet all unreal." The sensory trip is the new dope. If you take it you see the profane light.

True radiance begins with Byron the Bulb, the bright boy light bulb whose immortal beam screams "You're dead" in neon. His real name is Thomas Pynchon, the writer who staked his immortality on being the man who illuminated the death at the heart of all experience. What happened to Pynchon between *V.*, the wildly sophisticated survival manual, and *Gravity's Rainbow*, the brilliant analysis of how you died? What happened to a writer who was not profane enough to take his own advice: "Keep cool, but care?" What challenged Pynchon's balanced gravity? Pynchon does not say. As his publisher put it with terrific rightness, he keeps a "low profile."

But Pynchon offered a cautionary tale in *V.*, in the saga of Fausto Maijstral, who started out to be a priest and a poet. He married a woman he loved and had a daughter. He lost his faith, his work, his mind in an intimacy so disastrous it could only be described as world war. He wrote to his daughter, born, like Pynchon, in 1938: "The bombs arrived with you, child." The birth of a child, like the profane nativity in *V.*, is death, the baby twisting out of the antarctic birth canal like a devil of need who shows up your love as a sham, your limitations as awesome. At the bottom of Fausto's mind is the memory of *his* father who was wrecked by war, of *his* mother who wanted to jump with her baby Fausto into the sea. Is death the willingness to breed life?

For Pynchon had the clarity, the guts to see that what makes people kill and hate is not a lover's rejection but a beloved's responsiveness. Given a choice between exaltation or sensory amusement, people prefer the limited kick. What they cannot transcend is their gravity, the depression that has an umbilical force binding them back to the stern down of Father Death and pained Mother Greta. Pynchon goes still further. He makes the most radical possible statement of the refusal to give up depression in Blicero's hatred of the lover whose youth and devotion are a challenge to his own. "O Gottfried, of course . . . you are beautiful to me but I'm dying. . . . I want to get through it as honestly as I can, and your immortality rips at my heart—can't you see why I might want to destroy that, oh, that stupid clarity in your eyes. . . . When I see you so open, so ready to take my sickness in and shelter it, shelter it inside your own little ignorant love."

Love is a great reminder of limitations, of what you are not. The man who needs to dominate, control, and crush spends his life hating his finite powers and trying to limit love. Blicero ties Gottfried up, puts him in a dog collar, forces on him a cycle of contempt and humiliation to bind up Gottfried's feeling. Pynchon boxes in love to the s-m connection, where Blicero is your will to power and Gottfried your ability to love, each tying the other in knots. Through the novel Blicero is constructing the ultimate death-box, the V-2 rocket fitted out for Gottfried, who will enter its nose cone wrapped in an Imipolex G shroud. Gottfried soaring on his love for Blicero goes arching toward his death, while Blicero dives straight into the flames of the rocket launch. Blicero is faithful to his gravity!

Pynchon affirms the loneliness unto death, forces this *Liebestod* into a statement that there is no union even in death. Blicero does not die with Gottfried but rather makes sure each of them dies alone. The Radiant Hour for Pynchon is the hour of death, the fires of V-2 that liberate Gottfried and Blicero from the box of their own personalities, the shut trap of dominance and submission, into the molecular flow. What radiance Blicero and Gottfried achieve in their flaming deaths is the sparkle of illuminated filth, dirt gleaming in the streaked glow of the rainbow that is not the sign of God's covenant with Noah, but the mark of Pynchon's covenant with death.

Pynchon sold his soul to the devil for his own inviolability, his irrefutable alignment of all human endeavor on the axis of death. He is the artist of man's limitations, the best voice of a generation whose great discovery was exactly the finite nature of all human reality. Pynchon did his bit to limit life further by boxing experience into one either/or: the mechanical symbiosis of V. or no life at all. But Pynchon went still further in affirming limitation as the sole purpose of existence. Given our destructiveness, our need to kill, to sully life, our mission on earth, Pynchon concludes, must be to celebrate the devil. "Our mission is to promote death."

Kepler conceptualized gravity as the Holy Ghost for "physical and meta-physical reasons." It was God's love, he thought, that swept the planets around the sun and kept them in place and in harmony. Pynchon conceptualized gravity as a parabolic rainbow also for physical and metaphysical reasons. The rainbow is Death's hate, Death's grimace, the tragic mask of the heavens pulled down forever in one inviolable affirmation of depression. And in his myth of himself as death incarnate, Pynchon transcends his limitations, puts himself beyond the pale of human pain and cruelty. He allies himself with the ultimate aggressor, the impersonal force of the entropy god. In the throes of his pessimism, by *force* of his pessimism, Pynchon still pursues his own invulnerability.

The dream of vulnerability conquered is the dream of the age. Pynchon has an unbeatable sensitivity to the evil the dream contains, an analytic brilliance at extracting the villainy behind every smile, a stunning accuracy about every-thing wrong with emotional life in this culture now. He got caught between the dream and his hatred for it. His pain, his vulnerability, his great and ruined expectations keep breaking through his fierce intellectual hardness. Pynchon's own refusal to stop demanding that life be perfect caring or perfect emotionlessness, his inability to stop making conditions that life cannot fulfill, his own bottomless pain, weld into a pessimism so unassailable it becomes an argument against pessimism. Pynchon's indictment of every human impulse is his crucifixion on the modern dream. It is so intense it has a cautionary force against gravity. Pynchon's most eloquent moral is himself.

Pynchon is the devil who went beyond the grave to anatomize the remains of the modern soul. Like Death himself he is the ultimate collector, putting together the emotional, cultural, and historical life of his generation with a brilliance and depth that outstrips in scope what Thomas Mann did for the prewar world in *The Magic Mountain*, that equals James Joyce's compendium of his time in *Ulysses*. He plays Beethoven to Rilke's Schubert, developing from Rilke's encapsulated emotional statements operative definitions about the nature of science, thought, and civilization. Pynchon is quite simply the genius of his generation. He is the Antichrist who offered up his own destructiveness to illuminate yours. Pynchon is the one man who realized that the moralist of our time would have to be the devil.

The Importance of Thomas Pynchon

One of the many distinctions between American literature and English literature, especially in the nineteenth century, is that most of the American writers whom we would call great were not, while most actively producing their best work, what we would also call popular. I'm thinking of Hawthorne, Melville, James, Eliot, Stevens. There has usually been a time lag between critical and general acclaim. Not that criticism has, by itself, kept up to the mark. There is the conspicuous case of Melville, who wasn't taken seriously until 1921, and even Faulkner had the misfortune of being popular not with his best but with his second-best novels, like *Sanctuary*. His popularity, coming before literary critics could take credit for creating it, put them in no mood to be generous when they at first got round to him. The same condition, with certain variations, has been true of Robert Frost. Serious criticism is still in Frost's case exceptionally begrudging and self-protective. Even now he is looked into as if he aspired to be Yeats or Eliot, not as someone who proposes an extraordinary alternative to them and to the dominant so-called modernist line of the twentieth century.

Among the remarkable facts about Thomas Pynchon is that if we are to believe the best-seller list, the selections of the Book-of-the-Month Club, the reviews, and the committee for the National Book Awards, then presumably we are to believe that *Gravity's Rainbow* is a popular book and, at the same time, that it ranks with *Ulysses* and *Moby-Dick* in accomplishment and possibly exceeds them in complexity. Something peculiar is happening here. A writer is received simultaneously into the first rank of the history of our litera-

From *Mindful Pleasures: Essays on Thomas Pynchon.* © 1975 by Richard Poirier. Little, Brown, & Co., 1975.

ture and also as a popular novelist. Only Mark Twain has been given such praise before, unless Hemingway and Fitzgerald are counted, though not by me, as of the first order.

If what I've said is true of Pynchon's reputation, and even if it only seems to be true on the evidence of what the media and a lot of people want to believe, then we have to ask some questions about the culture in which we find ourselves, a culture which Pynchon himself seems to include within his imagination at once more abundantly and more playfully than anyone now writing. In his inclusivenss he is a kind of cultural encyclopedia. He is also, after Hawthorne, the American writer with the deepest kind of skepticism about the advantages of being "included" by the culture America has inherited and shaped. For the present he is probably less than grateful for the way the culture has decided to include him. He may regard his being "taken in" as a kind of conspiracy, a kind of plot. Not a plot against gullible readers, since they, after all, can be encouraged to own, even to like his books, without reading them, without ever encountering the dizzying and resistant complexities of his style. Rather, he might think of these developments as a plot against himself, and he might wonder what is going to happen to a writer who is hailed both as a genius and a romp, even when he knows that the mass of good amateur readers—the kind who belong to the Book-of-the-Month Club—not only don't but can't much like him. Who are They, to use one of his favorite words, who are the mysterious donors apparently with the power to create and therefore the power to perpetuate his fame? Just because his constituency is so hard to identify, its power over him must be hard to resist; he can't negotiate directly with the They who concocted and therefore control his audience, and They can force him into strange compromises, such as his reluctant acceptance of the National Book Award simply because to have turned it down, which he most likely would have done had it been given to him singly, would under the circumstances have been an insult to the co-beneficiary, Mr. Isaac Bashevis Singer.

Well, who *is* Pynchon's audience? First of all, a certain kind of educated young reader who was probably trained to read hard books during the early to mid-sixties and who is also sympathetically responsive to the cultural manifestations of the late sixties—in rock, adult comic books, drug and black styles, filmmaking; second, a number of academics, older than the first group but who nonetheless went through some of the same sequences of interest and development; third, a growing number of quite learned academic readers who enjoy puzzles, especially costumed ones, who relish intellectual play, and who admire Pynchon's Johnsonian capacities to "work up" a subject (like the Fashoda incident or life in London during the blitz) wholly remote from his own personal experiences—Pynchon as the essential classicist; fourth, the various readers who come from these three groups, but who are also in the book business, with its hunger for a great writer, any "great writer" except Norman Mailer or the good grey champion Saul Bellow; and fifth, a lot of people who take their cue from these various groups and who are enthusiastic about a phenomenon without the capacity to understand it, intellectually turned-on groupies who see in Pynchon's obscurities and his personal elusiveness—his refusal to come out of hiding in any way—a sign of radical contempt. He's a radical to whom the establishment has simply had to defer—or so it seems.

What is left out of this grouping is of course the central mass of educated general readers. And a good clue to their reactions, so far as Pynchon is concerned, can be found in what might be called the Anglo-Americans. This is a literary nation of educated general readers who can always flee from the petty tyrannies of a new interest to the thrones of literary and cultural conservatism: to the likes of *Saturday Review/World* and the journal of bully-boy arriviste gentility, *Commentary* magazine. Tepid, condescending, unwilling or unable to submit to the intense pressure of Pynchon's work, they admire (when they manage to admire him at all) only what is separably cute or charming or what is compact or economical, like *The Crying of Lot 49*, though even that, not to mention *V.*, is unavailable now, for example, in Great Britain. "Of course what I like is *The Crying of Lot 49*," is the thing to say, equivalent to saying of Henry James that "Of course, what I like is his novel *Confidence*," or of Faulkner (in French) that "What I like is your Faulkner's *Pylon*." It's an old European trick with our stuff, unfortunately imported to this country, with its large core of American Anglophilic readers. When it comes to *The Crying of Lot 49*, the verdict is assisted by the fact that it is the only one of Pynchon's three novels whose size and scope make is usable in class.

I, too, consider *The Crying of Lot 49* an astonishing accomplishment and the most dramatically powerful of Pynchon's works because of its focus on a single figure. But what is at issue here is something else—the *nature* of Pynchon's reputation. And generally the Anglophilic response of the good reader, of the amateur book lover to Pynchon is, measured against what is offered by his whole achievement, ironic evidence that though Pynchon may be treated with the condescension historically visited on other great American writers by the literary establishment contemporaneous with them, he somehow appears to have escaped the consequences of this. That is, despite the dereliction of a large central core of readers and of the upper-brow journals where they find reassurance, he has, again, simultaneously achieved public acclaim and enormous private respect.

I admit to a certain unfairness in these characterizations of the amateur

reader, an unfairness of which I would suppose other protective admirers of
Pynchon might also be guilty. Amateur readers may be unable to respond to
the relentless vitality of Pynchon's writing, but professional academic readers
can positively smother it. And perhaps it is better, like an amateur, to be simply
oblivious to what is being offered in his books than, like a professional, to
set about anxiously to pacify Pynchon's vitality by schemes, structuralist or
otherwise. But to believe this, as I've tried to suggest, is to overlook the curious
historical change in what it means to be an amateur reader. The trouble with
amateur readers now is that they are *too* literary rather than not literary enough.
They are too anxious, most simply, that the life imitated by a new novel should
resemble only what old novels have taught us to recognize as life. They are
not amateur in the positive sense of being open and alive; they are not able
to take advantage of their freedom from those premeditations, those utilitarian
impulses which necessarily corrupt most professional readers and most of us
who are teachers of literature. We're in a situation where neither the amateur
nor the professional reader seems capable of reading Pynchon for the fun of
it, for the relish of local pleasures, for the savoring of how the sentences sound
as they turn into one another, carrying with them, and creating as they go,
endlessly reverberating echoes from the vast ranges of contemporary life and
culture. The ideal reader of Pynchon probably would be more amateur than
professional, but amateur in a positive sense – capable of unscheduled responses
even while being generally learned and inquisitive. For that reason, what's
happening to Pynchon, as he is moved increasingly into position for a guidebook
study, is a cause not for celebration but for misgiving. This is a crucial and
instructive problem which tells us a good deal about a larger cultural impasse.
Pynchon really has, so far as I can see, no wholly safe constituency except
one – the academy – and unless academic writers and teachers are extremely
careful they will do to him the damage already done to Joyce and Eliot.

Put simply, the damage consists of looking at the writing as something
to be figured out by a process of translation, a process which omits the weird-
ness and pleasure of the reading experience as it goes along, the kind of experience which, say, we expect from Dickens without being worried about
it. The damage consists of treating each of the formal or stylistic or allusive
elements in a work as a clue to meaning, a point of possible stabilization. This
is an especially inappropriate way to treat Pynchon because each of these
elements is in itself highly mobile and dramatic. Each is a clue not to meaning
so much as to chaos of meaning, an evidence of the impossibility of stabilization.
We are confronted with what, in another context, I call a literature of waste.
This is not to say literature *is* waste but that in certain works there are
demonstrations that the inherited ways of classifying experience are no longer

a help but a hindrance. All of the formulas by which experience gets shaped or organized around us are themselves a part of the chaos of experience with which one has to deal. The rage to order, Pynchon seems to say, is merely a symptom of accelerating disorder.

Pynchon goes beyond his predecessors because he projects this notion of waste past literature and onto all available systems of classification. Joyce, for example, followed by Barth and Borges and doubtless others, was a great innovator in that he pushed literary parody to the point of literary self-parody, showing how the available conventions, styles, forms of literature were insufficient as a breakwater of order and elegance against the tide of life—to paraphrase Stephen Daedalus. Pynchon extends this perception from literature not only to science, to pop culture, to the traditions of analysis, but even to the orderings of the unconscious, to dreams themselves. In his works dreams are treated as so many planted messages, encoded by what he calls the "bureaucracy of the other side." It is as if human life in all of its *recorded* manifestations is bent toward rigidification, reification, and death. Echoing Norman O. Brown, Pynchon seems to say not only that history is itself a form of repression, but so, too, is the human impulse to make or to write history.

If this is any proper reading of Pynchon then it should constitute a warning to any one of us who wishes to order or regularize his work by whatever plot, myth, symmetry or arrangement. And yet we persist in doing so, because, finally, it is nearly impossible to feel about our cultural (even, sometimes, about our biological) inheritance the way he does. We don't know *enough* to feel as he wants us to feel. I don't mean that it is impossible to appreciate his radical perspectives, since we can do that even if we don't agree with him. I mean that we can't with Pynchon—any more than with Joyce or with the Eliot of the lovably pretentious notes to *The Waste Land*—possibly claim to be as conversant as he wants us to be with the various forms of contemporary culture. He may be as theatrically enlivening and entertaining as Dickens, but a reader needs to know relatively little to appreciate Dickens. Really to read Pynchon properly you would have to be astonishingly learned not only about literature but about a vast number of other subjects belonging to the disciplines and to popular culture, learned to the point where learning is almost a sensuous pleasure, something to play around with, to feel totally relaxed about, so that you can take in stride every dizzying transition from one allusive mode to another.

This means that we are in a true dilemma if we love Pynchon or any writer who resembles him. We don't want to stop the game, we don't want to get out of the rhythm, but what are we to do if we simply don't know enough to play the game, to move with the rhythm? We can't, above all, pretend

that such a writer is a regular fellow, the way Anthony Burgess does with
Joyce. Burgess's *Re Joyce* is both quite a bad book and an amusing object lesson.
With totally false casualness, Burgess has to lay before us an immense amount
of requisite learning in the effort to prove that Joyce can be read by Everyman. Burgess makes an obvious, glaring but nonetheless persistent error: he
confuses Joyce's material (much of which is indeed quite ordinary and common)
with what Joyce does to it (which is totally uncommon, unordinary, and elitist).
Another way of answering Burgess, or anyone who says that a writer like Joyce
or Pynchon is just a "good read," is to say that nobody in Joyce, and very
few in Pynchon, could read the novels that have been written about them.
This is particularly true of Pynchon, who loves the anonymous if he loves
anyone, loves the lost ones—and writes in a way that would lose them completely. These discriminations would not even need to be made, of course,
were it not for the stubborn liberal dream of literary teachers, especially in
the last five years, that literature is written for the people who are in it. It
makes as much sense to think that blacks should care about literature because
they find black experience in it as to say that shepherds should care about
pastoral poetry because there are shepherds in it. It is precisely this arrogant
overvaluation of literature that the truly great works have often tried to dispel.
As much in Shakespeare as in anything written now there is often some sensed
resentment about the way literature is itself exploiting life for literary purposes,
and Pynchon offers perhaps the most exhaustive and brilliant repudiation of
this exploitation in our language.

To know just how masterfully and how feelingly Pynchon reveals the
destructive powers of all systematic enterprise, however, one has first to know
things about which all of us are in some measure ignorant. Not many of us
know about Zap comics as well as about double integrals. Of course we are
all relatively ignorant whenever we sit down to read, and notably so when
we are reading works by writers who in any way resemble Pynchon, like John
Barth or Borges or Burroughs, like Melville or Joyce. But with these our
ignorance is usually a different kind. We can correct it by reading more closely
for internal evidence or by reading other novels or classical literature with
maybe an excursion into history or film. But we are always pretty much within
the realms of fiction, and even where fictional characters are modeled, as in
Joyce, on real people it matters little, if at all, that we know about these real
people. At most we need to know only a bit about the literary or classical
myths with which their fictional counterparts are implicated.

In Pynchon we find ourselves in a curious fictional world which is often
directly referring us back to the real one. This is of course always true of novels
to some degree. But in Pynchon the factuality seems willingly to participate

in the fiction; it disguises itself as fiction to placate us and the characters. Fact is consciously manipulated by "They" in order to create the comforting illusion that it *is* fiction, an illusion contrived to deceive Oedipa or Slothrop into *not* believing in the reality of what is happening to them. Crazy names like Pierce Inverarity turn out, when we do a little investigation, to be a compound of a quite famous, real-life stamp collector named Pierce, and of the fact that if you should go to Mr. Pierce for the kind of flawed and peculiar stamps so important in *The Crying of Lot 49* you would ask him for an "inverse rarity." What sound like crazy schemes turn out to have been actual experiments, such as Maxwell's demon, again in *The Crying of Lot 49*, or historically important institutions like Thurn and Taxis. With one very slight exception all of Pynchon's material in *The Crying of Lot 49* about that postal service is historically verifiable, and even a cursory glance into a dictionary will show that some of the figures in *Gravity's Rainbow* were historical, not only obvious ones like the chemist Liebig or Clerk Maxwell, or Frederick Kekulé, but also Käthe Kollwitz and Admiral Rozhdestvenski. Eventually we get to wonder at almost every point if perhaps we are being given not fiction at all, but history.

This is not simply to say that Pynchon's fictions have historical analogues or that he allegorizes history. Rather, his fictions are often seamlessly woven into the stuff, the very factuality of history. His practices are vastly different from such allegorizations as one gets in Barth's *Giles Goat-Boy*, different from Borges's inventions of fictional conspiracies which are analogous to the historical ones of the Nazi period, and different, too, from the obsessive patternings one finds in Nabokov, which are private, local, and while including certain aspects of American reality, never derived directly from them. In Pynchon's novels the plots of wholly imagined fiction are inseparable from the plots of known history or science. More than that, he proposes that any effort to sort out these plots must itself depend on an analytical method which, both in its derivations and in its execution, is probably part of some systematic plot against free forms of life.

The perspectives—literary, analytic, pop cultural, philosophical, scientific— from which Pynchon operates are considerably more numerous than those available to any writer to whom he might be compared, and it is therefore especially impressive that Pynchon insists not on keeping these perspectives discrete but upon the functioning, the tributary, the literally grotesque relationship among them. All systems and technologies, in his view, partake of one another. In particular, science directs our perceptions and feelings whether we know it or not, even while, as literary people, we may like to imagine that it is literature that most effectively conditions how we feel. Other writers have of course recorded the effects, and seldom recorded them as benign, of technology and science on human lives, and the techniques of literature have in this century shown some conspicuous indebtedness to the technique of machines, as in William Gaddis, who was a most important influence on Pynchon, and in other influences like Dos Passos, Joyce and Burroughs. But again, Pynchon is doing something different, something more frighteningly inclusive.

Perhaps he is the first writer to realize Wordsworth's prediction in the Preface to the third edition of the *Lyrical Ballads*. Writing in 1801, Wordsworth reveals a sense of the power of poetry and the capacities of the poet to incorporate into himself and into his work all other forms of human enterprise that can only be for us now a sad illumination both of his prophetic genius and of his noble but betrayed optimism. It is as if Pynchon set out to do what Wordsworth instructed the poet to do, but to show that the results were not the transfiguration of science but the transfiguration of man.

> Poetry is the first and last of all knowledge—it is as immortal as the heart of man. If the labours of men of Science should ever create any material revolution, direct or indirect, in our condition, and in the impressions which we habitually receive, the Poet will sleep then no more than at present; he will be ready to follow the steps of the Man of Science, not only in those general indirect effects, but he will be at his side, carrying sensation into the midst of the objects of the Science itself. The remotest discoveries of the Chemist, the Botanist, or Mineralogist, will be as proper subjects of the Poet's art as any upon which it can be employed, if the time should ever come when these things shall be familiar to us, and the relations under which they are contemplated by the followers of these respective Sciences shall be manifestly and palpably material to us as enjoying and suffering beings. If the time should ever come when what is now called Science, thus familiarized to men, shall be ready to put on, as it were, a form of flesh and blood, the Poet will lend his divine spirit to aid the transfiguration, and will welcome the Being thus produced, as a dear and genuine inmate of the household of man.

"Carrying sensation into the midst of the objects of the Science itself"— that alone would be a sufficiently original and remarkable accomplishment. Pynchon has had to go knowingly beyond that, however, because all of us have together gone *un*knowingly beyond it, passed *un*knowingly into a world where the effects of exposure to the implementations of science and technology are so pervasive as to have been invisible and inaudible. We have few ways, for example, of measuring the effect of the media within which we live except by the instrumentalities of the media. Pynchon does not set out to rescue us from this condition, in the manner of Lawrence. He is in fact as partial to technology and to science as he is to Rilke, Zap comics, Glen Gould, Orson Welles or Norman O. Brown. He no longer perpetuates the dream of Wordsworth that poetry or a radical esthetics derived from poetry provides a basis for understanding and resisting any of the other systematic exertions of power over human consciousness. Science, the analytical method, technology—all of these are not merely impositions upon consciousness. They are also a corporate expression of consciousness; they express us all as much as do the lyrical ballads. They express us more than does our late and befuddled resistance to them. Put another way, the visual and audible messages offered on the film called *Citizen Kane* tell us no more (and no less) about modern life than does the movie projector which shows the film or the camera which made it. These machines are a product of the human imagination which, if felt as such and studied as such, refer us to the hidden nature of human feeling and human need. In the instance of the movie projector we are referred specifically to the desire first to frame the human image—with all the slang connotations involved in the word "frame"—and then to accelerate it. The movie projector itself necessarily refers Pynchon back to "this strange connection between the German mind and the rapid flashing of successive stills to counterfeit movement, for at least two centuries—since Leibniz, in the process of inventing calculus, used the same approach to break up the trajectories of cannonballs through the air" (*Gravity's Rainbow*). It refers back to historically verifiable persons and developments and forward, from the time of *Gravity's Rainbow*, to future ones, to the encapsulated trajectory of men in space.

The Crying of Lot 49 is in many ways a novel about the effort and the consequences of "carrying sensation into the midst of the objects of the Science itself." That is precisely what Oedipa Maas does with the idea of Maxwell's demon, an idea proposed at the end of James Clerk Maxwell's *Theory of Heat* (1871). Maxwell hypothesized a vessel divided into two portions, A and B, by a division in which there is a small hole. He asks us to conceive of a being, subsequently known as Maxwell's demon, with faculties that allow it to follow the course of every molecule in the vessel. The being is situated beside a small shutter located in the dividing wall between the two portions of the vessel and he opens and closes this shutter so as to allow only the swifter molecules to pass from A to B and only the slower ones to pass from B to A. According to Maxwell this being "will thus, without expenditure of work, raise the temperature of B and lower that of A, in contradiction to the second law of thermodynamics."

Oedipa comes to picture herself as an equivalent of Maxwell's demon, only in her case she sorts out a vast array of circulating data all seeming to emerge out of the inheritance from Inverarity. She is one of the executors of his estate, and she would like to transform all of the random information that floods in on her into "stelliferous meaning," just as the demon operated as an agent of order in a system of random occurrences. She wishes, that is, to increase order and to decrease entropy in the system which is the life around her. By decreasing entropy, which is a measure of the unavailable energy in any system, she will forestall the drift toward death as the ultimate state of the entire system of life. However, by the end of the novel she has managed only to prove a point made by one of the later commentators on Clerk Maxwell, Leon Brillouin, in a paper published by *The Journal of Applied Physics*, entitled "Maxwell's Demon Cannot Operate." Brillouin contends that an intelligent being has to cause an *increase* of entropy before it can effect a reduction by a smaller amount. This increase of entropy more than balances the decrease of entropy the demon might bring about. In the words of W. Ehrenberg in his essay on Maxwell's demon in *Scientific American* (November 1967), "Similar calculations appear to be applicable whenever intelligent beings propose to act as sorting demons."

What are critics of Pynchon, like myself, but a species of sorting demon? And yet what are we to do with the random material of his books, what is Oedipa to do with the random and maddening material of her inheritance, if we do not all at some point become sorting demons? It is necessary to *know* about sorting demons before one can even know why one should break the habit. This is a way of saying that it takes a lot of work to know what's going on in Pynchon, even though what's going on finally lies importantly on the other side of such knowing, such "sorting" out. Really to see and hear his concerns, we must at least sense how Pynchon *feels* about his knowledge, we must participate in his Coleridgean anxiety about knowledge, about analysis, about any kind of sorting.

Even Clerk Maxwell and the great chemist Kekulé in *Gravity's Rainbow* are imagined as themselves haunted, visited, obsessed and paranoiac in their exploration, just as much as is the fictional heroine, dear Oedipa Maas. Thus, we learn in *Gravity's Rainbow* that the demon may not in its inception have been a model meant to demonstrate something in the physical sciences. Though it served for that, it might have been designed primarily as an encoded warning to all of us. Instead of being an example of how plots may be created from randomness, it was meant to tip us off to an ongoing plot that got carried into the twentieth-century, on to World War II and the present. In *Gravity's Rainbow* someone speculates — it is impossible to know who — that Liebig, a renowned professor of chemistry in the last century at the University of Geissen, was an agent whose task was to put Kekulé in a position where he could receive a dream from "the bureaucracy of the other side," the world of the dead—a dream of the shape of the benzene ring. This shape was to be the foundation of aromatic chemistry, which, along with theories of acceleration, made possible the rocket and the nosecone for its destructive reentry into our lives. Kekulé had entered the University of Geissen as an architectural student but he was inspired by Liebig to change his field.

> So Kekulé brought the mind's eye of an architect over into chemis try. It was a critical switch. Liebig himself seems to have occupied the role of a gate, or sorting-demon such as his younger contemporary Clerk Maxwell once proposed, helping to concentrate energy into one favored room of the Creation at the expense of everything else (later witnesses have suggested that Clerk Maxwell intended his Demon not so much as a convenience in discussing a thermodynamic idea as a parable about the *actual existence* of personnel like Liebig . . . we may gain an indication of how far the repression had grown by that time, in the degree to which Clerk Maxwell felt obliged to code his warnings . . . indeed some theorists, usually the ones who find sinister meaning behind even Mrs Clerk Maxwell's notorious "It is time to go home, James, you are beginning to enjoy yourself," have made the extreme suggestion that the Field Equations themselves contain an ominous forewarning—they cite as evidence the disturbing intimacy of the Equations with the behavior of the double-integrating circuit in the guidance system of the A4 rocket, the same double-summing of current densities that led architect Etzel Ölsch to design for architect Albert Speer an underground factory at Nordhausen with just that symbolic shape . . .). Young ex-architect Kekulé went looking among the molecules of the time for the hidden shapes he knew were there, shapes he did not like to think of as real physical structures, but as "rational formulas," showing the relationships that went on in "metamorphoses," his quaint 19th-century way of saying "chemical reactions." But he could visualize. He *saw* the four bonds of carbon, lying in a tetrahedron—he *showed* how carbon atoms could link up, one to another, into long chains. . . . But he was stumped when he got to benzene. He knew there were six carbon atoms with a hydrogen attached to each one—but he could not see the shape. Not until the dream: until he was made to see it, so that others might be seduced by its physical beauty, and begin to think of it

as a blueprint, a basis for new compounds, new arrangements, so
that there would be a field of aromatic chemistry to ally itself with
secular power, and find new methods of synthesis, so there would
be a German dye industry to become the IG.

This passage is at once portentously impressive and satirically comic. It
emanates from the voice of the novel—as if Pynchon were himself a demon
for sorting random sounds that pass through the cultural environment carrying information with them. And as always there is a hint of acute paranoia.
In Pynchon, however, as sometimes in Mailer or even Melville, paranoia is
often the precondition for recognizing the systematic conspiracy of reality. So
much so, that to think of oneself with any pejorative sense as a paranoiac
constitutes in Pynchon a kind of cop-out, a refusal to see life and reality itself
as a plot, to see even dreams as an instrumentality of a bureaucracy intent
on creating self-perpetuating systems.

Pynchon is a great novelist of betrayal, and everyone in his books is a
betrayer who lets himself or herself be counted, who elects or who has been
elected to fit into the scheme of things. But they are the worst betrayers who
propose that the schemes are anything more or less than that—an effort to
"frame" life in every sense—or who evade the recognition of this by calling
it paranoiac. To be included in any plot is to be to that extent excluded from
life and freedom. Paradoxically, one is excluded who is chosen, sorted, cate-
gorized, schematized, and yet this is the necessary, perpetual activity of life
belonging to our very biological and psychic natures.

This is a distinctly American vision, and Pynchon is the epitome of
an American writer out of the great classics of the nineteenth century—
Hawthorne, Emerson, and Melville especially. The vision is not, as has been
argued so often, one of cultural deprivation, but rather of cultural inundation,
of being swamped, swept up, counted in before you could count yourself out,
pursued by every bookish aspect of life even as you try to get lost in a wilderness, in a randomness where you might hope to find your true self. And it
is that at last which is most deeply beautiful about Pynchon and his works.
He has survived all the incursions which he documents, and he is, as I hope
he will remain, a genius lost and anonymous.

GEORGE LEVINE

Risking the Moment

Pynchon's novels disorient. They offer us a world we think we recognize, assimilate it to worlds that seem unreal, imply coherences and significances we can't quite hold on to. Invariably, as the surreal takes on the immediacy of experience, they make us feel the inadequacy of conventional modes of making sense—of analysis, causal explanation, logic. But Pynchon's language is so richly, sometimes so cruelly anchored in the banalities of the colloquial, the obscene, the trivial, the familiar, and it so miraculously spins from these things into high scientific and historical speculation, into melodrama, romance, and apocalyptic intensity, that the experience is not merely—if it is even primarily—intellectual. Yet critics almost invariably respond to the novels with thematic readings that reduce variety to a fairly conventional coherence.

Anticipating such readings, I'm sure, Pynchon made characters like Herbert Stencil and Oedipa Maas pretty good literary critics themselves. Writing about them thematically is like joining them, and that is part of the irony and experience of reading the books, too. A writer so busy implying connections, dropping allusions, thwarting conventional responses invites the sort of criticism Pynchon has been getting; and I don't pretend to stand outside or above it. Furthermore, any attempt to avoid the disorientation of his characters requires that we first join them in their desperate—and sometimes silly—quests.

More important than the possible resolution of the quests is the disorientation and almost visceral disturbance that come of being forced into

From *Mindful Pleasures: Essays on Thomas Pynchon.* © 1976 by George Levine and David Leverenz. Little, Brown, & Co., 1976. Originally entitled "Risking the Moment: Anarchy and Possibility in Pynchon's Fiction."

them. Such disturbance is a condition of growth for the characters and for the readers. Pynchon evokes the terror and anxiety of the disturbance as he describes the feelings of Oedipa, in the last moments of her novel, awaiting silently the crying, the annunciation—of what rough beast?

And there I go, making comfort out of anxiety by invoking a myth and poetic variations on it to "place" Oedipa's experience. The falsification is a serious one, even if the allusion points to something true about the novel. For if the invoked myth of annunciation is one way to talk about Oedipa's situation, it still misses the possibility that nothing is coming, that in fact the book will never yield its secret and threatens to be an elaborate joke, or that whatever is coming is neither divine nor demonic. Even Oedipa's sense of two possibilities—a real conspiracy or a paranoid fantasy—the binary options reminding us of the way Pynchon toys with computer mathematics, flip-flopping, ones and zeroes, misses the possibility of the now excluded middle, the "bad shit" that Oedipa had learned (probably incorrectly) "had to be avoided."

But no myth, no multiplication of intellectual possibilities can quite do justice to the energizing experience of sustaining uncertainty. The full significance of Pynchon's fiction is in its styles, in its language, since the language is called upon to sustain the uncertainty it is structured to deny, to imply what cannot be articulated in language. Pynchon denies resolution into myth by wandering among all the available myths, from those of the Greeks to those of modern science, technology, film, comic books, radio. Verbal and mythic virtuosity is not, in Pynchon, show-off obscuring of what might be made clear but, in a way, what the books are about; and like almost everything else in Pynchon's world, virtuosity is both a threat and a possibility.

Pynchon himself understands the connections between his own kind of virtuosity and the historical decadence with which his books are so much preoccupied. That connection is one of the dominant explicit concerns of *V*. The Whole Sick Crew, sinking into "Catatonic Expressionism," values "technique for the sake of technique . . . parodies on what other people had already done" (*V*.). And Victoria Wren "felt that skill or any virtú was a desirable and lovely thing purely for its own sake; and it became more effective the further divorced it was from moral intention" (*V*.). The technology of Pynchon's prose parallels the technology of sex and destruction that runs through the three novels. But the recognition of this connection does not entail retreat from virtuosity, or even a conscious attempt to connect skill with moral intention. The prose requires that we make our way beyond the categories of the virtuous to strain the very limits of virtuosity. Eigenvalue, frightened, imagines the End when all the Proper Nouns have been arranged in all their possible combinations, when the last technical manipulation of finite matter has been accomplished:

"the exhaustion of all possible permutations and combinations was death" (*V.*).
The Lost Ones of the Hereros are "Sold on Suicide" and attempt to renounce
all the things of this world.

But the renunciation can't be complete—never quite. "The trouble with
it is," says Pynchon's narrator, "that by Gödel's theorem there is bound to be
some item around that one has omitted from the list, and such an item is not
easy to think of off the top of one's head, so that what one does most likely
is to go back over the whole thing, meantime correcting mistakes and inevitable repetitions, and putting in new items that will surely have occurred
to one, and—well, it's easy to see that the 'suicide' of the title might have to
be postponed indefinitely!" [*Gravity's Rainbow*; all further references to this text
will be abbreviated *GR*]. The materials of the world seem finite, but there are
always surprises that will not fit the fictional structures language imposes. There
is always "Murphy's Law," crucial, I think, to the unpredictability of Pynchon's
prose: *"when everything has been taken care of, when nothing can go wrong, or
even surprise us . . . something will"* (*GR*).

The virtuosity of Pynchon's prose is a confrontation with the finite, the
determined world. It becomes at times a kind of litany aspiring to the infinite
sequence, implying always that there's more where that comes from. And it
implies that nothing is predictable in the particular, despite Pointsmanesque
conditioning and pervasive paranoia. With such ambitions, the prose must
also be self-consciously amoral, as though the ultimate morality is in a truly
Whitmanesque embrace of everything, of coprophilia, sadism, masochism,
gangbangs and daisy chains, genocide, incest, sodomy, fellatio, transvestitism,
torture, physical decay, murder, pie-throwing, decomposition, toilet bowls.
But not only these. It is a prose that seems almost desperate in the tricks it
will invent to keep from its own finitude, to find some sort of life in the very
decadence and de-animation of which it is a symptom. If, as many critics propose,
Pynchon not only describes but participates in paranoia, it is not the sort of
selective paranoia that sustains itself by screening out the details that don't fit.
It survives in the quest for the surprise or the aberration that nobody ever
noticed before.

The exhaustiveness of Pynchon's catalogues of waste moves him beyond
decadence because he challenges us to resist the entropic reductionism of the
systems we have been trained to impose on them. The question the prose
proposes for us at every moment is whether we are strong enough to accept
the details as they come to us. Pynchon anticipates the risk of such acceptance.
To live exclusively in and with the moment is difficult and dangerous not only
for readers but for characters within the fiction; characters who do this reject
relations to the past or thought of the future, lose the capacity for love.

Moreover, they tend to join in the very betrayals and de-animations, within the culture, that have driven them outside into the fragmentary moment. Benny Profane thus summarizes the effect of his experiences in *V.*: "offhand I'd say I haven't learned a goddamn thing" (*V.*). Tyrone Slothrop manages to unlearn everything his experience offers him, and betrays Bianca as Benny betrays Fina. His personality, his "temporal bandwidth," dwindles to zero as his memory goes with everything but the merest sliver of the present, and, consequently, even that. If we have to choose between facing each moment as it comes to us or making the present moment part of a pattern between past and future, we haven't, in Pynchon's world or ours, much choice.

But choices imply finality and systems, and if the terror for Pynchon's protagonists resides often in their discovering that they must make a choice, their lives remain full of unsystematic surprises. Experience belies the simplification of binary choices into which our logic and our language bind us. The strength thus required is somehow to honor *both* the moment and the memory, to allow almost any possibility while holding on to or creating a genuinely human self. But this, of course, is much easier to say than to feel. Like Oedipa, we must confront the worst possibilities, be driven to choice, if we are to avoid reduction to Tupperware and the plastic prose of a plastic culture; like her we must relearn the past, reimagine the possibilities of connection. Her husband, Mucho, is driven half mad by his power to see in the detritus of used cars whole lives of misery. Everything comes to him as intensely present and, metonymously, as ever more intensely past and future.

But unless we arrive with Oedipa at the point of taking the risk of that intensity, we are doomed to a kind of yo-yo LSD escape, or to enrollment among the members of the Firm. The effect is the same. If we do take the risk, we are driven by Pynchon's art into reconsidering our fundamental assumptions about the way things connect. The discontinuities, the surprises, the refusals of categories, the fake mythologizing—these all confront us with the possibility that art is most valuable, in a culture where power resides among the organizers, when it rejects the tradition of organic coherence we take as a universal standard. Might not that art be best—at this moment, in this place—that constantly pushes toward the possibility of fragmentation? Might it be that not order but anarchy is the most difficult thing to achieve in this culture? The pressure toward anarchy, in a world structured to resist anarchy at any cost, might release us, ironically, into a more humane order, where the human continuities with stones and mountainsides become visible and possible and not plastic reductions to SHROUD and SHOCK or even Imipolex G; where, then paranoia is not a mental disease but a vision, where either/or is not the option and Oedipa's "mixed shit" isn't shitty.

I'm not trying to reduce Pynchon into an "anarchist," though there are anarchists in each novel. The point is to recognize the risk-taking in his art as no mere decadent virtuosity (though it is partly that). There are thermodynamic surprises everywhere, shocks of possibility that can rip us out of our literary critical and human reductionism. The possibilities of an anarchic style and structure seem to me more centrally the "subject" of Pynchon's fictions than even entropy or charisma or the preterite and elect of Calvinism or paranoia. Thematic analysis is inescapable and essential (part of the pain of Pynchon's vision is that he does not pretend that we can escape system or language), just as anarchy is ultimately impossible in our world. But the moments are there beyond any patterns into which they may be made to fit. Pynchon can be so intellectualized that we ignore how deeply, viscerally painful, indeed nauseating, he can be; we ignore, too, what I regard as his most astonishing and overwhelming power, to imagine love out of the wastes of a world full of people helpless to love. These qualities live in the moments, not the patterns. For his characters and, I think, for us, the challenge is to penetrate the moments as they come and then find a way to live with them.

II

There is, obviously, no simple way to characterize Pynchon's prose, and no selection of passages can begin to account for its varieties. It is deliberately unstable, parodic, various, encyclopedic, fragmented (what *are* all those ellipses doing in *Gravity's Rainbow*? why does the narrator, in and later out of Slothrop's consciousness, stutter on "a-and"?). Though capable of traditional decorum, it is characteristically indecorous in its refusal to be locked into a mode. It is perfectly at ease in technical scientific and mathematical analysis, historical reconstruction and documentation, evocative and ominous descriptions, chitchat about films, metaphorical leaps from one area of discourse to another. But perhaps its most disorienting and testing quality is its almost sullen resistance to judging the various horrors it coldly narrates. It is almost impossible to locate the narrator, who refuses to protect us with his own disgust, or with ironies that don't cancel each other out.

One of the earliest completely uncomfortable moments in Pynchon's fiction is Esther's nose job, in the fourth chapter of *V.* Easy enough to talk about admiringly, the passage is physically discomforting and unpleasant, so much so that it requires, from me at least, an act of will to keep reading through it. Insofar as the revulsion is merely from the precision with which the plastic surgery is described, we can say that we have here only a virtuoso extension of the tradition of naturalistic fiction. But the experience is very different from that of naturalism. It is not merely clinical, but clinical and vulgar, and not merely that but clinical vulgarity observed as though it were funny—which it almost becomes. As the two-inch needles are shoved up Esther's nose to administer anesthetics, she discovers pain: "nothing before in her experience had ever hurt quite so much." To be given Esther's pain in such a context is, at least, to be protected by a confirmation of our own sense of a reasonable response to the physical manipulation; it is to make us feel satisfyingly that Esther made a mistake and is learning that she did. But at the same time, she is sexually aroused, in part by Nembutal, in part by the very manipulation that causes the pain. Schoenmaker's assistant, Trench, "Kept chanting, 'Stick it in . . . pull it out . . . stick it in . . . ooh that was good . . . pull it out' " (V.).

The scene becomes a kind of show, but a show in which we—and Esther—are forced to participate. The brutal playfulness is combined with an efficiency complete and routinized, so that the extremity of the experience is reduced both by the play language (" 'That boy,' you expected her to say"), and by the total professional detachment of Schoenmaker and the surgical description. Though we feel the extremity, we are not allowed by the language to come to terms with what we feel: "It was a routine operation; Schoenmaker worked quickly, neither he nor his nurse wasting any motion" (V.).

Schoenmaker's technical efficiency has its correspondence in the clinical textbook language used to describe it. As we begin to be impressed by the particularity and precision, then to marvel at the virtuosity, we begin to participate in the unnatural act Pynchon is forcing us to watch, to shift our focus from the human significance to the technical virtuosity. The moral enormity of the manipulation of a human being becomes routine, and the loss of normal focus is reinforced by the simile—a nontechnical intrusion—in which cutting bone is like cutting hair, and the man in the barber chair is merely a head, though belonging to a body, presumably, that gives high tips. The technical term "undermining," describing the procedure, may have a literary-symbolic resonance, but the voice is neutral, and the moment is wrenched free of the normal social and moral context of action.

For Esther, spectator and object, the experience is sexual and then, madly and convincingly, religious. Her selfhood is lost in her transformation into an object. And the next image is of Schoenmaker looking from the plastic mask of Esther as though she were a rock, for sculpting. "Your hump is now two loose pieces of bone, attached only to the septum," Schoenmaker tells Esther. "We have to cut that through, flush with the other two cuts." And the narrator's voice: "This he did with an angle-bladed pull-knife, cutting down swiftly, completing the phase with some graceful sponge-flourishing." "Graceful" is the

Pynchonian flourish, the word that forces the scene into virtuosity and releases the human subject into objecthood.

We can, of course, place this morally, and Pynchon gives us the context of the whole book to do it. We can connect Esther's rockhood with Mildred Wren's rock, with the rock of Malta itself, and with the progressive de-animation of V. and the society; we can connect Schoenmaker's surgical skill with the skill involved in the slaughter of the Hereros, with the high technology that threatens Profane and all the characters in the book. But to read this as a document of moral outrage is to read in what Pynchon has, to our discomfort, left out. The prose participates in the brutal virtuosity it describes. It recognizes, in part by allowing Schoenmaker to adopt a mock Nazi accent, how much it all has become a subject for cynical comic distance. Esther, after all, has asked for it. And beyond this, Schoenmaker is genuinely enthusiastic about his work, his skill, his flourishes, regardless of their human uses. Pynchon doesn't rescue us from the consequent disorientation. The narrator, like Schoenmaker, has something of the quality of the little boy showing off.

It is important to see how much Pynchon participates in the horrors he describes, how much he knows he participates, and how much, consequently, he must resist simple moral placing that allows him and us to judge, as though we were separate from what we see. Like Esther, we are separated only in that we are drugged; like Schoenmaker, we cannot help admiring the skill that happens to make victims. By giving us no easy position from which we might judge the experience, Pynchon forces us into it beyond morality. The more we admire the prose that can make us feel the pain, the more it implicates us in it. The writer who makes us feel that something quite horrible has been routinized and socially accepted participates in the technical joys and power lust involved in the activity. Moral judgment becomes irrelevant, and the question is whether the prose, in facing the tyranny of its own skills, can release Pynchon or us from them.

The special difficulties and graces of Pynchon's art are early put to the test in the wonderful third chapter of *V.*, "in which Stencil, a quick-change artist, does eight impersonations." The "impersonations" are of narrators who neither know each other nor care very much about the apparent subject of the narrative. Each narrator is one of the preterite, preoccupied with a private life into which the tourists intrude themselves briefly. Since the narrators' stories seem not to be connected, we, as readers, are seduced into piecing together the tourists' story, which looks very much like an exciting Edwardian spy adventure. We teach ourselves to see the continuity of character behind flaking sunburn, suggestive nicknames, blue eyeglasses, fatness. We might say that we become Stencil, or Stencilized, in our attempt to make order out of various fragments.

We may, at first, believe that once we have pieced together the narrative, we have "made sense" of the fiction; but we must soon recognize that in exercising our deductive skills, working on conventional assumptions of continuity and cause and effect, we have been tricked into acting out our own touristic assumptions about the nature of reality. We must understand that narrative tradition itself entails the exercise of a Schoenmakerian skill in rejecting unwanted material and shaping what is wanted. To "make sense" of the narrative we must exclude most of the evidence. We become tourists, like the characters whose fate most absorbs us, and though the natives tell us the story, we read it as though their lives don't matter. Entropy is high: the expenditure of energy and the rejection of material entailed in the reading creates order at great expense. To read the story right, we must come to terms with disorder.

Aïeul, the waiter, watches Goodfellow and Porpentine disappear from his life:

> I will see neither of you again, that's the least I can wish. He fell asleep at last against the wall, made drowsy by the rain, to dream of one Maryam and tonight, and the Arab quarter . . .
>   Low places in the square filled, the usual random sets of criss-crossing concentric circles moved across them. Near eight o'clock, the rain slackened off.

The best we can do if we are to participate in Stencil's preoccupation with V. is reconstruct the story he has obviously already constructed. That is, the fullest exercise of our ingenuity in decoding the narrative from the irrelevancies of the lives of the narrators can only put us where Stencil already is. But Pynchon gives us other options, if we choose to exercise them. We can decide that Maryam, and tonight's meeting with Aïeul, are as important as Porpentine and Goodfellow. We can recognize that the Arab quarter exists beyond the experience of the English characters, beyond the prose that invokes it. We can feel the ominousness of the precise physical details (the low places in the square filled, the raindrops making crisscrossing concentric circles) but take them as the expression of physical necessities rather than as meaning something for the spy adventure. The circles in the puddles can be taken as a figure for the crisscrossing concentric circles of the narrative. But the center, we know, is Stencil, not the natives like Aïeul. Only if we take Stencil's imagination as primary can we accept the circles as figuratively concentric. Otherwise, we must live with randomness.

Randomness, of course, is what neither Stencil nor we can live with.

Thus, we read the "irrelevant" details thematically, make them relevant not to the particular passage, but to the themes of the novel as a whole. There is comfort even in recognizing that the theme of tourism is important everywhere in *V.*, ironically, however, that theme justifies our ignoring Aïeul once we understand that he is there as a sign of the way tourists ignore the real life of the country, of the way empire exploits and denies the reality of what is natively there. Suppose we are left, however, with the reality of Aïeul and Maryam, whom we will never see, or with the rain flooding the Place Mohammed Ali. Suppose we refuse to connect the eight different narratives. Suppose they are juxtaposed only in Stencil's imagination. Do we know how to honor what we see but do not know?

Pynchon's prose works to make us see and to know, to know by seeing intensely, excessively. The prose has a passion for the lost and dispossessed, the preterite, as *Gravity's Rainbow* has retaught us to call them. It entails not placing but recognition; nothing is mean enough not to be recorded, everything matters. The traditions of nineteenth-century realism implied that the ordinary was latent with the extraordinary; in the romantic program of the realists, the ordinary is endowed with wonder. Ironically, Pynchon, in rejecting the realist tradition, carries out in his prose the extreme of the realist vision, allowing the ordinary, the base, the obscene to threaten us with significances we do not, perhaps need not, understand.

Pynchon has been criticized for not creating "real" characters and, especially, for creating loveless worlds. But traditional character is an imagination of order and structure that belies the pervasiveness of change, variety, aimlessness, waste. Character, in traditional fiction, is the clearest emblem of the elect—dominating and controlling the action of the world. And Pynchon creates character by imagining it as participating in the energies of the world created around it. He mocks (especially in the names) and uses the notions of character fiction has inherited, but as Fausto Maijstral insists, even the self is an invention.

Character is an abstraction that allows us to see through the moment, not to experience it. Explanation of actions in terms of motives, psychoanalysis, instincts, gets us off the hook of responsibility to each lived moment. The self is unintelligible as a stable "thing," except when it has *become* a thing; and it must be seen in relationship, or in the failure of relationship. The prose, in any case, gives us the experience of *being* before (if ever) it tries to explain it. Profane, looking into the desolation of the winter seascape "which meant nothing more than the turbulence of the screws or the snow-hiss on the water," needs no analysis. Our capacity to accept such moments depends on our capacity to resist the coherences of narrative or even of rational expectation. We enter Pynchon's moments, as Oedipa does, discovering new and terrifying realities behind the conventions of reality—that is, of selection and election—we have been trained to believe in.

One powerful and characteristic example of such a moment comes in Oedipa's encounter with the ruined old man who had left his wife in Fresno: "When [Oedipa] was three steps from him the hands flew apart and his wrecked face, and the terror of eyes gloried in burst veins, stopped her" (*Lot 49*). She imagines him as one of the lost and forgotten, living in a flop house:

> What voices overheard, flinders of luminescent gods glimpsed among the wallpaper's stained foliage, candlestubs lit to rotate in the air over him, prefiguring the cigarette he or a friend must fall asleep someday smoking, thus to end among flaming, secret salts held all those years by the insatiable stuffing of a mattress that could keep vestiges of every nightmare sweat, helpless overflowing bladder, viciously, tearfully consummated wet dream, like the memory bank to a computer of the lost? She was overcome all at once by a need to touch him, as if she could not believe in him, or would not remember him, without it. Exhausted, hardly knowing what she was doing, she came the last three steps and sat, took the man in her arms, actually held him, gazing out of her smudged eyes down the stairs, back into the morning. She felt wetness against her breast and saw that he was crying again. He hardly breathed but tears came as if being pumped. "I can't help," she whispered, rocking him, "I can't help." It was already too many miles from Fresno.
>
> (*Lot 49*)

Entering such a moment entails believing in the reality that nothing has taught Oedipa, or us, to see. The wreck with his wife in Fresno is recorded only in an insatiable mattress that absorbs the secret salts of the lost. Oedipa is discovering America, feeling the tenuousness of the discovery, the possibilities of despair, and the further possibility that despair is a way to avoid the responsibilities of caring.

Of course, there are more possibilities, but there remains also the inescapable experience of Oedipa and the old man. The language, whatever else it is, can only be an expression of a passionate concern, every precisely imagined detail intimating luminescent gods beyond, sad and lost lives within. It is merely a convention, and a disastrous convention within and outside of fiction, that we can care only for what we know well. The ruined old man makes only a brief appearance in *The Crying of Lot 49*. Oedipa risks caring for him.

By all this I only mean that in Pynchon's work I am far more disposed to trust the moments than any ideas I might invent to account for them. Good critics can and do assume that Pynchon is (a) paranoid or (b) mocking the traditional structures that imply paranoia; that he is (a) asserting the inevitable heat-death of the world and the futility of resisting it, even in its local manifestations, or (b) suggesting that life, in its extraordinary capacity to produce surprises, constantly resists the heat-death, as must we all; that there is nothing to be done, or that there is everything to be done; that he is on the side of the elect, or that he is on the side of preterite; that he is asserting disorder, or that he is implying some kind of transcendent order; that choices are binary or multiple. I keep thinking that I know what I believe on these matters, and then keep discovering that I don't. Rereading Pynchon I find it surprisingly difficult to account for particular passages in particular places, and yet a condition of their power that they be difficult to account for. My uncomfortable feeling is that not knowing is an important qualification for participating imaginatively in his fictions. Only by surrendering our demands for order can we be released into the terror of the moment, as Oedipa is released, and as she grows.

III

And what does it mean, in Pynchon, to penetrate the moment?

Leni Pökler tries it, as a matter of life and death. Somehow, however, her husband Franz has a "way of removing all the excitement from things with a few words" (*GR*), and for him this is instinctive. The removal of excitement is the removal of risk and is connected with the fact that, as Leni says, Franz is "the cause-and-effect man." Words that embody the imagination, causal explanation, participate in the large fictionalizing of experience that Walter Rathenau, speaking from the other side, calls "secular history," "a diversionary tactic" (*GR*). Secular history in Pynchon is, I think, the faithless construction of defenses that, as they justify by explanation the power of the empowered, participate in the plasticizing of life and death.

To get into the moment and experience it, it is necessary to find a way to withdraw from the secular diversions of language. Leni, of course, has no language to explain herself to Franz, nor, I think, does Pynchon. Both of them try very hard. Leni, like Pynchon, invokes the language of calculus, of "Δt approaching zero," but is rebuked by Franz: "Not the same, Leni" (*GR*). Calculus is used here as a metaphor, and Leni is putting it to uses for which it is not intended. Franz is thus not persuaded, and removes the excitement from things. Pynchon tries to put it back.

Here is how he describes the movement into the moment that Leni requires. Against Franz's need for "security," his language full of the fear of "consequences" that keeps us all from resisting, we have Leni:

> She tried to explain to him about the level you reach, with both
> feet in, when you lose your fear, you lose it all, you've penetrated
> the moment, slipping perfectly into its grooves, metal-gray but
> soft as latex, and now the figures are dancing, each pre-choreog-
> raphed exactly where it is, the flash of knees under pearl-colored
> frock as the girl in the babushka stoops to pick up a cobble, the
> man in the black suitcoat and brown sleeveless sweater grabbed
> by policeman one on either arm, trying to keep his head up, show-
> ing his teeth, the older liberal in the dirty beige overcoat, stepping
> back to avoid a careening demonstrator, looking back across his
> lapel how-dare-you or look-out-not-*me*, his eyeglasses filled with
> the glare of the winter sky. There is the moment, and its possibilities.

The central implicit image of the street demonstration is exactly right for the
attempt to describe the condition of passing from spectator to actor, from user
of words to thrower of stones. The risk is clear for any liberal reading as for
the liberal with the glare of the winter sky on his glasses (used, no doubt, for
much reading, and reflecting not absorbing experience). The options—active
(tossing the cobble), passive (resisting when captured and overwhelmed), or
withdrawal (seeing the human demonstrator in the language of "careening"
matter)—are imagined with the particularity that always offers more than can
be systematized (the flash of knees, the babushka, the black suitcoat and sleeveless
sweater, the dirty beige overcoat). The moment, however systematized our
reading of it, suggests almost infinite possibilities and particularities, and that
any verbal efforts to locate it will pass over far more than can be chosen.

This is one of those passages that resists the easy placing it tempts us to
make. One feels the urgency, even the moral power, of Leni's willingness to
lose her fear and penetrate the moment. But the moment remains obscure—
why here, in the presence of such courage and energy to freedom, is the
moment imagined as a kind of long-playing record? You slip "perfectly into
its grooves, metal-gray but soft as latex," and the dancing figures are "pre-
choreographed." Are we here, in the moment of freedom and risk, when the
life of the street penetrates the hothouse of cause-and-effect history and suburban security, back in some paranoid fantasy, unreleased even as we act
and choose?

Leni's is an act of faith because the primary restraining fact is the terror
of what lies behind the order of secular history. "What if there's violence?"
is always Franz's question when Leni tries to induce him to act. But the "if"
in Pynchon's world is an absurdity: all of secular history is an act of violence,

the transforming of life into waste. The possible act is, simply, acceptance of the moment on its own terms, finding one's own place, two feet in the water, moving, then, with the current and the spinning of the earth itself. But if my language makes it sound easy, Pynchon's does not. Leni hates the "street," which "reaches in, makes itself felt everywhere." "Rest" is impossible.

Part of the difficulty of Pynchon's fiction and of the prose from moment to moment is, I think, that he is constantly engaged in the struggle to make language, a kind of cause-and-effect hothouse constructed to resist the disorder of the street, lead us into the street, into the moment. And when we get there we may find a more terrifying order. But the risk begins in the terrifying break from Franz's kind of order. We have seen the terror in Oedipa Maas's story, and, as in that story, the release contains no assurance but the discovery of the lost. Whatever the reality, Tristero or paranoia, Slothrop's paranoia or the dissolution of antiparanoia, "personal identity" or "impersonal salvation," as Mondaugen sees the possibilities (GR) – each version is frightening and morally expensive.

The language describing Leni's attempt to penetrate the moment echoes the language describing the "anarchist miracle" of *The Crying of Lot 49*. In one of those wonderfully screwy Pynchonian inventions that manage to bear heavy weight despite apparent ridiculousness, Oedipa finds herself in the middle of a left-wing convention of deaf-mutes. She is dragged into a dance "by a handsome young man in a Harris tweed coat and waltzed round and round, through the rustling, shuffling hush, under a great unlit chandelier" (*Lot 49*). Playing with sound as he plays with words, Pynchon somehow reinforces the absurdity and counters it. All those assonating, dull "u's," the softening "n's," the deliberate quiet sibilance of "rustling" and "shuffling" help make perfect the craziness of the "unlit chandelier," dull and sibilant and literally senseless. Vision without light, sound without noise, movement without direction, and the joke is translated, though remaining darkly funny, into something more than a little frightening:

> Each couple on the floor danced whatever was in the fellow's head: tango, two-step, bossa nova, slop. But how long, Oedipa thought, could it go on before collisions became a serious hindrance? There would have to be collisions. The only alternative was some unthinkable order in music, many rhythms, all keys at once, a choreography in which each couple meshed easy, predestined. Something they all heard with an extra sense atrophied in herself. She followed her partner's lead, limp in the young mute's clasp, waiting for the collisions to begin. But none came. She was danced for half an hour

before, by mysterious consensus, everybody took a break, without having felt any touch but the touch of her partner. Jesús Arrabal
would have called it an anarchist miracle. Oedipa, with no name
for it, was only demoralized. She curtsied and fled.

(Lot 49)

All the normal empirical assurances are gone, and yet instead of chaos and
disorder there seems to be a higher order.

It remains problematical for me how seriously we are to take the implicit
otherworldliness, perhaps religiosity, of Pynchon's world. Oedipa's curtsy is
too wonderfully funny, and yet too precisely appropriate to be unambiguous.
Neither the deaf-mute's waltz nor Walter Rathenau's discussion from the
other side can be taken merely as a joke. Trying to explain why cause-and-
effect thinking won't work, Leni says, "not cause. It all goes together. Parallel,
not series. Metaphor. Signs and symptoms. Mapping on to different coordinate
systems, I don't know" *(GR)*. But whether the language is out of geometry,
mathematics, literature, none of it is equal to the experienced reality, which
takes metaphorical, comic and dramatic shape in Oedipa's dance and curtsy.

Leni's sense of the "pre-choreographed" experience of the moment echoes
Oedipa's overwhelming feeling of "a choreography in which each couple meshed
easy, predestined." Oedipa, dragged into the moment where Leni, as it were,
leaped in, is demoralized by this sense of mysterious order. It is as though
anarchy does not free Oedipa—she will not allow herself to be freed—from
the rigidly determined structure of her life. She is afraid of the freedom, terrified by the possibility that it might work, that by admitting the disorder of
the street she will be released from the fake order of the suburban hothouse.

Gravity's Rainbow, however is built as Leni's world is—parallel, not series,
metaphor, signs and symptoms, mapping on to different coordinate systems.
Leni dares the possibility of mysterious orders, and the anarchy and cacophony
of the narratives and fragments of *Gravity's Rainbow* may well be an anarchist
miracle of the kind Arrabal describes. But Oedipa approaches the language
of *Gravity's Rainbow* just before she returns to the dance in the hotel. Watching the old man in a fit of delirium tremens, she connects the DT's with Leni's
kind of dt, evoked in her attempt to describe penetrating the moment:

"dt," God help this old tattooed man, meant also a time differential, a vanishingly small instant in which change had to be confronted at last for what it was, where it could no longer disguise
itself as something innocuous like an average rate; where velocity
dwelled in the projectile though the projectile be frozen in midflight, where death dwelled in the cell though the cell be looked

in on at its most quick. She knew that the sailor had seen worlds no other man had seen if only because there was that high magic to low puns, because DT's must give access to dt's of spectra beyond the known sun, music made purely of Antarctic loneliness and fright.

(*Lot 49*)

Moments later she will be dancing with people who seem to hear that music. A book before, Pynchon had evoked that Antarctic loneliness for old Hugh Godolphin. A book later, Pynchon confronts the change "where velocity dwelled in the projectile" though the projectile is frozen over the heads of the audience in the Orpheus theater in L.A. In all these cases there is a connection among the terror of choice, and the possibility of change that will undermine or destroy the world we know, and the terror of a reality other than that we believe in. They all inhere in the vanishingly small instant that we must risk. The dt's, Vheissu, the rocket are all metaphors for the moment—"a thrust at truth and a lie" (*Lot 49*).

Pynchon's language risks the lie, sustains the faith (like Arrabal's in another world) of the high magic in low puns. Pynchon also seems to understand, as in Leni's failure to make the moment present to Franz (that, we shall see, is possible only through risk and surrender, not through persuasion), as in Oedipa's recognition that "I can't help," that language may suggest the possibilities it cannot present, may bring us within sight of "the pure light of zero" (*GR*). This is only possible if language does not protect us with the comfort of its structure, if the word can somehow put us in the presence of "whatever it is the word is there, buffering, to protect us from" (*Lot 49*).

The anarchists in the three novels work to get beyond words, and beyond the labyrinths words construct. The Gaucho, in *V.*, prefers to use a bomb than to assist in the absurdly elaborate, labyrinthine plans to steal the Botticelli. Arrabal believes in some spontaneous revolution, "automatic as the body itself" (*Lot 49*). And most explicitly, Squalidozzi (can we take him seriously with such a squalid name?), also Argentinian, espouses spontaneity and immediacy against the Argentinian, Borgesian need for building labyrinths. As he responds instinctively—resisting his own impulse to speculate on Argentina and anarchism—to Slothrop's hunger, Squalidozzi finds for Slothrop sausage and fondue before going on. And only then does he tell Slothrop: "Beneath the city streets, the warrens of rooms and corridors, the fences and the networks of steel track, the Argentine heart, in its perversity and guilt, longs for a return to that first unscribbled serenity . . . that anarchic oneness of pampas and sky . . ." (*GR*). Anarchy is the quest for a preverbal directness of experience, for something like Leni's absorption—"both feet in"—in the moment. But, Squalidozzi says, such moments, such "oneness," can only come, now, from "extraordinary times" (*GR*). Squalidozzi sees the war, "this incredible War," as a time when things might be "wiped clean" (*GR*). In this anarchist vision, close, I think, to the mood of the whole labyrinthine book opposing labyrinths, the war and the rocket become a kind of last chance to penetrate to a new reality, to break through to an unscribbled, a wordless moment.

Anarchy becomes the kind of aesthetic and political program of these novels, a risk whose possibilities Pynchon doesn't know, though he tries them out on different coordinate systems, metaphors, signs. And we come back to the risk of Leni's moment. The narrative of Franz's discovery of the need to enter the moment enacts as miraculously as anything in *Gravity's Rainbow* the wonders, the risks, the achievements of Pynchon's prose and brings us to the edge of silence, the shuffling dance under unlit chandeliers.

Franz's refusal to risk what Leni risks keeps him in the intellectual hothouse of his life. Only his daughter Ilse's presence threatens to break that vacuum "in one strong rush of love" (*GR*). But before Ilse can bring Franz back to the streets he had rejected with Leni, Franz "put as much labyrinth as required between himself and the inconvenience of caring" (*GR*). Intellectual hackwork—minor contributions to the technology of the rocket—is what consumes Franz's time and concern. Engineering skill protects him from knowing what goes on in the prison camp Dora, just behind the walls where he worked. The violation of Pökler's vacuum is the intrusion of that other world, like the world of the wrecked old man Oedipa encounters, into the world of technology and cause and effect. Understanding at last that his daughter has been in Dora, "beaten, perhaps violated," Franz manages at last to risk the loss of his security. Franz's penetration of the moment becomes an act of love, a wordless engagement with the hitherto invisible and silent lost ones, almost unbearable because, as for Oedipa, there is nothing Franz can do except risk and love.

The cleverness, the labyrinthine obscurities, the obscenities are here extended into what I need to call high seriousness, despite all the Pynchonian tricks to short-circuit solemnities. The passage is evidence that all of those tricks are part of Pynchon's intense vision of the high magic of lowness, of what happens when we suddenly learn to see what lies behind the wall, within the threatening moment:

> The odors of shit, death, sweat, sickness, mildew, piss, the breathing of Dora, wrapped him as he crept in staring at the naked corpses being carried out now that America was so close, to be stacked in front of the crematoriums, the men's penises hanging, their toes clustering white and round as pearls . . . each face so perfect, so

individual, the lips stretched back into death-grins, a whole silent
audience caught at the punch line of the joke . . . and the living,
stacked ten to a straw mattress, the weakly crying, coughing,
losers. . . . All his vacuums, his labyrinths, had been the other side
of this. While he lived, and drew marks on paper, this invisible
kingdom had kept on, in the darkness outside . . . all this
time. . . . Pökler vomited. He cried some. The walls did not dissolve—no prison wall ever did, not from tears, not at this finding,
on every pallet, in every cell, that the faces are ones he knows after
all, and holds dear as himself, and cannot, then, let them return
to that silence. . . . But what can he ever do about it? How can
he ever keep them? Impotence, mirror-rotation of sorrow, works
him terribly as runaway heart-beating, and with hardly any chances
left him for good rage, or for turning. . . .

Where it was darkest and smelled worst, Pökler found a woman
lying, a random woman. He sat for half an hour holding her bone
hand. She was breathing. Before he left, he took off his gold wedding
ring and put it on the woman's thin finger, curling her hand to
keep it from sliding off. If she lived, the ring would be good for
a few meals, or a blanket, or a night indoors, or a ride home.

(GR)

IV

Such a Pynchonian moment is of the sort that Profane and Slothrop
approach and retreat from. The wedding with randomness, the vision of the
other side is, like the crossing of the Δt into the pure zero, an act of caring,
of connection. The danger, of course, is that we will end with the "losers,"
among the waste. Another danger is the dissolution of self, the entering of
the moment so completely that all connections before and after are lost.
Unanchored to a past which had been invented and programmed for him,
increasingly losing his connection with a future that was only rocket, Slothrop
finds no way to make love a part of his life beyond that instant when it
happens. He cannot hold both the moment and the memory. Slothrop's orgasm
with Bianca comes in the shape of a rocket; like a rocket explodes, destroys, ends.

Of course, there is caring in Slothrop. He goes over to the preterite
without willing it, and he seeks a freedom that Pointsman's world cannot
allow. But the freedom is only negative, defined against the imprisonment of
Pavlovian, cause-and-effect science and fiction. Yet before he dissolves into

his world, Slothrop has a moment rather like Squalidozzi's "anarchic oneness of pampas and sky." The precariousness of such moments is enacted in
Slothrop's disappearance: the risk and the ambiguities remain. If Slothrop is
a failure, as, in his betrayal of Bianca, we see him to be, it is nevertheless
wrong to read past the richness and sense of possibility in the language of
Slothrop's last moment.

Slothrop, we are told, becomes a "crossroad." He half remembers from
his youth one of those catalogues of waste, struggling not to pass over anything
in the infinite series of the passed over: "rusted beer cans, rubbers yellow with
preterite seed, Kleenex wadded to brain shapes hiding preterite snot, preterite
tears, newspapers, broken glass, pieces of automobile" (*GR*). Slothrop is not
quite remembering the fragments of his past: "instructing him, dunce and
drifter, in ways deeper than he can explain, have been faces of children out
the train windows, two bars of dance music somewhere, in some other street
at night, needles and branches of a pine tree shaken clear and luminous against
night clouds . . ." (*GR*). His life has been full of barely apprehended moments
latent with the richness of other worlds. And so, in his last moment, he
achieves the anarchist ideal:

> and now, in the Zone, later in the day he became a crossroad, after
> a heavy rain he doesn't recall, Slothrop sees a very thick rainbow
> here, a stout rainbow cock driven down out of pubic clouds into
> Earth, green wet valleyed Earth, and his chest fills and he stands
> crying, not a thing in his head, just feeling natural.

It is difficult to mistake this language for the language of failure or of impending doom. Freed to be "simply here, simply alive," as Webley Silvernail, "guest
star," wishes despairingly we all might be, Slothrop cannot survive on the
terms of Pointsman's or Blicero's world. The moment becomes the enactment
of the anarchic visionary ideal that animates much of Pynchon's fictions.

Since it is an ideal it must, in Pynchon's world, dissolve, but if we are
willing to risk it, there may be at the center of each preterite moment a stout
rainbow cock and a wet valleyed earth. It is commonplace now to talk of
Pynchon as our poet of death, but like everything else we might invent to
say about him—perhaps more so—it is a falsification. Certainly, he rubs our
faces unsparingly in shit, as though we were all General Puddings. That,
however, is the price of attempting to articulate the inarticulable, of attempting to make present to us what our language will not let us see, of attempting
to disorient us so much that we will risk what each moment, unpenetrated,
hides from us. There are, amid the infinite possibilities that Pynchon's virtuosity
begins to suggest to us, alternatives to the way we currently imagine our lives.

Pynchon's world is prepolitical; it implies that every political program is, at best, one more warren in the labyrinths we build between us and the moments, the caring, we ignore. It is not, however, antipolitical. Like Leni Pökler, we must risk action and loss by penetrating the moment; it would be good if we could do it as Pynchon does, terrified but lovingly, for the risk is the possibility.

CATHARINE R. STIMPSON

Pre-Apocalyptic Atavism:
Thomas Pynchon's Early Fiction

The place of women in apocalyptic literature is problematic. They can be
ignored. They can act in the eschatological drama. As they do in *Revelation*,
they can serve as polarized symbols of the corrupt and the pure, the Whore
of Babylon and the Bride of Christ. The pressure of last things can even crush
sexual distinctions. As some paranoids find the categories of female/male
trivial in comparison to the grand precision of I/Them or Us/Them, so the
apocalyptic can abandon female/male for Elect/Preterite. Yet the pre-apocalyptic
fiction of Thomas Pynchon, before the splendid *Gravity's Rainbow*, grants a
privileged place to women. They are actors and symbols. Their characteriza-
tion—at once generous and warped, shrewd and regressive—provokes a mixture
of contempt for contemporary sexuality and reverence for an atavistic mode.

To restate the orthodox, Pynchon sets the angels of possibility dancing
on the pincushion of plot. Applauding the complex, he delights in asking if
similar events are coincidences, correspondences, or clues to a conspiracy. *The
Crying of Lot 49* mourns the contraction of America from a land of diversity
to one of binary choice. Yet, the early fiction, the first pages of the atlas of
Pynchon's alternate universe, offers simplicities as plain as a needle's point.
Among them is a relentless lament for the West. Its decline from the decadent
through the mechanical and inanimate to annihilation compels his imagination.
Perhaps all secular systems—"galaxy, engine, human being, culture, whatever"—
wear out. They are subject to the growing randomness and terminal uniformity
of entropy. The West has urged the process along. Politically, it has bred racist
colonial empires. It has planted not seeds of life, but the flag. Pynchon uses

From *Mindful Pleasures: Essays on Thomas Pynchon.* © 1976 by George Levine and David Leverenz.
Little, Brown, & Co., 1976.

and inverts sexual metaphors to picture the civilization he ferociously, inventively deplores. The coast of Deutsch-Südwestafrika is an "ash plain impregnated with a killer sea." The rituals and romances of the West reflect a pervasive belief that any sexuality, be it natural, human, or divine, is intertwined with death. Pynchon has taken up the burden of T. S. Eliot's lines:

> Where is the wisdom we have lost in knowledge?
> Where is the knowledge we have lost in information?
> The cycles of Heaven in twenty centuries
> Bring us farther from GOD and nearer to the Dust.

Another simplicity is Pynchon's sexual conservatism, which pervades the early fiction and which reveals itself in the conventional conviction that women, both in sacred and in secular realms, ought to be lovers and mothers. The womb is a gift to life and defiance of death. Such mediation between man and nature is a source of prestige and power. Like Mailer, Pynchon endorses a sexuality that links itself to reproduction. So doing, it may symbolize fertility itself. Part of his hostility towards homosexuality and such phenomena as sexual cross-dressing derives from the fact that they sever the libido from conception. They are barren in terms of the future of the race.

Healthy male sexuality must, at the least, promise fertility. Raunchy Pig Bodine romps towards legendary status, his raw energy that of a satyr in sailor suit. Pigs, Robert Graves says, were sacred to the Moon-goddess. Among the vilest characters in *V.* is the German Foppl. A savage warrior, then a savage settler in Südwestafrika, he personifies virility run wild towards sterility. Domineering, sadistic, violent, he delights in the rape of the living and dead. Sun to V.'s moon, he is the male counterpart to her chillier excesses. Though seen as indirectly as she is, through the accounts of others, he seems to take his joy in brutality. Pynchon, however, is no feminist. In his daisy chain of victimization, a sour adaption of a slang phrase for group sex, women are as apt to hurt men and men women. Both sexes wield the whip.

A healthy female sexuality is a primary agent of biological life. Goddesses offer supernatural aid and mythological support. A theme of *V.* is imagining what a goddess ought to be. Because he often hedges the context in which they appear, I am wary of Pynchon's explicit literary allusions. He warns readers not to confuse texts with life, one text with another, Pynchon with a predecessor. Nevertheless, even seen cautiously, Pynchon seems to use Robert Graves's *White Goddess* to help fashion a fit divinity. He mentions Graves, in one of his problematic passages, which is, on a superficial level, a description of Herbert Stencil. At the same time, Pynchon refers to J. G.

Frazer, whose anthropology appears to have provided some of the raw material about Mediterranean culture for *V.*

> He would dream perhaps once a week that it had all been a dream, and that now he'd awakened to discover the pursuit of V. was merely a scholarly quest after all, an adventure of the mind, in the tradition of *The Golden Bough* or *The White Goddess.*
>
> (*V.*)

For Graves, the White Goddess both generates life and inspires culture. He writes:

> [T]he language of poetic myth anciently current in Mediterranean and Northern Europe was a magical language bound up with popular religious ceremonies in honour of the Moon-goddess, or Muse. . . . [T]his remains the language of true poetry. . . . [T]he Moon-goddess inspired [poetic myths] and . . . demanded that man should pay woman spiritual and sexual homage . . .man's love was properly directed towards women. . . .Moira, Ilithyia and Callone—Death, Birth and Beauty—formed a triad of Goddesses who presided over all acts of generation whatsoever: physical, spiritual or intellectual.

To Graves, Pynchon adds a notion about goddesses that he derives from Henry Adams. (Both Stencil and Callisto in "Entropy" model themselves on Adams.) At the Great Exposition in Paris in 1900, wary of his subjectivity, Adams concludes:

> The woman had once been supreme; in France she still seemed potent, not merely as a sentiment, but as a force. Why was she unknown in America? . . . The trait was notorious, and often humorous, but any one brought up among Puritans knew sex was sin. In any previous age, sex was strength. Neither art nor beauty was needed. Every one, even among Puritans, knew that neither Diana of the Ephesians nor any of the Oriental goddesses was worshipped for her beauty. She was goddess because of her force; she was the animated dynamo; she was reproduction—the greatest and most mysterious of all energies; all she needed was to be fecund. . . . [S]ymbol or energy, the Virgin had acted as the greatest force the Western world ever felt, and had drawn man's activities to herself more strongly that any other power, natural or supernatural, had ever done.
>
> [*The Education of Henry Adams*]

If the two theologies, as it were, fail to cohere fully, they agree that the European past worshipped physical fertility; that the present may blaspheme.

V. bleakly follows Adams to name the American divinity: the machine. Fat Benny Profane ought to recognize a life-enhancing goddess. His pig eyes are set in "pig-pouches." However, in fantasy, his perfect woman is a robot:

> Someday, please God, there would be an all-electronic woman. Maybe her name would be Violet. Any problems with her, you could look it up in the maintenance manual. Module concept: fingers' weight, heart's temperature, mouth's size out of tolerance? Remove and replace, was all.

Benny is usually dumb about women, an intellectual sluggishness that fails to bar him from generalizations about them. As bleakly, *V.* refuses to follow Adams and Graves to name explicitly the European divinity. Instead, the novel names and blames her antithesis, the polymorphous and polymorphously perverse V. If she is fecund, she spawns the forces of antilife. As Moon-goddess, she retains only the power to destroy. She is Moria, without Ilithyia and Callone to balance her.

The symbol "V" obviously has many connotations. It can refer to victory; to the stain on a plate a German barmaid is washing in a beer hall in Egypt; to two vector lines (the writers and the twentieth century?) colliding to place vessels on a white, blank page; to Vheissu, a region that symbolizes gaudy glamour dressing a void; to the dominant chord on the major scale. Picturing female sexuality, it evokes the names of Venus and of the Virgin, each of whom, in her way, manifests it. "V" must also be read in conjunction with the letters "N," a double "V," and "M" and"W," each a triple "V." Think, for example, of "*V*egetation *M*yth." In single, double, or trinitarian form, the letter, the words it initiates, and the meanings of the words embody diametrically opposed values. They illustrate the "flip/flop" McClintic Sphere describes. Malta is the womb of the writer (often sententious) Maijstral; the tomb of the Bad Priest.

To trace Stencil tracing V. is to watch the twentieth-century West trying to grasp its antidivinity. His search inverts older, richer mythologies. He is a male Isis hoping to recover parts of the dismembered Osiris. Stencil is also the battered child of the century seeking its parents. The father is weak. His legacy is some facts, some friends, which the son may use but not redeem. The mother is vicious, an adulteress who has abandoned him at birth. The son is sterile. His "seeds" are dossiers, the compilation of which barely keeps him alive. Possibly mad, certainly neurotic, he is the fearful archivist of the period before the apocalypse.

V. first appears as Victoria Wren in Egypt in 1898. Her name is that of England's queen, an empire's goddess and symbolic mother. She wears an ivory comb, on which five crucified English soliders are carved. The comb connects her to the oriental goddess Kali, who both succours and devours. (Many Tibetans saw Queen Victoria as Kali's incarnation.) Victoria, as V. figures do, succours only pain. Her sexual loyalties are dubious, her conspiratorial ploys enigmatic. Accompanying the pretty Victoria is her ugly sister Mildred. Few children appear in Pynchon's early fiction, but when they do, their presence signals the possibility of grace. Lovers of children, like lovers of nature, treasure the animate. Though Mildred is plain, she is good. The two sisters symbolize the terrible split between beauty and humanity. Bongo-Shaftesbury, the wired man, repels the child. She also cherishes a rock, which foreshadows Malta, the rocky womb that will bring forth a spirit of survival and workable myth.

That a Victoria will dominate V., while a Mildred disappears, is a clue to the moral that waits, beastlike, at the heart of the labyrinth of story. Victoria will appear as Veronica the Rat; Vera Meroving; Veronica Manganese, and as the Bad Priest of Malta. As she changes, those features that betray the benign goddess will grow. Her body will become more and more opulently mechanical. At her machinelike worst, she will parody the dynamo Americans worship. Her costume will become more and more masculine, not a sign of freedom, but of decline. Her politics will become increasingly reactionary. Her sadism will become both rawer and more refined. If good women in Pynchon use fingernails to stimulate male lovers and to express the pleasure of orgasm, V. rakes them over male flesh. Sometimes a V. will be openly cruel. In Foppl's home in Africa, her surrogate sister sings her theme song. Hedwig Vogelsang's charming lyric also exemplifies Pynchon's ability to adapt the devices of musical comedy to fiction.

> Love's a lash,
> Kisses gall the tongue, harrow the heart;
> Caresses tease
> Cankered tissue apart.

V. delights not in simple sadistic activity but in any destructive hurly-burly of the will. Pynchon's characters dabble with the notion, which they ascribe to Machiavelli, that human actions, the aggregate of which is history, are the result of the interplay of two forces: virtú and *fortuna*, will and fate. V., vain enough to wish to play goddess of fortune, relishes the exercise of an amoral virtú as well. However, V. can be a voyeur. In Florence, during a political riot:

> She saw a rioter . . . being bayoneted again and again. . . . She stood . . . still . . .; her face betrayed no emotion. It was as if she saw herself embodying a feminine principle, acting as complement to all this bursting, explosive male energy. Inviolate and calm, she watched the spasms of wounded bodies, the fair of violent death, framed and staged, it seemed, for her alone in that tiny square. From her hair the heads of five crucified also looked on, no more expressive than she.

Finally, V.'s Catholicism will become more pronounced. "Meroving" echoes the Merovingians, rulers of part of France who were Catholic converts. Pynchon treats Catholicism with some distaste. It harms men because it tempts them towards manipulation. Offering themselves as priests of salvation, they actually seek control. Catholicism harms women because it urges them to conceptualize and to live out a tension between the natural and the supernatural; to fear the natural and to prefer the supernatural; to discharge sexuality, if they must, in a falsely romanticized motherhood. The Church tells women they can be whores or saints or earthly mothers. Pynchon says each woman can be all three. V.'s religiosity has two benefits for her: a "seed-time" for the narcissistic self-dramatization in which she expertly indulges; a chance to sublimate sexuality into role-playing as the Bride of Christ, to transform energy into repressed lasciviousness.

The section about V. in love crystallizes her nastiness. To measure her best is, in a dialectical judgment, to measure her worst. The style reflects Pynchon's ability to write about that which he dislikes, a paradox of the rhetoric of *contemptus mundi*. The site of V.'s passion is Paris during an explosion of cultural modernism, a mark of Pynchon's distrust of the street of his century. V. loves a fifteen-year-old dancer, Mélanie l'Heuremaudit (cursed hour). *Her* last romance has been with her father. Though lesbianism is an entry in Pynchon's edition of *The Decline and Fall of the West*, he finds it less appalling than the context in which it occurs. When Mehemet, a gabby Mediterranean sailor, tells Sidney Stencil about sapphism in a Turkish harem, the tale is meant to be cute.

For V. and Mélanie are narcissists, substituting self for others as objects of love, and fetishists, substituting things for persons as objects of love. Male characters also have fetishes. Mantissa (half-weight, a trivial addition) adores Botticelli's Venus enough to steal it. But female fetishism is more sinister, if only because Pynchon assigns women that normative task of acting out and symbolizing natural fertility. The trinity—V., Mélanie, Mélanie's image—mocks the Moon-goddess trinity—birth, death, and beauty. Mélanie's physical death, a probably suicidal impalement on a sharp pole as she dances, mirrors the Western nexus of sex, art, and fatality. V.'s own death is equally appropriate. She does not wish it. Weakly, she asks a group of children on Malta to help, not to torment her. However, the spargefication she endures at their hands, in her guise as Bad Priest, is a result of forces she has cheered. If Germans were not bombing Malta, there would be no packs of bestial children roaming through its ruins.

The "Epilogue" of V. is a last reminder of the penalties that may follow if the goddesses of fecundity are abandoned. In June 1919, Sidney Stencil is leaving Malta. The boat that has brought him is taking him away, another connection between a beginning and an end. A powerful waterspout suddenly appears. It is analogous to the earthquake and tidal wave of 9 July 1956 that killed forty-three persons who had "run . . . afoul of the inanimate" in the Aegean. It lasts long enough

> to lift the xebec fifty feet, whirling and creaking, Astarte's throat naked to the cloudless weather, and slam it down again into a piece of the Mediterranean whose subsequent surface phenomena— whitecaps, kelp islands, any of a million flatnesses which should catch thereafter part of the brute sun's spectrum—showed nothing at all of what came to lie beneath, that quiet June day.

Syntactical ambiguity permits the reference to Astarte, one of the great fertility goddesses, to serve two functions. Throat naked, she personifies the spout. Next, she is the figurehead of the boat. The inanimate, which might once have been animate, shatters the inanimate, which might once have been an icon of the living body of myth. A simpler reading might be that the goddess is permanent enough to exact revenge.

V. also concerns women who inhabit a quotidian world. Pynchon grants their behavior a degree of motivation. They lack the elusiveness of V. that arises from Stencil's faulty perceptions; her function as a symbol; and the inexplicability of remnants of the divine. Pynchon, though he suspects tight schemes of cause and effect, grants that culture influences personality. In "Entropy," for example, Aubade shatters the windows of the hermetic apartment in which she and Callisto live. Trying to hasten their heat-death, she longs for "the hovering, curious dominant of their separate lives . . . [to] revolve into a tonic of darkness and the final absence of all motion." She is both French and "Annamese." The child of colonial mating, Pynchon suggests, will be perverse. Fortunately, *V.* avoids the tiresome satire of middle-class American women, be they housewives or government girls, that mars "Entropy" and other of the early stories.

The women in *V.* are judged according to the degree that they resemble V. The more like her they are, the worse they are. The novel's first scene bluntly introduces Americans who have fallen away from the good traditions of the goddesses. One Beatrice, who is a barmaid in the Sailor's Grave in Norfolk, is the sweetheart of "the destroyer U.S.S. Scaffold." Another Beatrice, who owns the bar, sets up artificial breasts to serve beer to sailors to prove her maternal care. In New York, robust Mafia Winsome, a racist Jacqueline Susann, preaches a theory of Heroic Love that reduces love to lust. She also uses contraceptives, to Pynchon less a legitimate act of self-protection than a morally and psychologically illegitimate separation of sex from love and of sex from reproduction. Her dithering husband thinks:

> If she believed in Heroic Love, which is nothing really but a frequency, then obviously Winsome wasn't on the man end of half of what she was looking for. In five years of marriage all he knew was that both of them were whole selves, hardly fusing at all, with no more emotional osmosis than leakage of seed through the solid membranes of contraceptive or diaphragm that were sure to be there protecting them.

Esther Harvitz, despite some self-assertion, succumbs to the ministrations of Schoenmaker, disillusioned plastic surgeon. His great love is over: a feudal, homosexual adoration for a pilot in World War I. When Esther has her nose job, Schoenmaker amputates the physical sign of the goddess. Mehemet has described Mara, the spirit of woman, for us:

> In her face is always a slight bow to the nose, a wide spacing of the eyes. . . . No one you'd turn to watch on the street. But she was a teacher of love after all. Only pupils of love need to be beautiful.

In contrast, Rachel Owlglass has promise. Her fetishistic desire for her MG is an aspect of collegiate adolescence she will outgrow. Though kind to members of the Whole Sick Crew, she is aloof from its decadence. She opposes Esther's abortion because, she believes, it will stunt Esther's capacity for heterosexuality. Her own heterosexuality is active. She offers Benny, whom she pursues, the chance to experience the comminglings of love. She projects a physical desire stronger than ego. In one of the novel's sloppiest passages, she croons to her crotch: " '. . . when it talks we listen.' " If not in literal fact, then in act, she also mothers: tucking men into bed; washing their faces. Pynchon's Jewish men want to sit *shivah* for the lost of the world; his Jewish women want to nurture and feed them. What wisdom Rachel has she attributes to the more irrational lessons of prelapsarian biology. She murmurs to a seduced Benny:

> "[Women] are older than you, we lived inside you once: the fifth rib, closest to the heart. We learned all about it then. After that it had to become our game to nourish a heart you all believe is hollow though we know different. Now you all live inside us, for nine months, and when ever you decide to come back after that."

Pynchon offers women another acceptable role: that of Marina, a daughter. She can inspire the tender chivalry of the good father. If Paola teaches Pappy Hod the mysterious plenitude of sex, in a surrogate daughter/father relationship that avoids incest, he reveals to her the virtue of forgiveness. Paola will also bring relics of the European goddess to America: the ivory comb. The name she has taken while pretending to be a black prostitute, Ruby, has already connected her to V. and the sapphire V. stitches into her navel. Yet Paola purifies the comb. She gives it to Pappy, an act of domestic fidelity. She will return to Pappy and live in Norfolk where, like Penelope, she will be faithful and "spin." Only the double meaning of the "yarn" she will create—fabric and fable—hints that the wife may not be wholly tamed.

A curious element of the structure of *V.* is that malign V. carries much of its symbolic weight, but the characters most often on page are male. Sailors on leave; anarchists in exile; foreign service officers planning counterespionage; explorers on expeditions—the good old boys and the old boys dominate the action. Two wistful comments, by Rachel and by Brenda Wigglesworth, offer a partial explanation. Boys are permitted more adventures than girls, more "Diesels and dust, roadhouses, crossroads saloons." Pynchon's picaresque reflects that social truth. Brenda anticipates Oedipa Maas: banal enough to drink sloe gins and own seventy-two pairs of Bermuda shorts, she is courageous enough to drive around Europe alone and witty enough to recite and to dismiss a poem that summarizes the action of the novel itself. Pynchon deploys her as literary critic.

However, male characters do more than occupy the bulk of narrative space. Pervasively, they provide point of view, even if points of view within the novel undercut and buffalo each other. So Stencil sees Mondaugen seeing Foppl seeing a black woman. The passage is horrible.

> Later, toward dusk, there was one Herero girl, sixteen or seventeen years old, for the platoon; and Firelily's rider was last. After he'd

had her he must have hesitated a moment between sidearm and bayonet. She actually smiled then; pointed to both, and began to shift her hips lazily in the dust. He used both.

(When men, usually in a lurid homosexual compact, take on a "feminine role," they impersonate such apparently voluptuous submissiveness.) At times the author himself distances us, through the tactical use of direct address, from a woman character. He writes about Rachel at a party:

> You felt she'd done a thousand secret things to her eyes. They needed no haze of cigarette smoke to look at you out of sexy and fathomless, but carried their own along with them.

Some men are granted moral authority as well. Dahoud and Pig both have the snappy one-liner, "Life is the most precious possession you have." McClintic Sphere cites a credo for dignified survival. A black jazz musician who plays at the V-Note, his figure points to a custom of white American male writers in the 1950s and early 1960s: the transformation of jazzmen and blacks into savants; the use of national outsiders as cosmic insiders. Within V. itself the race the West has sought to exterminate provides the texts of its salvation. In his Triumph, driving in the wind, a persistent symbol of spiritual verve in the novel, McClintic thinks:

> Love with your mouth shut, help without breaking your ass or publicizing it: keep cool, but care.

Readers reading my reading of Pynchon, in the mirror game of criticism, may justly say that *The Crying of Lot 49* reverses such structural features of *V.* An elusive, probably malign man, rich Pierce Inverarity, is a core symbol. A woman claims narrative space and the prerogatives of point of view. Oedipa Maas is a twenty-eight-year-old California housewife. Her most mythic role has been as a solipsistic Princess in the Tower. Though an unlikely candidate, she assumes the traditionally male tasks of executor of a will; interpreter of literature, a "whiz at pursuing strange words in Jacobean texts"; and questor. She sets out with only the fuzziest notion of what her job might be. She inhabits a polluted land, the urbanized California of housing tracts, factories, shopping centers, and suicide strips blithely known as "freeways." Construction has numbed nature as much as American society since World War II has narcotized sense and sensibility. Natural language, the frame of civilization, is running down, the victim of entropy, sloth, and the media. In Vesperhaven House, old Mr. Thoth (the Egyptian god of learning and writing) is nodding out in front of Porky Pig cartoons on TV. Rulers, such as the corporate officials of Yoyodyne, are corrupt. Oedipa must ask the right question, but the lesson of earlier quest narratives and of the drama of Oedipus himself is how hard it is to ask the right question; how hard it is to interpret oracular answers; how dangerous it might be to have the answers.

Nevertheless, the sexual conservatism of *V.*, if softened, infiltrates *The Crying of Lot 49*. Pynchon sexualizes ability to give Oedipa the weapons of "gut fear and female cunning" (*Lot 49*). That cunning exposes itself in Oedipa's ability to respond to the sea: the symbol of a teeming, insatiable, omnipotent womb. As she drives to a picnic at a lake Pierce has built, she thinks:

> Somewhere beyond the battening, urged sweep of three-bedroom houses . . . lurked the sea, the unimaginable Pacific, the one to which all surfers, beach pads, sewage disposal schemes, tourist incursions, sunned homosexuality, chartered fishing are irrelevant, the hole left by the moon's tearing-free and monument to her exile; you could not hear or even smell this but it was there, something tidal began to reach feelers in past eyes and eardrums, perhaps to arouse fractions of brain current your most gossamer microelectrode is yet too gross for finding. Oedipa had believed . . . in some principle of the sea as redemption for Southern California. . . . Perhaps it was only that notion, its arid hope, she sensed as this forenoon they made their seaward thrust, which would stop short of any sea.

During her quest, Oedipa discovers the Tristero. An underground mail delivery system, it works in opposition to "legitimate" authority. So doing, it includes both criminal and revolutionary; extreme right and extreme left; Mafia enforcer and saint. As she deciphers codes about the Tristero, she becomes increasingly celibate in body and isolated in spirit, but she also releases a suppressed capacity for maternal tenderness. Psychological motherhood marks her moral growth. In a scene that resembles a slum Pietà, she cradles a dirty old sailor suffering from DTs, as if he were "her own child."

She may become a supernatural mother as well. As revelations buffet her, she wonders if she can hold to a central truth. In a grim metaphor, Pynchon asks if we are not all like Prince Myshkin; if we are not epileptics in the confrontation with spectra beyond the known sun. Oedipa meditates:

> I am meant to remember. Each clue that comes is *supposed* to have its own clarity, its fine chances for permanence. But then she wondered if the gemlike "clues" were only some kind of compensation. To make up for her having lost the direct, epileptic Word, the cry that might abolish the night.

The capitalization of "Word" is vital: it is a translation, linguistically and conceptually, of the Greek "logos," an animating and renewing principle of reason in the cosmos. Oedipa thinks of it once again. After calling upon God, during the dark night of her soul, she remembers

> drifters she had listened to, Americans speaking their language carefully, scholarly, as if they were in exile from somewhere else invisible yet congruent with the cheered land she lived in. . . .And the voices before and after the dead man's that had phoned at random during the darkest, slowest hours, searching ceaseless among the dial's ten million possibilities for that magical Other who would reveal herself out of the roar of relays, monotone litanies of insult, filth, fantasy, love whose brute repetition must someday call into being the trigger for the unnamable act, the recognition, the Word.

The Tristero may be carrying not simply letters, i.e., written communications, but Letters, pieces of the Word.

Pynchon may be going on to give "the Word" special meaning. Some theoreticians of Logos—the Stoics, the Jewish philosopher Philo, the early Christian apologist Justin Martyr—though of the divine principle as germinating, seminal, the "*spermatikos logos.*" Justin writes of "the seed of reason . . . implanted in every race of man." He mentions the "spermatic word." The Tristero may be delivering it. Pynchon, exploiting the puns natural language is heir to, literalizing a sexual metaphor, may want us to think of mail as male. If so, as Oedipa succumbs to the languid, sinister attraction of the Tristero, she represents the female body being pierced and receiving some sacred seed. Towards the end of her quest:

> The toothaches got worse, she dreamed of disembodied voices from whose malignance there was no appeal, the soft dusk of mirrors out of which something was about to walk, and empty rooms that waited for her. Your gynecologist has no test for what she was pregnant with.

One of the novel's ambiguities is whether she is carrying the child of life or of death. The former will add to and renew this world. The meritorious chance of our redemption may prevail. Bearing it will give Oedipa a salutary public significance. The numbers 49, apparently arbitrary, may prove symbolic: 4 the number of spring, 9 of lunar wisdom. If she is bearing the child of death, it will either add to her isolation or generate disease. Her pregnancy, as it were, will either be meaningless or of morbid public significance. The odds are on this possibility. If Oedipus must marry his mother and father his own siblings, parentless Oedipa must leave her husband and mother sterility.

Oedipa never reaches the Pacific. Only one character does: Randolph Driblette, the director of a Jacobean tragedy. He drowns himself. The closest she comes to the symbol of female fertility is to stand near the shore on old railroad tracks, ties, and cinderbed. She simplifies her choices to one: does the Tristero exist or not? Making sense of her clues, has she discovered or manufactured a reality? If Oedipa has invented the Tristero, then Pynchon's early feminine metaphor for it, a malign and pitiless stripper, is another image for her hidden self. She commits herself to the Tristero and goes to the auction at which some possibly relevant information about it will be sold. The atmosphere is grim. The room is locked; the men inside have "pale, cruel faces"; the auctioneer is like a "puppet-master," a priest of "some remote culture," a "descending angel." The narrative abandons the questor in the Chapel Perilous.

In V., Benny Profane experiences the loss of vital myth. The affirmation of such absence is one of the longest cries in twentieth-century literature. Sitting in Little Italy in New York, amidst the garish shoddiness of a Catholic saint's day celebration, he tries to tell a girl about his job.

> He told her about the alligators; Angel, who had a fertile imagination too, added detail, color. Together on the stoop they hammered together a myth. Because it wasn't born from fear of thunder, dreams, astonishment at how the crops kept dying after harvest and coming up again every spring, or anything else very permanent, only a temporary interest, a spur-of-the-moment tumescence, it was a myth rickety and transient as the bandstands and the sausage-pepper of Mulberry Street.

If the early Pynchon were to offer a vital myth, it would have to be flexible enough to verify urban life; radical enough to regenerate the decaying world; tough enough to withstand the testing acids of irony, burlesque, and parody. It would also respect nature. Spring, taking on the role of Paraclete, would descend with tongue of flame. Ordinary women would be fertile. Goddesses would protect the natural bounty of the womb. Like the moon, women would have a dark side that would haunt the imagination of men and remind them of their fragile mortality. However, the early fiction dramatizes the mortifying betrayal of such roles, which some women will and others resist.

MELVYN NEW

Profaned and Stenciled Texts:
In Search of Pynchon's V.

There is a sentence in Montaigne's essay "Of the Inconstancy of our Actions," which Charles Cotton has translated, "It is impossible for any one to fit the pieces together, who has not the whole form already contrived in his imagination." The point is well taken, particularly when we approach a modern fiction such as Thomas Pynchon's *V.*, where the seeming failure of the modern imagination to contrive a whole form scatters the world into pieces that do not seem to fit. As always, Montaigne serves to warn us that however much we enumerate and authenticate the differences between our modern age and the past, there are abiding similarities which, if nothing else, should caution us against the danger of too severely dichotomizing past and present. It is a danger into which modern literature, and in particular a work like *V.*, has led us, and into which we, as critics of literature, have hastened like proverbial lemmings. For it seems to me more and more apparent that however much we analyze literature, and however much we analyze ourselves in the act of analyzing literature, we do return at last to Montaigne's fundamental dilemma: the whole consists of constituent parts, and the parts are organized only by the whole.

Nor should Montaigne's use of the term "imagination" deceive us, for the word carries none of our connotations of untruthful or fictional. Rather, imagination is simply the capacity of the mind to order the fragments into a particular cohesiveness. Moreover, the literary critic is perhaps privileged among men in that the human avocation of exercising the imagination, or ordering the fragments, is as well his vocation. Despite every attempt by recent critics,

From *Georgia Review* 33, no. 2 (Summer 1979). © 1979 by the University of Georgia.

that is by certain structuralists, to deny this aim of criticism, I have read nothing in their actual analyses of texts that does not reduce itself to Montaigne's apothegm. Criticism continues to be, I believe, the urge to order parts into intelligible wholes, whether it be diverse works into historical or political or generic schemes, or the elements of a single work into a particular meaning—even when that meaning is assigned multiple facets. Nor is this wrong; rather, it is the response, of all others, the most human and most comprehensive: the necessity to incorporate the diverse elements of our experience into our own system, so that we have mastered it and removed its threatening aspect.

The problem is that Montaigne's world shared an imaginative system of order no longer available today, so that the emphasis of modern man falls upon "our own" rather than upon "system." It is, to some degree, a useful distinction, particularly when used to describe literature caught in the interface between Christian and secular world views. On the one hand, we have a literature that describes a God-ordered world in which events and characters are moved by an intervening hand toward a conclusion which verifies that order; on the other, a literature that describes a man-centered world, where characters and events determine an outcome which at most verifies a personal order but may indeed try to suggest that no verifiable order is available. In my own work on eighteenth-century fiction, I have found it convenient to label the first fiction, *romance*, and the second, *novel*, and to suggest that eighteenth-century fiction is best comprehended as a displacement of romance by the novel, mirroring the eighteenth-century displacement of Christianity by a secular world view.

The validity of such a dichotomy, however, depends upon ignoring the underlying similarity between Christian and secular man, brought out so well by Montaigne's sentence. By focusing on whether the whole form is received and accepted (that is, Christianity) or individual and problematic (that is, secular), we tend to slight the insistent need represented by both to fit the pieces together, to imagine or contrive the whole. The acceptance of or conversion to one particular system is ultimately little different from the individual search for order, except insofar as the individual quest may be viewed as more dangerous or more glorious, depending upon one's viewpoint. Certainly it becomes more urgent, more insistent, the multiplicity of available systems producing precisely that fearful, anxious, depressed state so descriptive of modern man. Psychologically, we can point to clinical depression as the failure of the individual's symbol system to incorporate a particularly threatening fragment; and paranoia, so dominant a subject in all Pynchon's writings, may be seen as a total breakdown of the system. Politically, so astute an observer of modern society as Jacques Ellul considers the need for a system to order the events of life the single most important condition that makes possible the control of mass societies. And in literary criticism, the frenetic activity of the Age of Criticism attests again to the urgency we feel to order existence. In short, the problem is one of consciousness itself, laboring to secure its relationship to the fragments that surround it. The literary work we hold in our hand is one such fragment; the insistence with which we feel the need to understand that work, in actuality to master and subdue it, is the human need to incorporate all fragments into an imagined whole.

Let me pursue this subject one step further. There has been much in recent criticism concerning "open" and "closed" texts, and several critics have found Pynchon's works useful in examining the issue. In a fine essay by Frank Kermode, for example, *The Crying of Lot 49* is used to illustrate what Kermode perceives to be a fallacy in the work of the structuralists. His complaint seems to me twofold; on the one hand, the critic always tries to close a work, at least to the extent that it no longer remains an unincorporated fragment:

> Making sense of other somewhat arbitrary symbolic universes, understanding their construction, is an activity familiar to all critics. Certainly it involves choices, a limitation of pluralities. The activity of the critic . . . seeks order, and is analogous to the social construction of reality. What Oedipa is doing is very like reading a book.

On the other hand, all worthwhile texts (not simply modern ones) remain ultimately open, Kermode notes, if only because of the multiplicity of readers and hence of possible systems of organization:

> the category of the *lisible* virtually melts away, since all such books [books "worth reading"] assume that they will be competently read— "produced"—not, of course, because they are complex riddles, but because they know, as if by introspection, that it is a property of narratives (doubtless often neglected) to be plural, self-examining, incapable of full closure, as indeed the history of interpretation confirms.

For Kermode, then, there exist not two kinds of texts but two kinds of readers: "Probably the basic issue is between those who think that textual simulacra of order and system must be ideological (nauseous) and those who take them to be responses to a more radical need for satisfaction. . . ." I find these insights quite valuable and, as I hope to show, not merely coincidentally supported by a reading of a Pynchon novel; but for the moment, I would like to approach the same conclusion from a different direction, that of generic distinctions.

The form of romance, as I briefly suggested above, tends toward a closed text in that its aim is to verify or convert to an accepted system. In contrast, the novel tends toward an open text because it offers a problematic or individualistic validation. But again, the dichotomy has its danger, for insofar as every reader works to close a work he "writes" a romance; and insofar as he is unable to convince other readers (or less often, himself) that he has closed the work (that is, that he has produced a reading which satisfies the reader's own system), he "writes" a novel. From the author's viewpoint, we might argue that every literary work is the result of the author's need to fit the fragments into a whole form, whether in defense or repair of a received system, or an attack upon it, or in search of a new one; and of the susceptibility or resistance of the imitated materials to that form. His success in this activity is ultimately the measure of self-satisfaction, since the impetus is an unfulfilled need; but the author must become a reader in order to make that measurement, and of course as a reader at different times he may feel his system of ordering his experience more or less successful. Generic distinctions between fictions, then, exist on two intersecting axes: (1) the tendency, but not the success or failure, of the work to endorse or attack a received system, to create or refrain from creating a new one; and (2) the success or failure of the individual reader to close the work to his own (and others') satisfaction. Values on the first axis are derived from the usual methods of literary analysis; values on the second from psychological need (self-conviction) and rhetoric (convincing others). A simple diagram might be useful at this point:

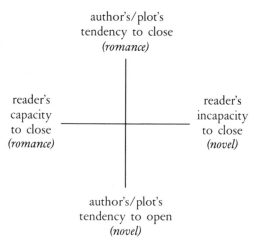

Worthwhile literature does not exist in the upper left-hand quadrant except as a society's sacred scripture, its meaning closed by its Divine Author and His priests. All other literature so closed would be simplistic or propagandistic and therefore no threat to the reader's capacity to integrate it. But it is important to note that all literature and all criticism move toward that quadrant, pushed by the incessant creative and critical urge to order the fragments. The revolutionary work that attacks one system is positing another which has proved more satisfactory to the author in organizing his world. The critic who attacks another's reading of a work is really arguing the failure of that reading effectively to integrate the work into his own system; his own reading is an attempt to satisfy that need. What fascinates us about great literature is precisely the fact that it always remains, if I may appropriate for my own purposes Northrop Frye's term, "secular scripture," occupying the other three quadrants where the conditions of human creation and human interpretation constantly resist and forestall the human need to order parts into whole forms.

Pynchon's *V.* leads one quite readily into an examination of the critical process because it is so profoundly concerned with the human need to order fragments. While Herbert Stencil searches for clues to the meaning of the woman V., accumulating his notecards, his sources, his linkages, we, as readers, parallel his activity, making our own accumulations, driven by the same urge to fit the pieces together, to arrive at the meaning of the novel *V.* Other critics have noted this parallel, including Richard Poirier, who asks at one point, "What are critics of Pynchon, like myself, but a species of sorting demon?" On the other hand, Tony Tanner, the best critic thus far of Pynchon, is also correct in seeing Stencil as a surrogate author:

> One aspect of paranoia is the tendency to imagine plots around you; this is also the novelist's occupation and there is clearly a relationship between making fictions and imagining conspiracies. . . . [Stencil] is the man who is trying to make the connections and links, and put together the story which might well have been Pynchon's novel.
>
> (*City of Words*)

Without doubt, both author and critic have traditionally been makers of plots, the one imitating a scene which reflected transcendent order and pattern, the other tracing (that is, stenciling) that reflection of transcendence within the imitation. We are reminded of Pope's embodiment of this particular vision of the world: "A mighty maze, but not without a plan," and surely the primary aim of artist and reader prior to Pope was to explain, to defend, to justify that plan. But Pope had written an earlier version of the line, far more apropos to the twentieth century that Pynchon and Tanner are writing about: "A mighty maze of walks," Pope first wrote, "without a plan." For Northrop Frye the two versions embody a fundamental clash between life and art, but one reconciled by art:

> The first version recognizes the human situation; the second refers
> to the constructs of religion, art, and science that man throws up
> because he finds the recognition intolerable. Literature is an aspect
> of the human compulsion to create in the face of chaos. Romance,
> I think, is not only central to literature as a whole, but the area
> where we can see most clearly that the maze without a plan and
> the maze not without a plan are two aspects of the same thing.
>
> (*The Secular Scripture*)

For Pynchon, as for many twentieth-century writers, the problem is not quite as simple as Frye suggests, primarily because the modern awareness that the constructs may well be only constructs and nothing more returns the human situation to intolerableness. The human compulsion to create may indeed be, as we suspect in Stencil's case, a paranoid activity, a failure rather than an achievement of human intellect.

To put it another way, when an author can embrace a construct that orders the world prior to his exploration of the maze of human experience, he is beginning with the romance, perhaps even with sacred scripture, and displacing it to varying degrees as his exploration leads him to challenge or deconstruct certain elements of his pattern. The modern writer, on the other hand, is inhibited by the perception that constructs are human creations, and that the maze may well be all there is. It is the message that Weissmann finds in Mondaugen's recordings of atmospheric noises: "DIE WELT IST ALLES WAS DER FALL IST"—"The world is all that the case is," the opening proposition of Wittgenstein's *Tractatus Logico-Philosophicus* (*V.*). At the same time, however, the author is motivated by the human compulsion to create that Frye talks about, so that however dedicated he is to the maze, and however hard he tries—through irony, ambiguity, discontinuity, and absurdity—to stay in the maze, ultimately he moves toward patterning the fragments into some version of Montaigne's whole form. From outer space we receive a message that there is no message in outer space. The music of spheres that Dryden heard so clearly in 1687—"From harmony, from heavenly harmony/This universal frame began"—in 1963 has become not silent but the paradoxical assertion of silence. This is precisely the paradox Pynchon explores in *V.*: the human inability to listen to the silence, whether as author or reader; the human need, in the generic terms I have set out, to displace the novel with elements of romance, to seek closure not merely of literature but of the existence imitated by literature. Pynchon's readers, Pynchon's characters, Pynchon himself—all search for the meaning of the mysterious woman V., for the romance within the novel.

The characters in *V.* are defined or define themselves in relation to certain private constructs, all of which share in Pynchon's overarching construct of an entropic progress from animateness in inanimateness, from life to annihilation. Because Pynchon builds an historical perspective into his pattern, there develops as well a series of legatorial relationships that penetrate the private constructs and perhaps serve as one hopeful signpost in an otherwise bleak landscape. Every construct except one, Victoria's relationship with Mélanie, is created by a male and embodies a female, usually—but not solely—associated with the ubiquitous letter V. Finally, and most obviously, Pynchon divides his world into past and future, the foreign-service world of stenciled plots and counterplots, and the nautical world (including the Whole Sick Crew) of Benny Profane, adrift in the "dreamscape of the future." Pynchon had worked with a similar division in his first published story, "Entropy," and he returns to its images late in *V.*:

> "If there is any political moral to be found in this world," Stencil once wrote in his journal, "it is that we carry on the business of this century with an intolerable double vision. Right and Left; the hothouse and the street. The Right can only live and work hermetically, in the hothouse of the past, while outside the Left prosecute their affairs in the streets by manipulated mob violence. And cannot live but in the dreamscape of the future."

The senior Stencil goes on to inquire: "What of the real present . . . ?" If the present does exist in *V.*, I would suggest it is found in the interpenetration of past and future, in those legatorial relationships by which the future assumes the "burden of the past," and in sexual (procreative) relationships where the past accepts its necessary implication in the future. From these moments of interpenetration, successful or otherwise, we can discover something about the manner in which fiction is written and read, for in many ways the work of art is the only "real present"—the only moment we can experience that is free from the constructs of past time and the random meaninglessness of the future. Significant art provides that freedom, and significant criticism teaches us to relish it, to find, that is, the present text between stenciled and profaned ones.

There is an episode in *V.* which can serve us as a paradigm for the entire work and the generalizations I have been deriving from it. Vheissu is first mentioned in the cryptic telegram Hugh Godolphin sends to his son Evan in 1899. The telegram is first intercepted by the foreign service in Florence and immediately becomes part of "The Situation," as Stencil *père* refers to it. Vheissu is a possible code word for another "V."—Venezuela—and perhaps yet another, Vesuvius. As such, it locks into Herbert Stencil's search for V., one more clue to the labyrinth in which he labors. More important, however, are the responses of Godolphins, father and son, to that Vheissu which is neither Venezuela nor Vesuvius but a vividly described "lost civilization" reached by the explorer-father in 1884:

> He had been there. Fifteen years ago. And been fury-ridden since. Even in the Antarctic, huddling in hasty shelter from a winter storm . . . there would come to him hints of the perfume those people distill from the wings of black moths. Sometimes sentimental scraps of their music would seem to lace the wind; memories of their faded murals, depicting old battles and older love affairs among the gods, would appear without warning in the aurora.

The image at first, setting aside "fury-ridden," might be that of any secret romantic place, a valley of delicacy and warmth, protecting one against colder, harsher realities. It is a deceptive image, however, as Godolphin, speaking to Victoria, immediately makes clear:

> "It's not," he continued, "as if it were unusual in any supernatural way. No high priests with secrets lost to the rest of the world. . . . No universal cures, nor even panaceas for human suffering. . . . There's barbarity, insurrection, internecine feud. It's no different from any other godforsakenly remote region. . . . Except . . . The colors. So many colors."

It is this constantly changing surface of Vheissu that both attracts and repels, and Godolphin's tone is one of reverent awe mingled with horror, as he describes the iridescent spider monkeys, the mountains that change color from one hour to the next "as if you lived inside a madman's kaleidoscope," the shapes "no Occidental ever saw." Everything about Vheissu is surface, is skin: "Like the skin of a tattooed savage. I often put it that way to myself—like a woman."

The image of the woman is a crucial one, trying Vheissu to the other constructs in V., all of which, including Malta, are feminine. Godolphin explores his relationship to Vheissu as female at some length:

> "But as if the place were, were a woman you had found some- where out there, a dark woman tattooed from head to toes. And somehow you had got separated from the garrison and found your- self unable to get back, so that you had to be with her, close to her, day in and day out . . ."
> "And you would be in love with her" [Victoria interjects].

"At first [Godolphin answers]. But soon that skin, the gaudy godawful riot of pattern and color, would begin to get between you and whatever it was in her that you thought you loved. And soon, in perhaps only a matter of days, it would get so bad that you would begin praying to whatever god you knew of to send some leprosy to her. To flay that tattooing to a heap of red, purple and green debris, leave the veins and ligaments raw and quivering and open at last to your eyes and your touch."

On the one hand, Godolphin expresses a sadistic sexuality that is one of Pynchon's dominant images for European colonialism, a persistent rape, a constant violation of the procreative penetration in which Pynchon finds some hope for modern man. By extension, it is the much larger failure of man's procreative urge in the twentieth century, and of course *V.* is filled with images of this failure, from Benny Profane's nailing of prophylactics on the cabin doors, to Esther's abortion, to the sterile advice of the bad priest (*V.*'s World War II disguise on Malta). On the other hand, the image is connected to *V.*'s death as well, since she undergoes a similar vivisection later in the work, and to Mantissa's love affair with Botticelli's "Venus," one of the main episodes in this chapter. It is thus significant that when Godolphin again speaks about Vheissu it is to his old friend that he explains his despair in the face of the ever-changing surface of life and his desperate attempt to penetrate that surface, to find the soul beneath Vheissu. He had sought his answer at the Pole because, as he explains,

"I had begun to think that there, at one of the only two motionless places on this gyrating world, I might have peace to solve Vheissu's riddle. Do you understand? I wanted to stand in the dead center of the carousel, if only for a moment; try to catch my bearings."

The desire to tear into the tattooed surface of things in order to discover the soul beneath, and the desire to stand in the dead center of the carousel are in reality one and the same — the urgent need, in all human beings, to master the flux of life's variegated surface, its inexorable movement of the future into the past. But when the image again shifts from temporal to spatial, when in the "entirely lifeless and empty place" at the polar ice cap, Godolphin scrapes through the earth's surface to discover the answer that must lie beneath, he finds only the frozen form of one of Vheissu's spider monkeys. For Godolphin it seems a sign, much like the message from Mondaugen's sferics, that there is no meaning to his explorations; that the end of the search, the answer at the dead center, is that there is no answer, that at the core is only the dazzling play of surface colors, just as when he pictures the flayed native woman all he can see is a "heap of red, purple and green debris."

If the vision of Vheissu's surface had made Godolphin "fury-ridden," possessed by the compulsion to solve its riddle, the experience of its heart drives him immediately to imagine a construct, to stencil a plot:

> "It was quite real; not like the vague hints they had given me before. I say 'they had given.' I think they left it there for me. Why? Perhaps for some alien, not-quite-human reason that I can never comprehend. . . . A mockery, you see, a mockery of life, planted where everything but Hugh Godolphin was inanimate."

The response is not a logical one, but in Pynchon's world it is the expected one. Precisely at the moment that Godolphin comes face to face with the "dream of annihilation," the nothingness which seems to be modern man's only logical discovery, he also discovers that Vheissu is evil, a plot planted by "them" to destroy "us." Penetrating the skin only to discover the same frightful surface beneath, Godolphin is unable to rest in meaninglessness but instead is driven to a construct, however malevolent, in which the personal struggle to order life is good and diametrically opposed to the universal mystery that mocks the struggle and is therefore evil. His perception is traditional, a part of the past: "If Eden was the creation of God, God only knows what evil created Vheissu." The sustaining belief of Stencil, which he repeats over and over to himself, "Events seem to be ordered into an ominous logic," is Godolphin's belief as well; Godolphin confronts the "dream of annihilation" with his own "dream of order," and in doing so imposes an ominous logic upon the tattooed surface, the colors of Vheissu.

It would probably not do to allegorize Pynchon, but the temptation is strong. Like Godolphin, we would like to impose our own "dream of order" on the ever-moving surface of *V.*, for like Vheissu, *V.* and all significant literary works can be considered a tattooed woman whose mystery we are driven to penetrate and possess. On one level, criticism is simply that process: we tear the work of art into its constituent elements, we delve below the surface (one of criticism's favorite metaphors) to the meaning supposedly hiding beneath the words or colors of shapes of the skin. But the process is always and necessarily unsatisfactory and incomplete: it is destructive, as is the love relationship in which the loved object is sacrificed to the needs of the lover. In the worlds of past and future this is perhaps all there is, and Pynchon mirrors this sacrifice in the various love relationships in *V.*, culminating in the sexual impalement of Mélanie, *V.*'s own object of love.

If there were nothing more, Pynchon's outlook would be bleak indeed.

But the work of art, like Vheissu, cannot be so easily destroyed, for within both there is no soul to kill but only the permanent, indestructible surface, the riot of colors and movement that repeats itself wherever one probes, however one approaches. This is the "real present" that Stencil has inquired after, and in which the human mind cannot seem to rest. The usual response we may call the second level of criticism in which, imitating Godolphin, we establish the construct to explain and order the fragments we have created into a whole form. The work of art, the object of love, is as resistant to this possession as to the earlier fragmentation, for between it and the construct is again the need of the possessor who exists only in the past and the future, while he betrays the present precisely by his urge to possess, to incorporate the work into his own system. The work of art remains alone in present time, impervious to its destructive or constructive lover, a continuous mockery of all attempts to profane or to stencil it. Among the many "lovers" in V., perhaps Mantissa alone understands the meaning of Vheissu. Driven by the desire to possess Botticelli's "Venus," after the first slash of Cesare's knife he thinks of what Godolphin has just told him; in that very instant he is "reminded of Hugh Godolphin's spider-monkey, still shimmering through crystal ice at the bottom of the world. The whole surface of the painting now seemed to move, to be flooded with color and motion." What sort of mistress would Venus be, he asks, and the answer comes back, "A gaudy dream, a dream of annihilation. . . . Yet she was no less Rafael Mantissa's entire love." Mantissa stops Cesare, and Venus is left, in the words of the chapter's title, hanging "on the western wall," violated but not penetrated, adored but not possessed.

Stencil, too, at the very moment when the secret of V. may finally be opened to him in Malta, follows a much weaker clue to Sweden, escaping that moment of ultimate despair when, in the act of penetration and possession we realize that we have mastered nothing, achieved nothing. The easy formulations that Pynchon tantalizes us with, such as "approach and Avoid," or McClintic Sphere's "keep cool but care" are obviously inadequate expressions of a very complex concept, but they are not wrong. The experiences of love and art are modern man's remaining contacts with the "real present," in which he cannot live and without which he also cannot live. Like the "real presence" of the older system, these "present" moments of penetration and possession awe and nourish us. We devour and are devoured in turn, the moments endure and allow us to endure. Victim and victor are intricately bound together in an eucharistic celebration, and as Stencil might suggest, the meaning of Vheissu without the "V" may well be "Jesu."

If Pynchon's analysis of the interpenetration of reader and literary work has taken me (through a circuitous if not devious route) to the communion table, it also leads down another street, toward the concept of priesthood, the dual role of embodying and promulgating God's word. Fausto Maijstral, we remember, wanted to be a priest, and in his own writings not only explores the priest's relationship to the writer, but as well passes on his gospel to his daughter Paola, and through her to Stencil. The woman V. ends her life disguised as the "Bad Priest," preaching her message of destructive chastity. And below the streets, Benny Profane encounters the story of Father Fairing, formerly of Malta, who preached Christianity to the sewer rats in Manhattan in the 1930s. What ties these characters together is the act of spreading the gospel, the legatorial act whereby the story is transmitted from the past into the future. In this respect, the most obvious priest is Sidney Stencil, who passes on to his son the legacy which dominates the novel: " 'There is more behind and inside V. than any of us had suspected. Not who, but what: what is she. God grant that I may never be called upon to write the answer, either here or in any official report.' " But Godolphin also serves the priestly role, and we can return to Vheissu in order to examine this second version of interpenetration.

Evan Godolphin had heard about Vheissu in the bedtime stories his father told him, and his recollections give us a rich picture of it:

> "He would sit in my room, before I went to sleep, and spin yarns about this Vheissu. About the spider-monkeys, and the time he saw a human sacrifice, and the rivers whose fish are sometimes opalescent and sometimes the color of fire. . . . And men in the hills with blue faces and women in the valleys who give birth to nothing but sets of triplets, and beggars who belong to guilds and hold jolly festivals and entertainments all summer long."

As a boy, feeling the need to separate himself from his father, Evan loses faith in the reality of this fantasy world, composed it would seem of elements of myth and medieval romance. But now, in Florence, he finds his faith dramatically restored; significantly, the cause he assigns is the effect:

> "I thought Captain Hugh was mad; I would have signed the commitment papers myself. But at Piazzi della Signoria 5 I was nearly killed in something that could not have been an accident, a caprice of the inanimate world; and from then till now I have seen two governments hagridden to alienation over this fairy tale or obsession I thought was my father's own."

The event Evan refers to is, on its surface, a comical one, a direct parody of the modern detective story but with roots in the coded amulets of romance.

Entering his father's room in search of clues, he had acted out the role of spy, searching the place from top to bottom:

> After twenty minutes he'd still found nothing and was beginning to feel inadequate as a spy. He threw himself disconsolate into a chair, picked up one of his father's cigarettes, struck a match. "Wait," he said. Shook out the match, pulled a table over, produced a penknife from his pocket and carefully slit each cigarette down the side. . . . On the third day he was successful. Written in pencil on the inside of the cigarette paper was: "Discovered here. . . . Be careful. FATHER."

The discovery is so improbable, so contrived, that surely Pynchon takes an ironic stance toward it; nonetheless, it is the stuff that "dreams of order" are made from, and Evan confirms the state of mind toward which he is moving when, leaving the apartment, he is nearly killed by the collapse of the stairway. After rescuing himself with cinematic acrobatics he first congratulates himself, but "a moment later, after he had nearly been sick between his knees, he thought: how accidental was it, really? Those stairs were all right when I came up. He smiled nervously. He was getting almost as loony as his father." It is this event that Evan refers to as "something that could not have been an accident," but of course there is no reason to believe that it is not. No reason, that is, unless one has already inherited and made his own the structure of one's father, for whom there are no accidents but only patterns, no future of random events but only the past in which "events seem to be ordered into an ominous logic." Evan's own analysis of his new perception combines significantly the ideas of legacy and communion:

> "Their [the Italians and the English in Florence] anxiety is the same as my father's, what is coming to be my own, and perhaps in a few weeks what will be the anxiety of everyone living in a world none of us wants to see lit into holocaust. Call it a kind of communion, surviving somehow on a mucked-up planet which God knows none of us like very much. But it is our planet and we live on it anyway."

And again, when he encounters Victoria quite by chance where the Via del Purgatorio and Via dell'Inferno intersect, he reaffirms the new vision he has come to: "He felt that belief in Vheissu gave him no right any more to doubt as arrogantly as he had before, that perhaps wherever he went from now on he would perform like penance a ready acceptance of miracles or visions such as this meeting at the crossroads seemed to him to be."

Through legacy, the interpenetrations of past and future generations, there comes about an acceptance of "dreams of order," or rather a participation in them, that seems to me one of Pynchon's more hopeful suggestions for the role of art in human affairs. Certainly when Mantissa speaks about it to Hugh Godolphin, he suggests at one and the same time the idealized role of father, priest, artist, and critic—what it is we would like to believe we do:

> "isn't it true that we spend our lives seeking for something valuable, some truth to tell to a son, to give to him with love? Most of us aren't as lucky as you, perhaps we have to be torn away from the rest of men before we can have such words to give to a son."

That the son gives nothing in return, that he "will take your gift and use it for himself, for his own life," passing "nothing back up" to the father, saddens Mantissa, but he sees it as part of a natural course. In fact, however, what Herbert Stencil and Evan Godolphin do return to their fathers is their commitment, however self-destructive, to the "dreams of order" they receive as a legacy, but which are simultaneously "dreams of annihilation" they are forced to pursue, "fury-ridden," because possession is never possible. Hugh Godolphin in 1922 can speak of Vheissu as something hardly remembered:

> "If anything gave me my Vheissu it was the time, the Pole, the service. . . . But it's all been taken away, I mean the leisure and the sympathy. It's fashionable to say the War did it. Whatever you choose. But Vheissu is gone and impossible to bring back."

But Vheissu we remember is the indestructible surface of things, and the same war that causes Godolphin *père* to forget it, is precisely the arena in which the dreams of order and annihilation clashed so violently together to usher in the modern era, the arena in which handsome, dashing Evan Godolphin crashes his plane, shattering his face to pieces. It is no accident that Evan is the last character we see in the novel. The horribly disfigured servant and lover of V. on Malta, he stands on the shore, tearful, calling something in English which no one understands, as Sidney Stencil heads out to see and death. Nor is it an accident that the good priest on Malta is named Father Avalanche, for the effect of the priest, the father, the artist, the reader, is always to overwhelm, to bury the future with his own constructs not through viciousness or even insensitivity but because it is the act of love by which the past speaks to the future about that elusive present which neither can penetrate nor possess, but where the "something valuable, some truth to tell to a son," is always located.

Quite obviously I have not resisted very successfully the urge to allegorize

Pynchon but rather, like Stencil and Godolphin before me, have sought for the romance within the novel, the structure which can give some order to the intolerable mysteries of *V.* In so doing I have undoubtedly violated the work but not, I think, in any manner that Pynchon did not expect and invite. If *V.* does indeed teach us something about the essential impenetrability and indestructibility of art, it instructs us as well about our own incessant need to deny and ignore those truths. Certainly Pynchon himself is no less a victim of the human need to order the fragments than are his readers, and perhaps his magnificent play of authorial self-consciousness—used primarily to comment ironically upon that need—is the best indication that he is the foremost victim.

But more than this, there is a very real dread in Pynchon's work that something has gone incredibly wrong in modern life and that the modes of possible amelioration, through the interpenetrations I have been analyzing, are no longer available. The tension between design and accident, pattern and fragment, is played out against a grave suspicion that the fragments cannot be ordered in any way that could satisfy man's need to understand the structure of life. Quite the reverse, as Stencil discovers: " 'sometime between 1859 and 1919, the world contracted a disease which no one ever took the trouble to diagnose because the symptoms were too subtle—blending in with the events of history, no different one by one but altogether—fatal.' " Where in earlier fiction patterns of belief made possible a competitive struggle against the randomness of life, Pynchon holds out to us the possibility that even if the fragments could still be ordered (and we are never certain that they can be), the result would be even more intolerable to man than the randomness that pursues him. It is Stencil who most persistently embodies the tension between accident and design, and hence it is fitting that he should summarize it in his last appearance in *V.*, just before he departs for Sweden to follow another clue:

> "V.'s is a country of coincidence, ruled by a ministry of myth. Whose emissaries haunt this century's streets. Porcépic, Mondaugen, Stencil père, this Maijstral, Stencil fils. Could any of them create a coincidence? Only Providence creates. If the coincidences are real then Stencil has never encountered history at all, but something far more appalling.
>
> "Stencil came on Father Fairing's name once, apparently by accident. Today he came on it again, by what only could have been design."

This is familiar ground, the climax of a series of puzzles and questions by which Pynchon has proved his own and the reader's implication in the need to order the fragments of life and art into whole forms. The "country of coincidence, ruled by a ministry of myth" may well be taken as fiction itself, moving between the poles of novel and romance, opened and closed structures. It is, however, the "emissaries who haunt this century's streets," the Benny Profanes, that mark a difference between the older struggle between design and randomness, and the modern one. In the past, assured that the mighty maze did indeed have a plan, the author and the reader, wherever they started and through whatever perils they journeyed, ultimately found their hope and their meaning in the simple phrase, "only Providence creates." But this hope has become the twentieth century's terror, for if Providence is creating and ordering the fragments of our time then Providence proves to be a malicious and malignant force. If in the past man comforted himself that the fragments could be ordered, in our own century the only comfort may be that they cannot. It would be better, in short, to agree with the sailor Mehemet, who tells the senior Stencil that nothing has gone wrong, that there is no disease in modern life, but only natural old age:

> "Is old age a disease?" Mehemet asked. "The body slows down, machines wear out, planets falter and loop, sun and stars gutter and smoke, Why say a disease? Only to bring it down to a size you can look at and feel comfortable?"

Sidney Stencil's answer is a painful one: "Because we do paint the side of some Peri or other, don't we," an allusion to Mehemet's earlier told story of a sinking ship and a man painting its side:

> " 'Come aboard,' we told him, 'night is nearly on us and you cannot swim to land.' He never answered, merely continued dipping the brush in his earthen jar and slapping it smoothly on the Peri's creaking sides. What color? It looked gray but the air was dark. This felucca would never again see the sun. Finally I told the helmsman to swing our ship round and continue on course. I watched the fellah until it was too dark: becoming smaller, inching closer to the sea with every swell but never slackening his pace. A peasant with all his uptorn roots showing, alone on the sea at nightfall, painting the side of a sinking ship."

I do not think this is Pynchon's final comment upon the nature of art and of man's constructs in general, but it is an important image and it haunts his other perceptions. The acts of communion and of priesthood, through which the dreams of order and dreams of annihilation were held together in uneasy compromise, are undone by a new pentecostal voice, "screaming" across the sky, that tells us the only order is annihilation. This paraclete offers no comfort, and the true voice of the artist is simply the measure of the apocalypse, the holocaust to come. Unless, of course, the poet tells lies, as Pynchon's poet, Fausto Maijstral, believes:

> Living as he does much of the time in a world of metaphor, the poet is always acutely conscious that metaphor has no value apart from its function; that it is a device, an artifice. . . . Fausto's kind are alone with the task of living in a universe of things which simply are, and cloaking that innate mindlessness with comfortable and pious metaphor so that the "practical" half of humanity may continue in the Great Lie, confident that their machines, dwellings, streets and weather share the same human motives, personal traits and fits of contrariness as they.
>
> Poets have been at this for centuries. It is the only useful purpose they do serve in society: and if every poet were to vanish tomorrow, society would live no longer than the quick memories and dead books of their poetry.
>
> It is the "role" of the poet, this 20th Century. To lie.

And the role, perhaps, of the reader as well.

MAUREEN QUILLIGAN

Thomas Pynchon
and the Language of Allegory

Wordplay is the generic basis of narrative allegory. The linguistic disposition of personification, one of the most trustworthy signals of allegory, indicates one reason why. Relying on the process of making inanimate nouns animate, it requires a curious treatment of language as language. The violation of grammatical categories necessary for personification emphasizes the very operation of language and, with such self-consciousness about the grammar, it is only logical for author (and reader) to become sensitive to other surface verbal structures. When the structure of personification is extended and becomes more than a mere figure of speech, verbal matter provides the most accessible resource for further exfoliations of plot. Mimicking not life but the life of the psyche, the author has less recourse to models of action in verisimilar reflections of the phenomenal world; he will therefore need that system of signs which retrieves for us the process of intellection itself. When language itself becomes the focus of his attention rather than the action language describes, the author may be said to write allegory. More than any other creator of narrative, the allegorist begins with language purely; he also ends there.

Take, for example, Thomas Pynchon. Pynchon initiates the action of *The Crying of Lot 49* with a pun. At the outset of the narrative, Oedipa Maas receives a notice that she has been named executor of a former lover's will. The narrator explains, "She had never executed a will in her life, didn't know where to begin, and didn't know how to tell the law firm in L.A. that she didn't know where to begin." Oedipa would prefer not to take on the responsibility until her lawyer manages to convince her with speculations about "what

---

From *Critical Essays on Thomas Pynchon.* © 1981 by Richard Pearce. G. K. Hall, 1981.

111

you might find out." Pynchon explains that "as things developed, she was to have all manner of revelations," and that furthermore, her decision to "execute a will" ends what is described as Oedipa's previously "Rapunzel-like role of a pensive girl, somehow, magically, prisoner among the pines and salt fogs of Kinneret, looking for somebody to say hey, let down your hair." Previously imprisoned in passivity or will-lessness, Oedipa, by accepting executorship of Pierce Inverarity's will, stumbles upon the possibility that the will might be in an important sense a testament, a text of words which might explain part, if not all, of the meaning of her world. One of her first actions is, significantly, to read the will more carefully, assuming that "if it was really Pierce's attempt to leave an organized something behind after his own annihilation then it was part of her duty . . . to bring the estate into pulsing, stelliferous Meaning."

When on the last page we discover that Oedipa arrives at a stamp auction improbably taking place on a Sunday, to hear the auctioneer's "crying" of lot 49, we are asked to remember that the forty-ninth day after Easter, or the seventh Sunday, is Pentecost, or the celebration of the day Christ reappeared to his disciples to endow them with the special linguistic abilities necessary for bringing his estate into stelliferous Meaning. Then they learned how to execute his last will and testament, by writing and disseminating the New Testament, or his Word.

By becoming the executor of Pierce Inverarity's last will and testament, Oedipa comes close to a kind of sacred discipleship. Pynchon signals this (perhaps only parodic) meaning in the same way Spenser does, by the tension he puts on the word "will." This word, peculiarly posed in its consistent association with "legacy," "estate," "testament," "test," "Word," points to the slippery verbal process at work in the narrative which is perhaps more obvious in Pynchon's names—Oedipa Maas, Pierce Inverarity, or Benny Profane (this last form V.)—all of which sound like the labels of personifications with often humorous, if not also obscene, connotations. Thus Oedipa is a female Oedipus who must solve Pierce's sphinxlike riddle (though not kill off her parents) and Pierce Inverarity's will appears to offer some way of piercing the verities of life.

While Edmund Spenser's typical punning is silent, almost subliminal, Pynchon brings the question of wordplay into the narrative itself, no doubt because he must work more obviously to educate the reader into taking seriously the methods necessary for reading his work. At one point in her quest, Oedipa meets a derelict who suffers from delirium tremens, which makes Oedipa speculate on the coincidence between the term for this disease, the "DT's," and the function of these letters in an equation for time differentiation.

Behind the initials was a metaphor, a delirium tremens, a trembling unfurrowing of the mind's plowshare. The saint whose water can light lamps, the clairvoyant whose lapse in recall is the breath of god, the true paranoid for whom all is organized in spheres joyful or threatening about the central pulse of himself, the dreamer whose puns probe ancient fetid shafts and tunnels of truth all act in the same special relevance to the word, or whatever it is the word is there, buffering, to protect us from. The act of metaphor then was a thrust at truth and a lie, depending where you were: inside, safe, or outside, lost. Oedipa did not know where she was. Trembling, unfurrowed, she slipped sidewise, screeching back across the grooves of years, to hear again the earnest, high voice of her second or third collegiate love Ray Glozing bitching among "uhs" and the syncopated tonguing of a cavity, about his freshman calculus; "dt," God help this old tattooed man, meant also a time differential, a vanishingly small instant in which change had to be confronted at last for what it was, where it could no longer disguise itself as something innocuous like an average rate; where velocity dwelled in the projectile though the projectile be frozen in midflight, where death dwelled in the cell though the cell be looked in on at its most quick. She knew that the sailor had seen worlds no other man had seen if only because there was that high magic to low puns, because DT's must give access to dt's of spectra beyond the known sun, music made purely of Antarctic loneliness and fright.

Probing shafts of truth, puns underpin the parallel systems of metaphors with which Pynchon structures the book, and as the lyric density of this passage suggests (predicting as well the basic metaphor of *Gravity's Rainbow* in the frozen projectile), wordplay may by its swiftness point to the mystery of quickness, being posed at the threshold between life and death.

Aside from making his heroine ask the fundamental question about all fiction—about all language—in her remark on the truth of metaphor, Pynchon signals his readers to read *The Crying of Lot 49* as a verbal structure which unfolds by bringing into prominence the very medium in which the action is being described. He asks his reader to pay attention to the book as a text, not primarily as a story involving characters who move through a realistically organized plot. Pynchon continually presents the possibility that Oedipa's increasing verbal consciousness is mere paranoia, a silly, meaningless game. As foil for the serious possibilities inherent in the shared initials, he provides

the name of Mucho Maas's radio station: KCUF. Yet, although he hedges
the seriousness of his method by constant undercutting jokes and ironies, he
continually reinforces the notion that there is "high magic" to puns, and his
testing of the possibility provides the mechanism at work generating the action.

   Gravity's Rainbow makes its foundation in a matrix of language seen from
a more generalized perspective than Pynchon's earlier focus on the simple pun
could allow. All allegory is rooted in a cultural context which grants to language
a significance beyond that belonging to a merely arbitrary system of signs and
it presupposes at least a potential sacralizing power in language. Out of its
magic phenomenality—out of language sensed in terms of a nearly physical
presence—the allegorist's narrative comes, peopled by words moving about an
intricately reechoing landscape of language.

   Offering a carefully global view of the state of humanity in mid-twentieth
century (characters from all continents are represented), *Gravity's Rainbow*
searches in words for a means of salvation. Part of the quest is a search for
the cause(s) of damnation which, at his most specific—printing an old-fashioned
pointing hand in the margin—Pynchon calls a "rocket cartel," where the operative word is not so much rocket as "cartel." That is, our damnation derives
from the operation of a businesslike multinational corporation of the "elect"
whose purpose is to keep the preterite imprisoned in a dehumanizing lack of
communication. This summary, to be sure, unfairly simplifies what is a vastly
complex exfoliation of patterns, plots, counterplots, paranoias, and possible
leaps of faith, through an interlacing web of connections between characters
(hundreds of them), none of whom, even those few whom Pynchon hints are
members of the "elect," know what is going on. Pynchon, like allegorists before
him, is concerned with process, not with "finalization" (Pynchon puts the ugly
word in quotes), and the process he makes his reader go through is immense,
dense, and confusing. Using a favorite device of allegorists before him inherited
from the grail romances, Pynchon interlaces the narrative, switching back and
forth between at first widely disparate characters, a process which, as he suggests
on the first page, "is not a disentanglement from, but a progressive knotting
into." If not all the relationships are clear at the end of the book, then they
are at least less blurry, and we are made to sense that there is, inescapably,
a connection among them all.

   If there is one central character in *Gravity's Rainbow*, it is Tyrone Slothrop
whose Puritan heritage links him with the Bible-toting American past, and
hence (though unintentionally) with the origins of allegory in American culture.
It is not only in this context, however, that Pynchon reveals his concerns for
language, although Slothrop is the character around whom hover a number
of obsessively persistent metaphors about the "text." When, for instance,

Slothrop's Russian counterpart, Tchitcherine, finds himself sent to the first plenary session of a committee on the Turkish alphabet, Pynchon focuses on a basic theory of language in mid-twentieth century, and reveals the central linguistic concerns underlying the narrative. Edward Mendelson has remarked that this episode seems at first "disproportionate and anomalous," yet upon consideration it appears as the book's "ideological and thematic center." Just as Pynchon reveals the underlying mechanism of wordplay pervading *The Crying of Lot 49* in Oedipa's discovery about that "high magic to low puns," so, in *Gravity's Rainbow* he also alerts the reader to the usually hidden springs of the narrative.

The conference is supposed to decide what shape a New Turkic alphabet should take to translate a previously oral language into literacy. Tchitcherine has been assigned to the °*1* committee, where, Pynchon tells us, °*1* seems to be "some kind of G, a voiced uvular plosive." The problem is that "there is a crisis of which kind of g to use in the word 'stenography.' " Pynchon explains:

> There is a lot of emotional attachment to the word around here. Tchitcherine one morning finds all the pencils in his conference room have mysteriously vanished. In revenge, he and Radnichy sneak in Blobadjian's conference room next night with hacksaws, files and torches, and reform the alphabet on his typewriter.
>
> (*Gravity's Rainbow*)

As this comic sabotage of writing implements hints, Pynchon is concerned with what happens to language when it gets written down; through alphabetization, the means of human communication get bureaucratized and language loses (at the same time it gains another) magic power. Thus: "On sidewalks and walls the very first printed slogans start to show up, the first Central Asian fuck you signs, the first kill-the-police-commissioner signs (and somebody does! this alphabet is really something) and so the magic that the shamans, out in the wind, have always known, begins to operate now in a political way." The shaman's sympathetic magic (whereby a name is as good as a toenail for casting spells) will not, however, outlast the bureaucratization of print. In the next episode, connected to the previous by an interlacing formula— "But right about now, here come Tchitcherine and Dzaqyp Qulan"— Tchitcherine discovers what he has helped to do. During what in middle Scots was called a "flyting match," a verbal battle in alternating spontaneous verse, Tchitcherine realizes that "soon someone will come out and begin to write some of these down in the New Turkic Alphabet he helped frame . . . and this is how they will be lost." When Tchitcherine prepares to record the Aqyn's sacred song about the Kirghiz Light, Dzaqyp Qulan asks, "How are you going to get it all?" " 'In stenography,' replies Tchitcherine, his g a little glottal."

The Aqyn's song is itself about wordlessness, about a place "where words are unknown":

> If the place were not so distant,
> If words were known, and spoken,
> Then the God might be a gold ikon,
> Or a page in a paper book.
> But It comes as the Kirghiz Light—
> There is no other way to know It.

Having allowed the Kirghiz Light to take away his eyes, the Aqyn sings that "Now I sense all Earth like a baby." The scene in which the song is sung ends with a gesture reminiscent of a grade B cowboy movie convention—" 'Got it,' sez Tchitcherine, 'Let's ride, comrade,' " Pynchon tells us that later Tchitcherine will reach the Kirghiz Light, "but not his birth." And must later in the book Pynchon tells us, drawing the line of connection between Tchitcherine and Slothrop, "Forgive him as you forgave Tchitcherine at the Kirghiz Light." What we have to forgive Tchitcherine for, I think, is his having assumed that he had "got it" when he wrote it down. Language, insofar as it is just another bureaucratic system, is another instrument by which "they" stop true human communication. In focusing on the Kirghiz, Pynchon chose a people who went through the process of becoming literate at the time of World War II, a process lost in the mists of history for most of western civilization. By bringing Tchitcherine into the context of a tribal, oral society, directly out of the context of a committee on the New Turkic Alphabet, Pynchon pinpoints the loss of a primitive, holistic experience of the cosmos at the moment of original literacy. Edward Mendelson has emphasized the political operation of the alphabet; but what language gains in political power it loses in spiritual potency. The shaman magic has been translated into political action to be sure, but specifically into murder ("Kill-the-police-commissioner!"). When Tchitcherine brings the death of an oral society by bringing an alphabet, he cannot participate in the cosmic rebirth sung by the Aqyn.

The notion dramatized here, of violence done by the letter, Pynchon probably owes to theories about oral poetry first promulgated by Milman Parry and elaborated by A. B. Lord in *Singer of Tales*. The notion had been, of course, hotly debated at the time of Plato, so it is not necessarily new; but the theory was much debated in the 1960s and gave rise to a pervasive self-consciousness about the medium of written language. Developments in French linguistics have continued to reassert the prejudice against the written word implicit in theories of oral poetry. In perhaps the fullest summary of the complicated case against writing, Jacques Derrida lists all those developments in human culture which can be associated with the letter:

> All clergies, exercising political power or not, were constituted at the same time as writing and by the disposition of graphic power; . . . strategy, ballistics, diplomacy, agriculture, fiscality, and penal law are linked in their history and in their structure to the constitution of writing; . . .the possibility of capitalization and of politico-administrative organization had always passed through the hands of scribes who laid down the terms of many wars and whose function was always irreducible, whoever the contending parties might be; . . . the solidarity among ideological, religious, scientific-technical systems, and the systems of writing which were therefore more and other than "means of communication" or vehicles of the signified, remains indestructible; . . . the very sense of power and effectiveness in general, which could appear as such, as meaning and mastery . . . was always linked with the disposition of writing.
>
> (*Of Grammatology*)

Pynchon's association of writing with political power is not, therefore, some idiosyncratic ideology; his attitude is of his age. Derrida is, as I understand him, trying to find a rhetoric of writing which will allow him to go beyond the epistemology of Presence, while Pynchon is firmly mired in the problems of Presence—that is, of trying to decide how humanity can witness its own existence in relationship to itself, to the planet, and to whatever overall purpose there might (or ought to) be behind such an existence. But Pynchon would, I think, agree with Derrida's assessment of the "violence" of the letter, without, however, celebrating it. More important, what Pynchon indicates has been lost to the letter is something he attempts to reconstitute for his reader in *Gravity's Rainbow*.

The details of the New Turkic Alphabet scenes, Mendelson shows, are taken from an article in a scholarly journal. As this bit of arcane lore hints, Pynchon has done a surprising amount of homework in all areas covered by the book; how much of it is fact and not fiction will take scholars some time to discover. In the meantime, Pynchon's reader often finds himself feeling paranoid long after reading the books when he stumbles on some fact he had thought was part of the (wildly improbable) fiction. It is as if these discoveries were meant to be part of the reader's experience of the book, and the effect is more than mere satire of the contemporary scene; it becomes a process whereby the work of art reaches out to shape one's immediate response to life. The time bombs of particular historical detail comprise one method Pynchon uses to get beyond the covers of his book.

But Pynchon remains the captive of the very print he laments in the Kirghiz Light episode. His problem is to use language in such a way that it can free itself of its bureaucratizing control of experience. Part of his solution is the very bad pun. Thus Lyle Bland's lawyers are Salitieri, Poore, Nash, De Brutus, and Short; "So as the mustache waxes, Slothrop waxes his mustache." Macaronic as well, the puns cross cultural boundaries; hence the many references to the German lake, Bad Karma. Such idiot's delights as these can give way to more elaborate parodies of the usual methods of allegorical narrative, whereby Pynchon appears to have set up a whole story so he can make a pun; thus "hübsch räuber" can mean either "helicopter," or, without the umlauts a lady cannot pronounce, "cute robber." And this entire story appears as a mere aside in an otherwise recondite discussion of the meaning of "ass backwards" followed by an equally elaborate dissertation on the problems of translating "Shit and Shinola." One of the earliest examples of these extended tasteless excretions of style is the long series of variations possible in the syntactic context of the sentence "you never did the Kenosha kid" — a sentence which "occupies" Slothrop's consciousness on one of our first introductions to it.

The sheer silliness of this kind of punning wins for Pynchon's language a few laughs which dissolve the kind of seriousness bureaucratized by formal good taste. But Pynchon also has his own seriousness about this kind of word-play which may have been intended partly to provide a magic talisman in the style, to ward off (however unsuccessfully) the evil eye of criticism. Just as the narrator explains of the planted puns in Brigadier General Pudding's caprophiliac exercises — "But these are not malignant puns against an intended sufferer so much as a sympathetic magic, a repetition high and low of some prevailing form" — Pynchon's punning indicates the magic potency of language to indicate an otherness beyond the merely mundane. Puns in *Gravity's Rainbow*, as in *The Crying of Lot 49*, ground the book's structure in polysemy rather than in a parallel system of metaphors. Language is less controlling when it is not controlled to mean only one thing, but many. Making a different argument about the puns, George Levine has remarked that "language may suggest the possibilities it cannot present. . . . This is only possible if language does not protect us with the comfort of its structure, if the word can somehow put us in the presence of 'whatever it is the word is there, buffering, to protect us from.' " Because bad puns are in a sense anomalies of structure, they may be pointers to truth, may be initially so uncomfortable a signal of the author's medium that we are forced to see the use of language in a different way. And that may be to accept the use of language as magic.

In the only moment of pure salvation in the book, a witch named Geli Tripping loves Tchitcherine so well that she is able to cast a spell on him to make him give up his hate and relax into love. Pynchon comments: "This is magic. Sure—but not necessarily fantasy." Like the gaiety of her tripping with Slothrop, her magic is sympathetic; making a doll of her lover she chants a charm so that he, blinded by love, does not recognize his African half-brother, whom he had intended to kill. Some shaman magic is not just political.

Another kind of verbal play does not provide salvation, merely escape. Trapped at a menacing upperclass dinner party, Roger Mexico and Seaman Bodine manage to nauseate the diners into not noticing their departure by offering alliterative alternatives to the printed menu, such as "fart fondue" and "vegetables venereal." Again the humor is sophomoric, but sophistication in the context of the dinner party is suspect, and sophomores are closer to the baby the Aqyn had become than those who make the sounds of well-bred gagging heard throughout the dining room. If the effect of this wordplay, and of things like General Pudding's more-than-naked midnight lunches, is repellent, they at the same time are signatures in the book's style signaling that in *Gravity's Rainbow* Pynchon attempts to escape the bad kind of bookishness that haunts Slothrop.

As a scion of an old Puritan family that ran a lumbermill in the Berkshires, which "converted acres at a clip into paper," Slothrop is at the mercy of an ancestry that produced "toilet paper, banknote stock, newsprint—a medium or ground for shit, money, and the Word." It is the cause of his paranoia: "Did They choose him because of all those word-smitten Puritans dangling off Slothrop's family tree? Were They trying to seduce his brain now, his reading eye too?" Yet inherited paranoia is the only road Slothrop can take:

> He will learn to hear quote marks in the speech of others. It is a bookish kind of reflex, maybe he's genetically predisposed—all those earlier Slothrops packing Bibles around the blue hilltops as part off their gear, memorizing chapter and verse, the structure of Arks, Temples, Visionary Thrones—all the materials and dimensions. Data behind which always, nearer or farther, was the numinous certainty of God.

Slothrop's relationship to this ancestry is just as ambivalent as Pynchon's use of Puritan theology. The nostalgia implicit in noting that an earlier kind of paranoia had resulted in faith in the "numinous certainty of God," while

modern day paranoia discovers a rocket cartel, marks the difficulty faced by
any modern day allegorist. If, as Foucault has argued, the notion of "resemblance"
empowered Renaissance thought to find linked analogies in a harmonious
cosmos, then slender church steeples now resemble "white rockets about to
fire." Unfortunately, the impotently subversive advice that Pynchon has a pine
tree offer Slothrop during a hallucination late in the book—"Next time you
comes across a logging operation out here, find one of their tractors that isn't
being guarded, and take its oil filter with you"—will no more atone for the
sins of his Puritan ancestors than it will stop present exploitation of forests.
Yet Pynchon grants to one of Slothrop's forebears the authorship of a tract
on "preterition" which articulates the basic metaphor of salvation in the book.
William Slothrop, a happy pig farmer in western Massachusetts, "felt that what
Jesus was for the elect, Judas Iscariot was for the Preterite." Slothrop wonders:
"Might there have been fewer crimes in the name of Jesus, and more mercy
in the name of Judas Iscariot?" Perhaps this heresy was the "fork in the road
America never took"—although, with this reference to Frost, Pynchon may
be implying that the other road would not have made that much difference.

Slothrop is not the only character in the novel concerned with deciphering
codes; all of the characters are more or less engaged in acts of interpretation.
Foremost among those worshipping a text is Enzian, the half-Russian, half-
African, half-brother of Tchitcherine who searches for the elusive 00001 Rocket,
assuming it to be scripture, only to realize fairly late that not the rocket, but
postwar ruined Europe is the text:

> There doesn't exactly dawn, no but there *breaks*, as that light you're
> afraid will break some night at too deep an hour to explain away—
> there floods on Enzian what seems to him an extraordinary under-
> standing. This serpentine slag-heap he is just about to ride into now,
> this ex-refinery, Jamf Ölfabriken Werke AG, *is not a ruin at all.*
> *It is in perfect working order.* [. . .] all right, say we *are* supposed to
> be the Kabbalists out here, say that's our real Destiny, to be the
> scholar-magicians of the Zone, with somewhere in it a Text [. . .]
> well we assumed—natürlich!—that this holy Text had to be the
> Rocket [. . .]
> But, if I'm riding through it, the Real Text, right now, if [. . .]
> the bombing was the exact industrial process of conversion, each
> release of energy [. . .] plotted in advance to bring *precisely tonight's*
> *wreck* into being thus decoding the Text, thus coding, recoding,
> redecoding the holy Text . . . If it is in working order, what is it
> meant to do? [. . .]

> It means this War was never political at all, the politics was all
> theatre, all just to keep the people distracted . . . secretly, it was
> being dictated instead by the needs of technology.

While Pynchon carefully discounts the validity of personifying technology (later
capitalized) as the force that caused the war—that causes all ills—his use of
the terminology of textual interpretation here is more than mere metaphor.
Enzian's moment of illumination ends with a one-sentence paragraph that
belongs as much to the author as to the character: "Somewhere, among the
wastes of the World, is the key that will bring us back, restore us to our
Earth and to our freedom"; on this desperate hunch, which sounds more like
an article of faith, hangs not only Enzian's but Pynchon's search for salvation.

The metaphor of the Text is so widespread throughout the book that if
it does not order the kind of reading the book itself receives, then, at the very
least, it makes of all the characters, readers. Natural descriptions are turned
into its terms; thus ice on a building side "of varying thickness, wavy, blurred"
is "a legend to be deciphered by lords of the winter, Glacists of the region,
and argued over in their journals." But textual interpretation is not just the
province of cold scholarly journals. Of the many signs appearing throughout
the red districts of Berlin during the war that read "An Army of Lovers Can
Be Beaten," Pynchon explains, "They are not slogans so much as texts, revealed
in order to be thought about, expanded on, translated into action by the people."
Like the alphabet which translates the shaman's magic into the political sphere,
a holy text not only states a truth but incites action. The action here, of course,
as in the immediate response to the New Turkic alphabet, would be killing.
Yet the text is also ambiguous. Reversing the Spartan notion of comrades in
arms, the text would mean that lovers would not fight wars. Language in
Gravity's Rainbow, as in other allegories, has power to cause evil as well as
good, and ambiguity can cut both ways.

Blicero, just before he debauches Enzian, discovers that the relation between action and words is the thinnest of lines: "Tonight he feels the potency
of every word: words are only an eye-twitch away from the things they stand
for." Elsewhere the narrator hints that at a similar moment, Slothrop is hovering at the threshold of some epiphany of the center—a threshold which,
however, we are warned he will never cross:

> Is it, then, really never to find you again? Not even in your worst
> times of night, with pencil words on your page only Δt from the
> things they stand for? And inside the victim is twitching, fingering
> beads, touching wood, avoiding any Operational Word. Will it really
> never come to take you, now?

That any word might be "operational" is the important point here. All of Pynchon's antics are aimed at making the reader aware of the potent possibilities of language in the realm of action—which then become capable of leading us back to earth and our freedom. That endpoint may itself be wordlessness, but the road back can only be through the tortuous twistings of human reason, tracing all the labyrinthine systems of signs, one of which may be the key, the text.

> Each plot carries its signature. Some are God's, some masquerade as God's. This is a very advanced kind of forgery. But still there's the same meanness and mortality to it as a falsely made check. It is only more complex. The members have names, like the Arch- angels. More or less common, humanly-given names whose security can be broken, and the names learned. But those names are not magic. That's the key, that's the difference. Spoken aloud, even with the purest magical intention, *they do not work*.

Such a "theory" has all the limits of the unreliable character who offers it, but Pynchon's invocation of the magic of language here recalls the shaman magic of the Kirghiz Light episode; all of his references are self-consciously primitive. Yet, if it is at basis a very learned sophistication which allows him to know word-magic as archaic anachronism, still, at the same time, Pynchon appears to suspect that self-consciousness serves humanity poorly. Whatever the road back, however, it will have to take into account this pervasive (perhaps decadent) self-consciousness, as *Gravity's Rainbow* does. So imprisoned in bookishness that raindrops appear to Slothrop as "giant asterisks on the pavement, inviting him to look down at the bottom of the text of the day, where footnotes will explain all," Pynchon's reader and Pynchon's communication itself are prisoners of the book; all the filmic metaphors cannot turn the print on the page into anything else.

Pynchon's drive to get to the ineffable through the anomalies of language (such as the magic correspondences indicated by puns, silly or otherwise) owes little directly, I should think, to any one theorist of language; but that texts like *The Crying of Lot 49* and *Gravity's Rainbow* can now be written and read derives absolutely from the context of a widely felt concern for the being of language in the last half of the twentieth century.

This context was, of course, long in the making; Freud, whose *Interpre- tation of Dreams* in particular elevated the status of the play on words to the level of a nearly "magic" key for unlocking the secrets of the psyche, was a seminal figure in its creation. But the revolution in linguistics has been most responsible for the renewed interest. While as a linguist Noam Chomsky has posited that to describe the process by which man learns language is to describe what is essentially human about human nature (turning *homo sapiens* into *homo significans*), the method of French linguistic analysis in its application to many other heretofore unverbal areas of human endeavor has made it necessary, as Foucault has put it, to ask what must language be "in order to structure in this way what is nevertheless not in itself either word or discourse." Language once again is perceived as interpenetrating the nonverbal world. Further, linguistics' insistence on structure, as an invariable relationship within a totality of elements has also, as Foucault points out, opened up "the relation of the human sciences to mathematics," and so it has helped to close the gap between language and the purer forms of semiological systems that was created in the seventeenth century. At the very least, language-related studies have begun to regain some of the status they lost to mathematics.

Pynchon witnesses the fact of this closed gap by scattering very complicated equations throughout his text (which have sent his illiterate—in this sense—readers scurrying for basic textbooks in thermodynamics and information theory); his characters are technicians, engineers, research psychologists, and, furthermore, they live in their work. It is not just that the "hard" sciences offer systems of metaphors not usually found in modern novels, but that the book broaches the question of the interrelationship between disparate value systems. If church steeples look like rockets about to fire, rockets also look like church steeples. Pynchon has a sense of humor about the problem, of course. Challenged by a successful rival, the statistician Roger Mexico defensively says at one point, "Little sigma, times P of s-over-little-sigma, equals one over the square root of two pi, times e to the minus s squared over two little-sigma squared. . . . It is an old saying among my people." It would be possible to see this Gaussian formula for normal distribution as Mexico's comment on his rival's "normality"—it corresponds to the narrator's general sense of Jessica's betrayal of Mexico. If this is how we are to read it (after having checked the relevant text, or asked a friend who knows), then mathematics has been made to comment. The fundamental point about the equations, however, is that they, along with words, maps, service manuals, technical blueprints, even the flight of birds and the patterns of ice may all "also be read." All must be read, interpreted, and perhaps acted upon, for all these signs may be part of the "holy text," which will inform its readers (both inside and outside the book) of the truths that make human existence meaningful.

In a sense *Gravity's Rainbow* merely fleshes out in narrative form our concern for the Word. The plethora of questions our present culture has about language — as summarized here by Foucault — is the context which informs the shape of Pynchon's text:

> What is language? What is a sign? What is unspoken in the world, in our gestures, in the whole enigmatic heraldry of our behaviour, our dreams, our sicknesses — does all that speak, and if so in what language and in obedience to what grammar? Is everything significant, and, if not, what is, and for whom, and in accordance with what rules? What relation is there between language and being, and is it really to being that language is always addressed — at least language that speaks truly?
>
> *(The Order of Things)*

Pynchon's characters are obsessed with these very questions, and the rushing answerlessness of the tone also marks Pynchon's narrative, which flips from question to question as it rushes from quest to quest. The answers, if any, are promised in the interfaces of the work itself, in its own way of re-doubling back upon itself so that its own labyrinthine structure mirrors the polysemous density of what may again be merely a paranoid vision of reality. But the sheer weight of the narrative does not allow one to dismiss its vision as "mere" paranoia — which is momentarily personified in the text as an "allegorical figure . . . (a grand old dame, a little wacky, but pure heart)." Paranoia may be dictionary-defined as insanity, but it is a "sickness" which appears to speak the only hope of salvation:

> The rest of us, not chosen for enlightenment [. . .] must go on blundering inside our front-brain faith in Kute Korrespondences [. . .] kicking endlessly among the plastic trivia, finding in each Deeper Significance and trying to string them all together like terms of a power series hoping to zero in on the tremendous and secret Function whose name, like the permuted names of God, cannot be spoken [. . .] to bring them together [. . .] to make sense out of, to find the meanest sharp sliver of truth in so much replication, so much waste.

All of the principal characters, as interpreters or readers of signs, have a difficult task; engaged in reading not merely as an aesthetic exercise, but as a holy activity, they attempt to make sense of the world so that they can live it it.

In his description of the strange, enigmatic, and dense linguistic context of the late twentieth century, Foucault considers the position literature occupies.

It is one of many different possible dispositions to language which are all, however, parallel:

> For philologists, words are like so many objects formed and deposited by history; for those who wish to achieve a formalization, language must strip itself of its concrete content and leave nothing visible but those forms of discourse that are universally valid; if one's intent is to interpret, then words become a text to be broken down, so as to allow that other meaning hidden in them to emerge and become clearly visible: lastly, language may sometimes arise for its own sake in an act of writing that designates nothing other than itself.
>
> *(The Order of Things)*

Literature is that language which "arises for its own sake": having begun his whole discussion of the fluctuating *episteme* with a text from Jorge Luis Borges, Foucault implicitly makes it the paradigm for modern literature, of that species of language which "addresses itself to itself as a writing subjectivity, or seeks to re-apprehend the essence of all literature in the movement that brought it into being . . . all its threads converge upon the finest of points . . . upon the simple act of writing." The "ludic denial" of anything extraneous to the artistry itself in such writing is more than "art for art's sake," it is an insistence on language which "has nothing to say but itself, nothing to do but shine in the brightness of its being." But unlike Borges' or Nabokov's art for which Foucault's description is quite apt, Pynchon's language with all its self-reflexive qualities is more than self-referential. The language of *Pale Fire* only doubles back upon itself and encapsulates, within itself, a closed system, pivoting on the solipsistic neatness of the allegorical critic. Pynchon's readers are radically unlike Kinbote, who knows what "other meaning" he is going to find in his chosen text; and they spend more time reading the world than they do books, unlike the self-consciously literary characters who dominate Borges' stories. If Pynchon's characters do not even know what the text is, suspecting that in fact anything may be part of the readable text, they for that very fact inhabit an allegorical cosmos—where nothing is mere ornament nor all the ludicrousness merely ludic.

All of Pynchon's characters are readers, but Oedipa in *The Crying of Lot 49* is the protagonist who is presented most consistently as a reader. Oedipa's texts are not the pervasive metaphors of *Gravity's Rainbow*; they are real. First there is the text of Inverarity's will; she reads this over "more carefully" when she suspects that it may have something to teach her. Then, of course, there is the text of *The Courier's Tragedy*, a copy of which she spends much of the book's action trying to locate. Oedipa is dogged by misprints, multiple editions; she tracks down the history of Trystero through a series of footnotes in obscure texts. Puzzled by hieroglyphs of all sorts, she admits her incapacity to read them. We learn that the mysterious bidder at the final auction is initially a "book bidder," that is, one who sends in bids by mail which, in the context of the Trystero stamps, is suspicious. Even punctuation becomes important. After she at first misreads the letters W.A.S.T.E. stamped on a trash basket as a single word, she notices the periods between the letters and understands it to be an acronym.

Her problems in reading, however, are not merely problems of making out the words. She does not know how to read what the words mean. She considers alternate readings of her situation:

> [Pierce] might have written the testament only to harass a one-time mistress, so cynically sure of being wiped out he could throw away all hope of anything more. . . . He might himself have discovered the Tristero, and encrypted that in the will, buying into just enough to be sure she'd find it. Or he might even have tried to survive death, as a paranoia.

As a reader, Oedipa comes up with a binary choice: "Behind the hieroglyphic streets there would either be a transcendent meaning, or only the earth." And her binary alternatives are the same ones the reader of *The Crying of Lot 49* is faced with: "Another mode of meaning behind the obvious, or none. Either Oedipa in the orbiting ecstasy of a true paranoia, or a real Tristero." The problem posed Oedipa in the will's "code" is the same problem Pynchon's text poses for the reader. She is either mad or there is some redeeming system of communication. We are never told; the book ends before the crying of lot 49.

The clues in the number 49, the Pentecostal references, and the whole religious vocabulary pose the choice as one between a secular madness, modern paranoia, or a surprisingly traditional Christianity. The central moment of linguistic revelation in the book, when Oedipa offers to mail a letter for a derelict she finds on the street and later helps up to his impoverished room in a flop house, is a moment of remarkable *caritas*; a one-time frequenter of Tupperware parties, she can physically cradle someone who would seem to be beyond her reach on the social spectrum.

The total action of *The Crying of Lot 49* may, in fact, take place between Easter and Pentecost. Oedipa drives into San Narciso on a Sunday (and Pynchon mentions the fact twice, on [successive] pages); the concluding auction takes place on a Sunday. The action of the book could easily take seven weeks, although, characteristically, Pynchon does not give any definite proof. The possibility is only suggested, just as all other possibilities are suggested. If the first Sunday were to be Easter, it might explain Oedipa's sense of being "parked at the centre of an odd religious instant. As if, on some other frequency, or out of the eye of some whirlwind rotating too slow for her heated skin even to feel the centrifugal coolness of, words were being spoken." Pynchon could easily have given us a glimpse of Easter bonnets, bunnies, any secular signal, however improbable it might have been to catch sight of someone on a Sunday in San Narciso, but he does not. He dangles the possibility before us; but if this is one of the unspoken words in the book, it is for us, as for Oedipa, out of earshot. We can only guess.

We cannot know for sure that Oedipa is going to learn from the mysterious bidder on lot 49; we are granted, for that matter, no ultimate certainty that the dragon will stay dead at the end of the first book of *The Faerie Queene*; we know, in fact, that Archimago and Duessa are loose once again to do the dragon's work. The conclusion is inconclusive; the Redcrosse Knight leaves his Una to mourn. The choice of what we are to conclude about the significance of Oedipa's experience is ours and ours alone. And the ultimate effect of noticing the parallel between action and reading, both open-ended, is to enforce the reader's sense of his own need to decide, to impose his own conclusions on the story. If the Redcrosse Knight has slain his dragon, there are hints that other dragonets will live to grow and become foes of other heroes in other places. Pynchon's last ominous paragraph, as Oedipa is locked into the auction room, reveals not only Oedipa's heroism in being there in the first place but the power of the discovery which may lie just beyond the covers of the book.

In *Gravity's Rainbow*, Pynchon's technique differs from his organization of the reading experience in *The Crying of Lot 49*. He presents the reader not with a binary choice but with a number of alternatives. No longer a question of choosing ones or zeroes, the process of reading *Gravity's Rainbow* is, as Edward Mendelson puts it, "to read *among* the various probable interpretations of the book." His methods of signaling this process, however, include all the usual allegorical techniques for alerting the reader to the significance of his own interpretative activities. In the final book, "The Counterforce," Pynchon focuses on the need for the reader to participate more fully in the books's proliferation of meaning. It is not just that the main character Slothrop simply evaporates from the action, although by this loss of novelistic focus the reader is left at somewhat looser ends than he would have been had Slothrop continued to center his attention; rather Pynchon gives his reader a fictional part to play. No longer merely offering options, as in the cryptic invitation

to choose the infant prince's smile—"which do you want it to be?"—Pynchon
anticipates the reader's anticipations: "You will want cause and effect. All right."

After accepting the reader's challenge he proceeds to give a hilariously
improbable account of one character's arrival at a specific place at a specific
moment in time. Pynchon does not merely parody novelistic techniques of
verisimilar plotting, his indication of his reader's need for cause and effect puts
the reader in a class with the Pavlovian Pointsman, a repellant character who
dominates the opening book, "Beyond the Zero," by his inability to understand
the statistician Roger Mexico's neglect of causation. What in fact causes Thanatz's
appearance at a certain place in time is not only improbable, it concerns the
lack of continuity between cause and effect. Thanatz has been rescued off the
wandering Nazi ship *Anubis* by a Polish undertaker, who, inspired by Ben
Franklin's experiments with the electricity of lightning (an investigation of
cause and effect), tries to get hit by lightning. Thanatz is fascinated because,

> Well, it's a matter of continuity. Most people's lives have ups and
> downs that are relatively gradual, a sinuous curve with first deriva-
> tives at every point. They're the ones who never get struck by
> lightning. No real idea of cataclysm at all. But the ones who do
> get hit experience a singular point, a discontinuity in the curve of
> life—do you know what the time rate of change *is* at a cusp? *Infinity*,
> that's what! [. . .] You're *way* up there on the needle-peak of a
> mountain and don't think there aren't lamergeiers [. . .] waiting for
> a chance to snatch you off. [. . .] they'll carry you away, to places
> they are agents of. It will *look* like the world you left, but it'll be
> different. Between congruent and identical there seems to be another
> class of lookalike that only finds the lightning-heads. Another world
> laid down on the previous one and to all appearances no different.
> Ha-*ha*! But the lightning-struck know, all right! Even if they may
> not *know* they know.

It turns out that the undertaker is not interested in all these fanciful explanations of the causes of the effect of discontinuity; the interest is rather that of
the narrator, who introduces his own obsessions as a contrast: the undertaker
thinks getting hit by lightning will help him in his job, where he might have
to deal with the bereaved families of lightning victims. "You are perverting
a great discovery to the uses of commerce," Thanatz tells him.

The galloping absurdity of the account of causation here—which includes
little men with "wicked eyebrows" wearing Carmen Miranda hats—undermines
the reader's faith in the legitimacy of asking for such explanations. Signaled
to read in terms other than the fidelity to normal causation, the reader will

read Thanatz's comment about commerce in relation to an immediately preceding (but otherwise unconnected) interpolated story about a light bulb named Byron, through which Pynchon examines the perversions of the discovery of electricity to the uses of commerce, a story that, in fact, can itself be read to examine the spiritual life of men caught in the grid of economic coercion. Pynchon raises the question of cause and effect to alert the reader to its inapplicability for reading *Gravity's Rainbow*. Connections between events in the book are not causal, but are cued by verbal subjects—light bulbs-(electricity)-lightning-enlightment-(spiritual knowledge of other worlds, other possibilities for human communication). Lightbulbs communicate with each other more efficiently than human beings do in *Gravity's Rainbow*.

The point of the episode of the Polish undertaker is not therefore to supply a cause for an effect but to make a thematic commentary on previous action. It does of course deposit Thanatz at the proper place at the proper moment, so that he can be whisked away by the Russian police, which abduction begins a tortuous series of transfers so that he finally ends up with the Schwarzkommando headed by Enzian, whom he can tell about Blicero's firing of the Rocket, giving information they (and we) have long awaited. But the links in this chain of cause and effect only operate to survey the horrible results of such thinking. Thanatz becomes one of the many displaced persons created by the War. Shipped about like cattle, they are treated no differently from the wartime inmates of the concentration camp Dora. The War was supposed to end such treatment; in part it was "caused" by the attempt to "effect" an end to such suffering. Ironically, one effect of the War is to continue to cause it.

The most obvious manipulation of the reader as reader occurs when Pynchon uses the "you" form of address, but he also involves the reader with "we," not to mention his presentation of fictional characters as readers, or mirrors in which the reader must see himself reflected. The "you" address operates a first as a translation of the German "Mann," the French "on"—Pynchon avoids the prissy-sounding British "one." But the "you" soon operates to mean "you-reader." Thus a long reflection that begins as Enzian's reverie about being a rocket engineer becomes an argument aimed at the reader's own collusion in the rocket mentality, a collusion he shares simply by being a citizen of the American twentieth century.

> Here's Enzian ramrodding his brand-new rocket through the night.
> [. . .]
> Russian loudspeakers across the Elbe have called to you. American rumors have come jiving in to the fires at night and summoned,

against the ground of your hopes, the yellow American deserts, Red Indians, blue sky, green cactus. How did you feel about the old Rocket?

On the next page the "you" modulates to "we":

But remember if you loved it. If you did, how you loved it. And how much—after all you're used to asking "how much," used to measuring, to comparing measurements [. . .] and here in your common drive to the sea feel as much as you wish of that dark-double-minded love which is also shame, bravado, engineer's geopolitics—"spheres of influence" modified to toruses of Rocket range that are parabolic [. . .]

. . . not, as we might imagine bounded below the line of the Earth it "rises from" and the Earth it "strikes" No But Then You Never Really Thought It Was Did You Of Course It Begins Infinitely Below The Earth And Goes On Infinitely Back Into The Earth it's only the *peak* that we are allowed to see, the break up through the surface, out of the other silent world, violently.

Changing into the impersonal after this, only two pages later does the discourse touch home base in Enzian's consciousness. The modulations between "you," "we," and the impersonal, objective third person are not terribly troublesome; save for the fact that the "you" form of address is informal diction and therefore a bit unusual (part of what reviewers would call Pynchon's "voice"), the various forms of address pose no vast problems in experimental styles. But the "you" does pull the reader into the action, insisting more forcefully on his identification with the character in question, here Enzian, than would a more orthodox form of approach.

One of the things the reader has in common with Enzian and with all the other characters who are, in this, like Enzian, is the search for Slothrop. Just as Slothrop disintegrates, characters go in search of him. In one of the cinematic climaxes of the plot, Enzian meets Katje, who is hunting for Slothrop as some sort of expiation for her sins against him. They converse about him, exchange cryptic evaluations of each other's natures. Caricaturing the girl-spy survivor that she is, Katje begins to flirt with Enzian:

"Flirt if you want, " Enzian now just as smooth as that Cary Grant, "but expect to be taken seriously." Oh, *ho*. Here's whatcha came for, folks.

Here Pynchon manipulates celluloid romance conventions as deftly as ever Jean de Meun manipulated the conventions of allegorical romance and to the same effect; each questions the reader's involvement in the narrative. Has Pynchon caught us agape with all our voyeuristic tendencies showing? Did we really come for this kind of confrontation? Or is it that, so programmed by the signals, basing our responses on our previous experience with similar cues, we all react to "that" Cary Grant in the same way? Pynchon, of course, disappoints our expectations; there is no seduction scene. But the disappointment of expectations functions much as Langland had made it function; the reader must look for other causes of the effects.

In the last complete segment of the book, Pynchon disappoints the narrative arc he has set up in the Enzian-Katje confrontation. Even the search for Slothrop is abandoned and appears to have been something of an illusion. The final counterpointed episodes which flash at an exponentially increasing rate, announced by Joycean newspaper headlines, are prefaced by a piece which includes an unlocatable conversation between a "spokesman for the counterforce," and a reporter from the *Wall Street Journal.* "We were never that concerned with Slothrop qua Slothrop," the spokesman says.

> INTERVIEWER: You mean, then, that he was more a rallying-point.
> SPOKESMAN: No, not even that. Opinion even at the start was divided. It was one of our fatal weaknesses. [I'm sure you want to hear about fatal weaknesses.] Some called him a "pretext." Others felt that he was a genuine, point-for-point microcosm. The Microcosmists, as you must know from the standard histories, leaped off to an early start. [Brackets are Pynchon's]

In such a way does Pynchon begin literally to demolish a critical commentary on Slothrop. Yet soon the spokesman, having begun the parenthetical observations, concludes a longer confession in brackets which enacts the process of selling out to commercial interests. The confession invokes the search for Slothrop as the quest for the grail, a quest, however, inverted and scrambled by the spokesman's guilty self-consciousness.

> [Yes. A Cute way of putting it. I am betraying them all . . . the worst of it is that I know what your editors want, *exactly* what they want. I am a traitor. I carry it with me. Your virus. (. . .) Between two station-marks, yellow crayon through the years of grease and passage, 1966, and 1971, I tasted my first blood. Do you want to put this part in?] We drank the blood of our enemies. (. . .) The sacrament of the Eucharist is really drinking the blood of the enemy. [Pynchon's brackets]

Troublesome for many reasons, not the least being that the time scheme (1966–1971) is far removed from the main action of the book (which takes place in and around 1945), this passage ultimately addresses the reader as an "editor" whose virus the spokesman carries. And the question "Do you want to put this part in?" is a real one, posing for the reader the choice of how he wants to read this book. The bracketed passage breaks the connection between Slothrop and the Eucharist; not to put it in, to avoid it as a parenthesis, is offered as the reader's option. Yet to do so would be to make the reader an editor who somehow is responsible for spreading infection. The choice is difficult.

As if to underscore the connection between Slothrop and the Eucharist, Pynchon refines and comments on the blood of this passage in the next episode, which concerns the passing on of a legacy to Slothrop from Seaman Bodine. Bodine had given Slothrop a shirt soaked in the blood of John Dillinger. Bodine remembers their last conversation in our final glimpse of Slothrop:

> "They wouldn't want you thinking he was anything but a 'common criminal'—but Their head's so far up Their ass—he still did what he did. He went out and socked Them right in the toilet privacy of Their banks. Who cares what he was *Thinking* about, long as it didn't get in the way? A-and it doesn't even matter why we're doing this either. Rocky? Yeah, what we need isn't right reasons, but just that *grace*. The physical grace to keep it working, Courage, brains, sure, O.K., but without that grace? forget it. Do you— please, are you listening? This thing here works. Really does. It worked for me, but I'm out of the Dumbo stage now, I can fly without it. But you, Rocky. You. . . ."

Tinged with the rhetoric of a sentimental war picture, just as all Pynchon's revelatory moments are protected against their own seriousness by a self-conscious infection with the conventional diction of film (that repository of our American mythic consciousness), this apotheosis of John Dillinger as some sacrificed revolutionary whose blood has magic powers connects the blood-drinking spokesman of the counterforce with the story of the Passion; then also a revolutionary had hit the toilet privacy of the banks and had been executed as a criminal. Bodine's curious stutter (A-and) also associates his voice with the narrator's, both of whom use the stutter of sincerity—shy, inarticulate, American sincerity (like that Gary Cooper)—throughout the book. Pynchon does not duck the charge of mass hysteria in the vision of the mob compelled to soak up Dillinger's blood, but he also allows Bodine to say "there *was something else*." If that need for "something else" is the experience which Christian mythology attempts to fill, Pynchon has already indicated how it cannot provide a universal redemption. In the first book, during a lyrical description of the Advent evensong he had offered this:

> Listen to this mock-angel singing, let your communion be at least in listening, even if they are not spokesmen for your exact hopes, your exact, darkest terror, listen. There must have been evensong here long before the news of Christ. Surely for as long as there have been nights bad as this one—something to raise the possibility of another night that could actually, with love and cockcrows, light the path home, banish the Adversary, destroy the boundaries between our lands, our bodies, our stories, all false, about who we are [. . .] sure somebody's around already taking bets on that one, while here in this town the Jewish collaborators are selling useful gossip to Imperial Intelligence, and the local hookers are keeping the foreskinned invaders happy, charging whatever the traffic will bear, just like the innkeepers who're naturally delighted with this registration thing, and up in the capital they're wondering should they, maybe, give everybody a *number*, yeah, something to help SPQR Record-keeping . . . and Herod or Hitler, fellas (the chaplains out in the Bulge are manly, haggard, hard drinkers), what kind of a world is it [. . .] for a baby to come in tippin' those Toledos at 7 pounds 8 ounces thinkin' he's gonna redeem it, why he oughta have his head examined. . . .
>
> But on the way home tonight, you wish you'd picked him up, held him a bit. Just held him, very close to your heart, his cheek by the hollow of your shoulder, full of sleep. As if it were you who could, somehow, save him. For the moment not caring who you're supposed to be registered as.

The choice Pynchon offers here and elsewhere in *Gravity's Rainbow* is the recognition of the need for "something else," for that *allos* or Other which could reveal another world laid down over this one, where hookers, collaborators, bureaucrats barter away their own humanity in the *agora* or marketplace. Bodine cannot hold the vision or pass it on to Slothrop: "Then as he'd feared, Bodine was beginning, helpless, in shame, to let Slothrop go." And Slothrop evaporates completely after this, remembered only in a parenthesis "(Some believe that fragments of Slothrop have grown into consistent personae of their own. If so, there's no telling which of the Zone's present-day population are offshoots of his original scattering [. . .]" and a dependent clause, "It will all go on, occupation or not, with or without Uncle Tyrone."

Slothrop's evanescence, either mere disappearance or transcendence, poses the reader a choice. It is more complicated than the choice Oedipa's dilemma poses the reader because she, at least, shares the need to choose, while readers are very much on their own in interpreting the significance of Slothrop's failed quest. In great part, the choices readers make define not so much the book they have been reading, as themselves. David Leverenz has chosen, "Slothrop can't scream any more, and that's his final perdition." Scott Sanders sees Slothrop as "the most spectacular instance of Mondaugen's Law in operation" where Mondaugen's Law states that "the narrower your sense of Now, the more tenuous you are" and thus for him, Slothrop disintegrates into the freedom of death. Others define Slothrop's disappearance from the book less definitely in the negative. George Levine argues that "if Slothrop is a failure, as, in his betrayal of Bianca, we see him to be, it is nevertheless wrong to read past the richness and sense of possibility in the language of Slothrop's last moment." Suffice it to say that Slothrop's demise poses the reader a problem. Pynchon himself gives no final interpretation. Against Mondaugen's Law, which appears to define his dissolution as nonexistence, there is the language (which Levine invokes) of Slothrop's vision of the rainbow: "Slothrop sees a very thick rainbow here, a stout rainbow cock driven down out of pubic clouds into Earth, green wet valleyed Earth, and his chest fills and he stands crying, not a thing in his head, just feeling natural. . . ." Against his cartoon romp in an Oedipal nightmare, there is the last memory of Seaman Bodine. Slothrop's disappearance positions the reader in the same place as the elliptical end of *The Crying of Lot 49* did—in the same place, we must add, that Melville leaves his reader, that Jean de Meun and Hawthorne leave theirs—choosing among interpretations.

It would be easy to cite examples of the peculiarly personal choices all of Pynchon's readers have made. All interpretations, all criticism is subjective choice of one sort or another, of course, but Pynchon's readers consistently testify to a crucial sense of personal identity involved in their decisions. "If we are willing to risk it, there may be at the center of each preterite moment a stout rainbow cock and a wet valleyed earth." "We are not determined, unless . . . paradoxically, we *choose* to be." "To the Pynchon who throws shit in my white male established American face and then calls it mine, I respond first with confused intimidation, even guilt, and then with annoyed dismissal. . . . True, my participation in this language intricates me into the vision I so roundly disapprove of. . . . But he hooks me nevertheless." "As readers . . . we have survived. But we have more of the knowledge that is required if we are to act freely outside the world of writing—in the world where acts have consequences, time is real, and our safety is far from certain."

We could dismiss this personal testimony as merely a prevailing fashion in criticism; the persistence of the note of personal choice among critics who, having different specific interpretations of the book, generally disagree, would suggest that if Pynchon doesn't attract this kind of reader to begin with, he certainly makes his readers self-conscious about the personal revelation involved in their reading of the book. The emphasis on choice, on a choice that locates the reader as an ethical decisionmaker outside the realm of the book in his relation to his world, suggests that *Gravity's Rainbow* has done its work well. Whether we choose with Levine to see Slothrop's final dissolution as visionary transcendence, or with Leverenz as an ultimate perdition, we must choose. "*Gravity's Rainbow* invites its readers to make quantum leaps towards relationship in the very act of reading."

Tzvetan Todorov has written of the quest of the Holy Grail that "the quest of the Grail is the quest of a code. To find the Grail is to learn how to decipher the divine language." The grail is not found in *Gravity's Rainbow*; there is no pot of gold beneath its parabolic arch. There can, it seems, be no final decipherment of its language, divine or otherwise. It is, of course, we who are sitting beneath the rainbow's end, when the narrator invites us— "Now, everybody"—to join in in song, just as if, as in the *Queste*, the grail is within each of us.

While Todorov's argument, that the act of finding the grail is to learn to read the divine language, compellingly connects reading and action, this connection takes place legitimately only in the area of critical response. We can judge characters by their response to the Grail: Galahad is better than his father at least in this, because Lancelot cannot find the holy vessel. Pynchon's technique is to make the problem of choice a part of the text itself. To be able to make a decision about Slothrop's nature, about the judgment we are supposed to make of his quest and his presumed failure in it, is to be able to read the significance of the language which surrounds that quest, language especially significant by virtue of its self-reflexive saturation with metaphors drawn from Slothrop's own experience of reading signs. Lost in a comic book fantasy, we must judge Slothrop's reading to have been at one point surely very trivial. But his persistent concern with texts, along with all the other characters' obsessions with reading, makes us judge his success or failure in terms of how well he reads the signs about him. One must respect his ability to balance multiple interpretations, and to see how each leads to another and how they all interconnect—as in his figure-ground perception of the Nazi swastika, or his seeing a crossroad's resemblance to the underside of the V-2 rocket. Our interpretation must operate by such progressions as well, for his reading instructs ours. Whether Slothrop's last moments are to be dismissed as true transcendence or a kind of Mucho-Maas dematerialization is something, however, which the text forces us to decide on our own.

This burden of choice is perhaps the most intolerable weight the reader of allegory must bear. All his intellectual efforts at constructing a coherent meaning for the text, faithfully following its exfoliations that never proceed by a neat series of cause and effect, attending to the text's tortuous verbal complexities at the same time he must keep the actions of the characters in view for whatever helps to understanding they might offer—all these efforts do not result in a controlled display of objective meaning (although one can be quite surprised by the formal symmetries of allegory's self-reflexive artistry), they result instead in a weighty self-consciousness not merely at the end of the narrative but at each stage of the reading experience where the text constantly invites and then exposes the reader's imposition of meaning. Reading is always a process of selective editing, but only allegories directly ask "Do you want to put this part in?" implicitly querying at the same time "And what does it say of you that you want to put it in or leave it out?" The indictment appears to come from the author-narrator of the work, but the point is not that the author, Langland, Melville, Hawthorne, Spenser, or Pynchon, is out merely to trick the reader. To say that the author selects this or that device to create the effect is only a short-hand way of expressing the intentionality of the narrative form itself. Having set himself the task of writing an allegory (whether or not he calls it by such a name), that is, of investigating the possible permutations of truth he might be able to detect in his language, the author poses questions—do puns reveal the divine design? are words "true" or do they lie?— which make the reader share in the scrutiny of the verbal medium. By virtue of the fact that the immediate focus of the narrative is the language in which it is written, not only must the reader come to terms with the language in which such questions are asked, but he must also recognize that his answers— or such answers as seem to be indicated by the text—can be made only in language. This circular process ends in a self-consciousness the only way out of which may seem to be an arbitrary act of choice. Language does or does not lie. And if a reader chooses not to choose, he or she is left with a series of infinite regressions. Such a negative capability may, however, be purely the privilege of authors; for even if the reader chooses to accept the infinite regressions for what they are—inconclusive—that in itself is a choice. While this may seem the more honest response, the objective one that stays true to the text's own balance of interpretation, the mere posing of the text demands something more of the reader. There is always the implication, which Dante carefully points out at the opening of his allegory, that nonchoice is worse that damnation.

Those who never chose, who never made the act of self-definition by deciding what it was they believed in, are condemned to spend eternity chasing elusive banners in the vestibule of the inferno. Not even hell will have them.

MARCUS SMITH AND
KHACHIG TOLOLYAN

The New Jeremiad:
Gravity's Rainbow

Every reader of *Gravity's Rainbow* (henceforth GR) quickly becomes aware
of Pynchon's deep involvement with American Puritanism, and Scott Sanders
has already claimed that "the mental structures implied in Pynchon's fiction
reproduce dominant features of Calvinist and Puritan doctrine." The controlling
idea of GR is that the world's present predicament—the system of global terror
dominated by ICBMs—threatens to fulfill in historical time the apocalyptic
and millennial visions which prevailed in the Puritan culture of colonial New
England. Curiously, critics have failed to observe that this and related issues
of Puritan doctrine are elaborated in GR within a formal framework that is
an astonishing and brilliant reworking of the old Puritan jeremiad. Pynchon's
complex vision of crisis and apocalypse is best understood in the context provided by the historical studies of Perry Miller and Sacvan Bercovitch, and by
Frank Kermode's theoretical study of narrative, *The Sense of an Ending*.

A standard definition of the jeremiad is given by Shaw in his *Dictionary
of Literary Terms*: "A mournful complaint, an expression of sorrow, a lamentation denouncing evil. *Jeremiad* . . . refers to any literary work which contains
prophecies of destruction or complaints about the state of society and the
world." However, the jeremiad of early American literature is neither as simple
nor as static as this definition suggests. Perry Miller noted twenty-five years
ago that the jeremiad is "the one literary type which the first native-born
Americans . . . developed, amplified, and standardized. . . . [and which was] for
the second generation the dominant literary form."

From *Critical Essays on Thomas Pynchon.* © 1981 by Richard Pearce. G. K. Hall, 1981.

Pynchon's awareness of the early jeremiad tradition is clearly established by the text of GR. After the title page, with its illustration of clouds, the opening sentence—"A screaming comes across the sky"—intimates a typical jeremiad symbol of God's wrath coming out of the heavens to punish errant humanity. The connection is confirmed and clarified a few pages later when Slothrop is bracketed by the first two V-2 rockets to fall on London; his mind slips away to the past, to his family's history in New England. In this genealogical reverie we are three times presented with the Hand of God symbol: it is chiseled on Constant Slothrop's tombstone, and "that stone hand pointing out of the secular clouds" has haunted "all of the Slothrop blood one way or another, the nine or ten generations tumbling back . . . except for William the very first. . . ." In the last paragraph of this sequence, Pynchon directly fuses Puritan past and London present (it is September 8, 1944) in a vivid metaphoric linkage: ". . . slender church steeples poised up and down all these autumn hillsides, white rockets about to fire, only seconds of countdown away . . . *this is how it does happen—yes the great bright hand reaching out of the cloud. . . .*" This image is reinforced by virtually every subsequent reference to the Rocket.

Jeremiad imagery also dominates the terrifying conclusion of GR. "The last image" on the movie screen at the Orpheus Theatre when the film ends is "a bright angel of death," and as the rocket poised above threatens to descend, the readers are asked to sing "a hymn by William Slothrop, centuries forgotten and out of print":

> There is a Hand to turn the time,
> Though thy Glass today be run,
> Till the Light that hath brought the Towers low
> Find the last poor Pret'rite one . . .
> Till the Riders sleep by ev'ry road,
> All through our crippl'd Zone,
> With a face on ev'ry mountainside,
> And a Soul in ev'ry stone.

The imagery—the Hand of God, the Hourglass of Mutability, God's obliterating Light, the Towers of New Jerusalem, the Apocalyptic Horsemen—is a compilation of typical jeremiad figures.

Pynchon, like Joyce in *Ulysses*, parodies the major forms of rhetoric used in his encyclopedic narrative; the jeremiad rhetoric is no exception. Mother Slothrop's tipsy intimations of apocalypse—"Naughty Malline's on her *third* martini"—are voiced in her letter to Ambassador Kennedy:

> It isn't starting to break down, is it, Joe? Sometimes, you know
> these fine Boston Sundays, when the sky over the Hill is *broken*

into clouds, the way white bread appears through a crust you hold
at your thumbs and split apart. . . . You know, don't you? Golden
clouds? Sometimes I think—ah, Joe, I think they're pieces of the
Heavenly City falling down. I'm sorry—didn't mean this to get so
gloomy all so sudden, it's just . . . but it *isn't* beginning to fall apart
is it, my old fellow Harvard-parent? Sometimes things aren't very
clear, that's all. . . . and it's very hard at such times really to believe
in a Plan with a shape bigger than I can see.

It would be possible to fill a small catalogue with such passages from GR.
We offer these specific instances in order to establish that Pynchon—whose
first American ancestor wrote a theological tract—is quite familiar with the
imagery and rhetoric of the early colonial jeremiad, and to suggest that their
use at such critical points as the beginning and end of GR is a signal that he
is concerned with many of the basic matters which preoccupied the early
jeremiad writers.

Like the old Puritan preachers, Pynchon begins by forcing on us a vision
of the Imminent End, the nearness of the day when human history will reach
its apocalyptic fulfillment. But whereas the old jeremiads depended upon the
concept of a blessed Covenant between God and the Puritans, GR is "a demonic
inversion of the divine covenant" [Frank D. McConnell, *Four Postwar American Novelists: Bellow, Mailer, Bareth and Pynchon*. University of Chicago Press,
1977]. This inversion allows no a priori, special dispensation for a saved remnant
of the Elect; in Pynchon's scheme there is only a preterite condition for the
entire human race over which the V-2 Rocket and all its more recent successors
are suspended. Rare moments of "special dispensation" are possible but neither
guaranteed nor permanent. The Rocket operates by a dynamic of predestination—one which does not function on a scale of heavenly time outside human
history but moves in an arc of gravitational as well as historical inevitability,
and which carries it from Blicero's launching of a specific rocket, the 00000,
in the spring of 1945, directly to the moment when the Rocket "reaches its
last unmeasurable gap above the roof of this old theatre, the last delta-t."

These matters tie GR to the Puritan tradition of the jeremiad, but the
depth and importance of the connections—and the implications they have for
contemporary theories of narrative—must be considered further, in light of
several major scholarly texts. Perry Miller's work, especially *The New England
Mind: From Colony to Province*, is the starting point. Miller is almost exclusively concerned with the theme of declension in the seventeenth-century
jeremiad, the long and intensifying lament over the failure of the Puritans to
achieve the New Jerusalem. He describes the different forms of the jeremiad
and their appeal to different generations of Puritans. For the first generation,

the jeremiad consisted of "a recital of afflictions" followed by a "prescription" which maintained a "scrupulous distinction between physical afflictions . . . and sins." Here, the prescription is based on the "implicit recognition of a causal sequence: the sins exist, the disease breaks out; the sins are reformed, the disease is cured."

Although GR resembles this first phase of the jerermiad in that it, too, can be read as a catalogue of the afflictions of the western world just before, during and after World War II, it remains much closer to the later type of the jeremiad, which Miller ascribes to the middle of the seventeenth century. A second, less optimistic generation of Puritans saw sin as an affliction, not a cause. This fundamental shift had profound psychological consequences:

> The subjective preempted the objective: a universal anxiety and insecurity had become no longer something which, being cause, could be allayed by appropriate action, but rather something so chronic that the society could do nothing except suffer—and perpetually condemn itself.

Miller emphasizes that such a major shift in formal convention is accepted, indeed embraced "by a generation [only when] it makes sense of experience which previously has been ignored."

Some serious contemporary scholars claim to find the popularity of a grim catalogue of afflictions like GR incomprehensible. Much of that popularity is due to the fact that this contemporary jeremiad takes into account un-acknowledged anxieties, temptations and fears which are primarily *collective* in nature. The two hundred and twenty characters and innumerable subplots of GR serve as a vehicle for articulating collective fears, the like of which a single prophetic voice had the authority to articulate in the Puritan jeremiad. Despite structural differences, GR remains, like the second form of the jeremiad, a form for "conceiving the inconceivable." Furthermore, whereas the Puritans' jeremiads were also used to make "intelligible order out of the transition from European to American experience," GR addresses itself to anxieties and afflictions that become global rather than local when the American *returns* to Europe at the end of World War II.

Pynchon views the jeremiad-narrative as a form that has the capacity to deal with the condition of apocalyptic dread in the contemporary world, which is a place in which violence is no longer linked to the human will but rather to a set of technocratic systems that have gained ascendancy and autonomy. This dread is a new avatar of the spiritual anxieties which haunted the Puritans on a religious level; it is rendered palpable in the technological forms that threaten us, but it would be a serious mistake to see the technological side of Pynchon's work as its only, or even as its most important aspect. He knows that even our collective responses to fear tend to be technocratic, to involve both science and bureaucracy; to counter a general dread, we tend to generate precisely the kind of structure which feeds our fears. Pynchon's adaptation of the jeremiad uses the vocabularies of scientific and bureaucratic organizations, but these remain embedded in a larger fiction which envisions its central task as the Puritan authors of the jeremiad saw theirs: to bespeak doubts and apprehensions about the American dream, to question the fraying but still powerful sentiment that America—and the technology of Western culture—have a favored place and mission in history. The prolonged incantation-catalogues of GR, which list and lament the details of American technological might, spring as the purging incantations of the jeremiads sprang, "from something deeper than pious fraud, more profound than cant: they were [and are] the voice of a community bespeaking its apprehension about itself."

Though useful, Miller's analysis—and ours—must be modified by more recent studies, especially the work of Sacvan Bercovitch, who has convincingly demonstrated that the early jeremiads not only stressed the declension from the millennial dream but just as persistently and continuously projected a vision of redemption and fulfillment. His elegant and massively documented study, *Horologicals to Chronometricals: The Rhetoric of the Jeremiad*, achieves a "paradigm shift" in our understanding of the jeremiad and the Puritan imagination. Basically, Bercovitch shows that from the very beginning the jeremiad operated within a complicated and sophisticated double time scale. On one level (and Miller's study is focused primarily on this level) the jeremiads articulated the imperfect and provisional world of events in historical time, which impeded the New Jerusalem. Bercovitch (drawing on a passage from Melville's *Pierre*) labels this the "horological" dimension. The various disasters and setbacks which occurred on this mundane temporal level, however, were always coordinated and synchronized with a second level of perfected time, the "chronometric." For Bercovitch the jeremiads, throughout the seventeenth century and beyond, use a double time perspective that alternated "between the provisional and the predetermined . . . between the horological, the imperfect time of mankind, and the chronometrical, the 'original Heaven's time' unaffected 'by all terrestial jarrings.' " This effort "to impose chronometrical upon horological . . . motivates the rhetoric" of the jeremiads and "implicitly affords a synthesis of the human and the divine," even as it articulates "a vital and enduring aspect of the colonial imagination." In Bercovitch's study the jeremiad emerges not only as an incessant lamentation but also as a visionary form "peculiar and essential to the New England orthodoxy" characterized by "its unshakable optimism." Despite the deepening sense of declension, the increasing disparity between ideal and fact in the Puritan society, the Jeremiads continue to "restructure experience in terms of the one reality where horological and chronometrical can be made to synchronize, the realm of the imagination."

Such synchronization, achieved in the realm of the imagination, has been labeled "consonance" by Frank Kermode in his major theoretical study of fiction, *The Sense of an Ending*. He borrows the term from an American sociologist who studied religious groups that prophesied apocalypse and, when it did not arrive, restored the prophecy by recalculation rather than abandoning it. Starting with this, Kermode goes on to claim that the need for consonance is psychological and fundamental, and fictions about ends—like the Biblical Revelations—are ways of maintaining our sense of our lives as potentially meaningful, even when they seem overwhelmed by the provisional and the contingent:

> To maintain the experience of organization we . . . need many
> . . . fictional devices. . . . [The order of fiction become] our way
> of bundling together perception of the present, memory of the past,
> and expectation of the future in a common organization. Within
> this organization that which was conceived of as simply successive
> becomes charged with past and future: what was *chronos* becomes
> *kairos*. . . . *chronos* is 'passing time' or 'waiting time'—that which,
> according to revelation, 'shall be no more'—and *kairos* is . . . a point
> in time filled with significance, charged with a meaning derived
> from its relation to the end.

Being itself the End, Apocalypse is the most special of such *kairoi*.

While Bercovitch's concept of horological/chronometric is rooted in a specific historical moment, Kermode's *chronos/kairos* though derived from a study of the Bible as fiction, is made into a more abstract pattern applicable to all sorts of narratives. Both patterns contrast the provisional with the predetermined, the imperfect moments of daily life and historical time with privileged moments—especially endings which promise to transcend the merely temporal. (It is a terminological accident that Kermode's *chronos* is comparable to the horological dimension of Bercovitch, and not to his chronometrical.)

These accounts of the double time-schemes of the imagination are directly relevant to GR, despite the fact that upon an initial reading one is struck by the vehemence with which its author appears to reject all but the horological dimensions of history, which he chronicles in such proliferating and accurate detail. Pynchon does suggest that the Puritan obsession with some other-worldly chronometric dimension as the locus of perfection has constituted a fatal denial of the here-and-now. Furthermore, he asserts that the German (and by extension, Western) obsession with rocketry is a catastrophic secular attempt at transcending our earthbound condition. By using this analogy, Pynchon locates at the root of our own century's malaise the ruthlessly expansive European energies that brought the Puritans (and the death of the Indian) to America, and then gave the death-dealing, space-traveling V-2 Rocket and its descendants to the West.

These are large themes, sharing one common thread: the rejection of the horological dimension of history whose evils are seen, paradoxically, as being the result of a cruelly energetic and ceaseless attempt to transcend the horological, to achieve an ideal chronometric dimension. Pynchon contemplates this rejection in a very literal-minded fantasy in which the original sin of Puritanism is redeemed by a dream of history-as-film, one that can be run backwards:

> Ghosts of fishermen, glassworkers, fur traders, renegade preachers, hilltop patriarchs and valley politicians go avalanching back from Slothrop here back to 1630 when Governor Winthrop came over to America on the *Arbella*, flagship of a great Puritan flotilla that year, on which the first American Slothrop had been a mess cook or something—there go that *Arbella* and its whole fleet, sailing backward in formation, the wind sucking them east again . . . back across an Atlantic whose currents and swells go flowing and heaving in reverse . . . a redemption of every mess cook who ever slipped and fell when the deck made an unexpected move, the night's stew collecting itself up out of the planks and off the indignant shoes of the more elect, slithering in a fountain back into the pewter kettle as the servant himself staggers upright again and the vomit he slipped on goes gushing back into the mouth that spilled it.

But this image of history-as-vomit, as powerful as it is ugly, can not be reversed in the real, horological time of GR, which finds analogies to the deadly colonization of America by the Puritans in the extinction of the harmless dodo birds on the Dutch-colonized island of Mauritius, and in the German genocide of the Hereros in Southwest Africa, as well as in the crushing of the Indians of the Pampas and the destruction of the oral culture of the Kirghiz in Central Asia; the catalogue of such sins and the resulting afflictions fills the pages of GR, which, like much of Whitman's work, proceeds by enumeration. There can be no doubt as to Pynchon's judgment of these events. Europe, powered by the dream of transcending earthly limits and the horological dimension itself, has wreaked havoc on the rest of the world, and, incidentally, on its own citizens, since the seventeenth century: "Christian Europe was always death, Karl, death and repression." Despite the general applicability of the term "Christian Europe," it virtually never means Catholic Europe in GR;

rather, it almost always refers to Protestant Europe and its expansion since the seventeenth century.

Rejection of the horological does not suffice, either in the jeremiads described by Bercovitch, or in GR. In addition to rejection by fantasy reversal and by angry enumeration, Pynchon seeks to bring us to an awareness of a dimension of time which, while it is unlike the Puritan notion of "heaven's time," nevertheless retains an analogical relationship to the chronometric dimension of the old jeremiads. In the grim world which GR creates with such scrupulous care, the kind of hope embodied in any alternative can only be tentative.

GR is a fiercely polemical but honest narrative, which is to say that it presents will full force the powerful horological reality which it will attempt to deny, qualify, or at least bypass. History is no mere straw-figure here; it is irreversible and one-directional. Those who submit to it be accepting its end-oriented momentum develop a particular kind of self, as Mondaugen, a V-2 engineer and icy cynic, suggests when he states his horological view of human *persona*-lity:

> personal density . . . is directly proportional to temporal bandwidth
> . . . the more you dwell in the past and the future, the thicker
> your bandwidth, the more solid your persona. But the narrower
> your sense of Now, the more tenuous you are.

The basic terms of GR's discussion of the possibility of freedom from history's curse are established here: past and future (the horological) vs. the chronometric Now.

"Now" is the most insistent word in GR (closely followed by "here"). Around it Pynchon weaves his sense of the chronometric as it is or can be possible for contemporary man. What is at stake in GR is nothing less than the question of what hope is possible, and where, in a world where the alternatives seem to be the crushing weight of history or the corrupting attempts to achieve transcendence by clinging to a belief in a post-apocalyptic time or to a trans-global "elsewhere," a place to which the Rocket and its accompanying technology will take us. Pynchon's massive work erodes the possibilities offered by history, Puritan religion or technological achievement, but as these are undercut, the idea of what we shall call the "chronometric Now" is offered as a fragile possibility that is ever-recurring and usually ignored. Such an idea becomes possible only when Pynchon displaces categories from the religious-transcendental plane into the mundane, and finds plausible equivalents for them. The "chronometric Now" is a reimagining of the possibilities open to us in a secular age.

Like most alternatives and solutions offered in literature, this one is elusive.

Its beginnings are to be found in *V.* (1963), Pynchon's most purely horological fiction, which is obsessed with history and historiography. There, *V.*
is not only a cipher for various entities—Virgin, Valletta, Venus, Virtù—but
also a graphic representation of the choice of fates (the arms of the V) made
possible in a particular historical moment (represented by the apex of the V).
The record of the past, which was a succession of such moments of choice,
is distorted. Official history offers us, in both *V.* and GR, a vectoral, one-
directional, deterministic version of past reality: it ignores the "might-have-beens"
which were available to individuals or to the colonial Puritans, and by obscuring the alternatives offered by the past also obscures the possibilities that
the present may still be offering Now, under the shadow of the Rocket.
Pynchon seeks to return us to those possibilities by eliminating the "normal"
tension in most openly moralizing fiction, between what is and what *ought*
to be, and replaces it with the double tension between what is and might have
been, on the one hand, and what is and *can* be, on the other. Inevitably, this
burdens his fiction with the dominant moods of loss and fear, since he continues to see the imminent apocalypse of a rocket-borne atomic dawn as the
likeliest conclusion of the horological predicament.

Given this vision, Pynchon hesitates as he returns us to his alternative,
the chronometric Now that is pregnant with possibility, yet it has been a
persistent hesitation, one that began to manifest itself in *V.* There, Rachel goes
to visit the plastic surgeon Schoenmaker who is about to operate on her friend
Esther. For Rachel, such an operation represents false hope and false possibility.
In depicting Rachel's anger at what she perceives as deception, Pynchon offers
us his vision of hope and the rhetoric proper to it by presenting us with a
denial of one and a parody of the other; like most postmodern authors, he
is embarrassed by warmth, optimism, or the naïveté of intense feeling even
as he endows an occasional character with them, and so he works by negatives
and eschews the lyrical (except for a few extraordinary passages in GR).

Rachel and the narrator consider time and reverse-time, world and mirror-
world (the young Pynchon tends to borrow authority from the discourse of
physics), and conclude that the plastic surgeon's waiting room is appropriately
equipped with mirror and clock:

> Were there many such reference points, scattered through the
> world, perhaps only at nodes like this room which housed a tran-
> sient population of the dissatisfied; did real time plus virtual or
> mirror-time equal zero and thus serve some half understood moral
> purpose? Or was it . . . only a promise of a kind that the inward
> bow of a nose-bridge or a promontory of extra cartilage at the chin
> [would alter?]

Rachel's anger at the plastic surgeon stems from her feeling that what is offered here is the false promise of escape by reversal: the offer to replace a hook nose with the "inward bow of a nose-bridge" is only an emblem of all the other false promises to reverse the temporal (clock) and spatial (mirror) realities in which the characters of *V.* (and of GR) are enmeshed. Like his fictional character, Pynchon is not simply "puritanical"; he does not so much reject the pleasure Esther may derive from her changed appearance as he rages at the fact that such "change" comes to be perceived as the only possible and effective way of shaping one's life. Later, Esther deals with a pregnancy by resorting to the "reversal" that abortion can provide. Again, Rachel's anger—and Pynchon's—is directed not at the choice of abortion but at the choice which Esther earlier refuses to make: passive about sex and birth control, she becomes pregnant. Responsibility she leaves to the plastic surgeon who has become her lover, and who does not care about her pregnancy either, since there are medical techniques for dealing with it. This whole set of episodes is perhaps chosen naively and with an eye to the main chance for a criticism of society, but the young Pynchon hammers at the point which is directly relevant to GR: there are "nodes" (in time and space) in which technology offers the possibility of a freedom that is false because it makes us all the more dependent on itself. Analogically, we are seduced by our visions of a total and predetermined historical design into yielding our control of the separate moments of life. In Pynchon's narratives, characters are constantly lured away from the fleeting possibilities of shaping a fragment of Self or a minute part of History.

All this inevitably sounds rather grandiose in the critic's paraphrase. Pynchon goes to great lengths to avoid the embarrassment of preaching and prophecy, which perhaps the Puritan practitioners of the jeremiad had less need to fear, in a less ironic society. Indeed, he has been so successful in masking the rhetoric of hope that most criticism has failed to see the maddeningly complex structure of GR as a working out of the promises and betrayals of nodal points as they occur within a preapocalyptic horological history. No other modern author, to our knowledge, has created a work so thoroughly infused with this sense of recurring but fragile possibility, made more poignant by the fact that it is all enclosed in a narrative shaped by the darker vision of the jeremiad.

The fate of Tyrone Slothrop is at one level an illustration of such possibility. Near the end of GR, one of Pynchon's several nameless narrators evokes "the story of Tyrone Slothrop, who was sent into the Zone to be present at his own assembly—perhaps, heavily paranoid voices have whispered, *his time's assembly . . .* " (author's emphasis). The sentence creates an analogy between the making of a self and of history-in-the-making, "time's assembly"; what motivates such an assertion is Pynchon's desire to force us to think analogically, to insist that no matter how powerful and impersonal the forces that shape history may be, our only participation in that shaping will come in the form of personal choices made at the "nodes," at the forking of the "V," at the instances the horological offers us, and which instances we can transform into the "chronometric Now" by perceiving them as offering rich possibilities. Slothrop's failure, as Pynchon makes quite clear, lies in part in his refusal of the moment. He accepts some adventures when they are offered to him in the ruins of postwar Germany, but none that demand from him the vulnerability of love and understanding. Though all of Pynchon's several narrators tend to be elusive in assessing behavior and judging characters, one of them is quite clear in condemning Slothrop at the point in which he accepts Bianca's playful sexuality, but rejects the rest: "Right here, right now, under the make-up and fancy underwear, she *exists*, love . . . But her arms about his neck are shifting now, apprehensive. For good reason. Sure he'll stay for a while, but eventually he'll go, and for this he is to be counted, after all, among the Zone's lost."

"Here," "now," "lost": these words are of more than local significance in GR; unlikely as it seems to many scholars accustomed to the more exalted strains of Puritan literature, Pynchon sees a direct path that connects the refusal of sexually expressive love, offered "here" and "now," to the sense of loss and damnation which informs both the Puritan jeremiad and his own modern version of it.

Thomas Schaub is the one critic known to us who has seen that "Pynchon reserves some of his bitterest reproach for those who acquiesce to the formalism that obscures the terror with which each moment presents us." The terror, Schaub makes clear, is the result of that mixture of fear, hope and uncertainty with which we face major choices, whereas the "formalism" (not a word we would have used) is the tendency to avoid choice by pleading that the pregnant moment is really a small part of a larger design, too great for us to alter. The failure of Slothrop's "assembly" of self and history, already mentioned, is ascribed on the same page to just such a fatalistic formalism: "His cards had been laid down, laid out and read . . . but they point only to a long and scuffling future, to mediocrity . . . to no *clear happiness or redeeming cataclysm*" (our emphasis). We underline the secular vocabulary of happiness and the phrase "redeeming cataclysm," with its overtones of the religious, because they are characteristic of Pynchon's language and emblematic of his commitments. He rejects end-oriented fictions (to use Kermode's descriptive phrase) and their designs of coherence, whether purely horological or chronometric, because neither leaves room and courage to choose the uncertain possibilities offered by the moment, even though they might lead to nothing more than the too-easily-dismissed "mediocrity."

We have lingered over Pynchon's preoccupation with moments of choice because it is in the pages where he considers the issue that he comes closest to revealing his many links with the Puritan vision and with the jeremiad. Of course he uses the form of the latter in order to reject the ghost that haunted the former, and haunts us still, but he needs 760 pages of encyclopedic narrative to exorcise this particular demon, to earn his right to insist on the wealth of promise in "here" and "now" without seeming facile. He not only enumerates the temptations of designs and end-oriented forms, including the Apocalyptic, but also catalogues other, more mystical temptations so eloquently that many readers, undergraduates in particular, locate Pynchon's vision in these prophetic musings about a way of living that

> will have no history. It will never need a design change. Time, as time is known to the other nations, will wither away inside this new one. The Erdschweinhöhle will not be bound, like the Rocket, to time. The people will find the Center again, the Center without time, the journey without hysteresis, where every departure is a return to the same place, the only place.

These lines are spoken by Enzian, a leader of exiled Hereros from German Southwest Africa who have survived the Second World War. In this passage, rich in echoes of T. S. Eliot's *Four Quartets*, Enzian dreams of the Eternal Center as an alternative to the proposal made by Josef Ombindi, a competing chief of the exiles. The latter wants his tormented people to escape the horological by committing a form of mass suicide, by refusing to reproduce. Enzian formulates his vision of escape from history and into timelessness, yet recognizes that this is perhaps an impossible and certainly a dangerous dream: "The Eternal Center can easily be seen as the Final Zero," he muses, "names and methods vary, but the movement toward stillness is the same." What makes GR a rich but perplexing book is Pynchon's insistence upon making his modern jeremiad an encyclopedia of all the "names and methods" by which modern man seeks to surrender to history, to absolute fictions, to any design that promises to shield us from the vulnerability of living with the moments of choice, the so-called "nodes" of *V.* and the "cusps" of GR. When Tyrone Slothrop speculates about his Puritan past and "the fork in the road America never took, the singular point she jumped the wrong way from," he links personal history to national history, and the landscape of postwar Germany to that of the jeremiads. As Schaub has written, "in the vernacular of *Gravity's Rainbow* all lives are a succession of such points, where the curves of history, place and heritage form the terrible intersection from which we must choose a direction."

Pynchon directs our attention to the "terrible intersections" inherent in

certain moments in a number of other ways. His relentless commitment to
the present tense is perhaps the major rhetorical strategy, employed in shifting
"now" from a simple adverb to the primary key of a new chronometric level
in GR. "Now," of course, is the ultimate term of the book's opening paragraph:
"A screaming comes across the sky. It has happened before, but there is nothing
to compare it to now." Pynchon has several paradigmatic options here—"but
never like this," "but this is different," "but this is it,"—yet avoids them all,
which forces us to conclude that his selection of "now" to close this opening
paragraph is deliberate and meaningful. Moreover, this first sentence prefigures
quite deliberately the line at the book's end, "Now everybody—." Later, Pynchon
closes one of his mocking songs about ninety pages from the end with the
lines, "Skies'll be bright-er some day!/Now *ev'*rybody—." Other instances, too
numerous to deserve mention, abound.

The final "Now everybody—" is uttered on the last page of the fiction,
when a fictional Rocket bearing an uncomfortable resemblance to a ballistic
missile is poised to descend on the people gathered in a motion picture theatre
(Pynchon's modern version of the theatre-stage, the "gran teatro del mundo").
This "Now . . ." compels a double reading, which, if we are right, clearly
establishes a synchronized time perspective for GR, analogous to that which
Bercovitch locates in the old jeremiads. The most immediate meaning of
"Now everybody—" is horological: the cataclysm is here. The end, so long
predicted, so richly deserved, is here, the Rocket is about to arrive. The
horological dimension is about to be fulfilled and the consequence will be the
end of history, and perhaps human life.

But "Now everybody—" is also injunctive, imperative, a command that
we shift our time sense from the horological, where we dwell in the past and
the future, in the hopelessness of the "one-way flow of European time," to
the chronometric Now. It directs us away from a preoccupation with false
polarities of choice such as that offered by the horological/chronometric. In
this sense, GR carries on the traditions of *V.*, in which the letter V symbolizes,
among other things already cited, the forking horns of a false dilemma. Similarly, Pynchon rejects the either/or situation in which Oedipa finds herself
trapped in *The Crying of Lot 49*, in which the minimum of hope allowed to
her is that, "at the very least . . . [she can wait] for a symmetry of choices to
break down, to go skew. . . . How had it ever happened *here*, with the chances
once so good for diversity?" As we have said before, "Here," like "Now," is
an insistent, recurring word in all of Pynchon's work. In this particular case,
it refers directly to America, whose paralysis in the face of false dilemmas
Oedipa is lamenting.

This interpretation, we have tried to show, bears directly on the major
critical question of GR, its apparently deep pessimism. On the horological

level, the charge is fully warranted. Pynchon offers no easy escape from the threatening nuclear apocalypse. Yet he does not utterly abandon us, the new Preterite, to the inevitable thunderclap. Instead he insists that we acquire a metahistorical perspective of the Now as a recurring and in this sense Eternal Center. This will perhaps restore us to our selves and to others, but it gives us no assurances on the horological level of "society," "history," and the "future," those dead tokens of exhausted positivism. Instead, GR imposes on us a relentless metahistorical sensibility. It catches us and throws us beyond the cataclysm. So that while we live near the End, perhaps because we do, we can free ourselves, paradoxically, of the systems which propel us and themselves to certain destruction.

It is the extraordinary ambition of GR to help its readers toward such freedom, and to the degree that it is fulfilled for some readers, this is a measure of its achievement as well. As Sacvan Bercovitch reminds us, such has been the ambition of great visionary authors working with other modes. Just as in "Book XI of the *Confessions* . . . Augustine directs man away from the horological towards a vision of the 'permanent and stable unity' of creation, perceptible through an *indivisible present* [our emphasis] that engulfs past and future," so Pynchon bids us attend, while waiting for the onrushing catastrophe, to the eternal Now-ness of the Earth and the cosmos. It is this insistence that justifies the presence of echoes of Rainer Maria Rilke's *Sonnets to Orpheus* throughout the text, a presence acknowledged explicitly in a citation:

> And though Earthliness forget you,
> To the stilled Earth say: I flow.
> To the rushing water speak: I am.

These lines, and others like it, written in the injunctive present tense and scattered throughout the second half of GR, return us to a new version of Augustine's "permanent and stable unity of creation," to a "here" which complements the "now" upon whose importance we have been so insistent. They are the locus of an escape, *not* from the horological dimension of history and *to* a transcendence located in some version of the chronometric, but one that is possible within the secular moment, is anchored to Earth and embraces the recurring present of the "chronometric Now."

It can be argued that Pynchon's vision of the social world is impoverished, and that the appeal to Here and Now involves the Earth and Love to an overwhelming degree, while ignoring Society, the relation of more than two people, the community which was Ecclesias to Augustine. At least one of us thinks there is truth to the charge, which invites further study; such study can begin with the consideration of a sentence from GR: "in each of these streets, some vestige of humanity, of Earth, has to remain. No matter what has been done to it, no matter what it's been used for . . . " Though the sentence is placed in a section which reports to the reader the bombing of Hiroshima, the word "humanity" receives less attention than "Earth," which quickly becomes the focus of the next sentence, with its ecological overtones. It is all too often thus in Pynchon's work, especially in GR. As a Marxist critic would be eager to point out, this jeremiad laments the damage social ideologies have done, but the solutions are private, involving Self, Love and Nature. This reflects, for good or ill, much of Pynchon's debt to Emerson's America and to the latter's mediation of the Puritan heritage.

We have not exhausted other features of the early jeremiad tradition that bear upon GR. Of these, the most important calls for a comparison of Pynchon and Cotton Mather, whose *Magnalia Christi Americana* Bercovitch regards as "the *magnum opus* of the seventeenth-century jeremiad." Despite its greatness, what stands out starkly is "the total isolation of the author from his audience." McConnell has rightly observed that Pynchon's notorious invisibility is "one essential context of the books," but Bercovitch's discussion of the "sharpening alienation of the ministers" in the late seventeenth century offers a tantalizing clue to the mystery of Pynchon's isolation and, more importantly, its purpose. The sense of declension in the colony was matched by a shift in the way the preachers regarded themselves:

> To the first generation, the word [watchmen] denoted the soci-
> ety's architect-guardians, men by whose "watch . . . you may be
> made conquerors." During the sixties the concept takes on the sterner
> implications of a *"watchfull shepherd"* warning his flock against temp-
> tations. Through the seventies the orthodoxy comes to see itself
> as a beleaguered watchman for God, a "gap-man" holding back the
> floodwaters of apostasy and berated by those he sought to protect.
> Thereafter, they retreat further and further from the world around
> them. Like the prophets who foretold their errand, they raise the
> voice of one crying in the wilderness.

In other words, the jeremiad writers retreated further into themselves, "back into the 'monument' of the individual mind and will." From the isolated self Cotton Mather (like Pynchon a polymath, linguist, scientist and lover of puns) created his *Magnalia*, drawing the seventeenth century's "most pronounced success out of *de facto* failure, through the individual's capacity at once to say No in thunder to reality and to internalize the mission of his society." Pynchon may appear to have utterly repudiated the notion of mission (except in its negative dimensions), but his isolation, too, is a feature of the old jeremiad tradition.

In the final part of his study, Bercovitch traces the jeremiad rhetoric through the works of various writers, religious and secular, from the eighteenth century through the 1960s. He finds the jeremiad developing both a positive and a negative legacy in American civilization. The positive stream runs through Jonathan Edwards, David Austin and others. Edwards is seen as "a radically innovative historical theorist: the first New World spokesman for a non-Augustinian 'optimistic view' of progress . . . " who replaces the imminentism of the older tradition with a "gradualistic apocalypticism" and "the God of National Salvation" who would "in due time restore" his people. Pynchon reflects this transition to a secular ideal and damns the form it has taken in Slothrop's furious recapitulation of his ancestors' economic history:

> They began as fur traders, cordwainers, salters and smokers of bacon, went on into glassmaking, became selectmen, builders of tanneries, quarriers of marble. . . . The money seeping its way out through stock portfolios more intricate than any genealogy. . . . They carried on their enterprise in silence, assimilated in life to the dynamic that surrounded them thoroughly as in death they would be to churchyard earth. Shit, money, and the Word, the three American truths, powering the American mobility, claimed the Slothrops, clasped them for good to the country's fate.

A darker side of the jeremiad tradition, according to Bercovitch, runs through Thoreau, Whitman and especially Henry Adams. Thoreau and Whitman "resolve the dichotomy between 'meaning' and fact [in American experience] through the visionary optimism that marks theocracy's last solitary watchmen." In other words, they internalize America and, like Mather, remove the chronometric ideal into their creations. *The Education of Henry Adams* "is the darkest outgrowth, the *fleur du mal*, of the jeremiad tradition," and Pynchon, of course, has brought Adams' vision of disaster forward into our own times, especially in *V.*, where this is openly acknowledged, but also in GR. Bercovitch argues that Adams, despite his caustic view of his times, "preserves the Utopia" glimpsed by the founding fathers "by placing all emphasis on an America rushing toward self-destruction in what might be called an entropic inversion of the work of redemption." Adams evokes the ideal of his grandfather, "the remote, majestic symbol of the 'moral principle' of an earlier age." Pynchon does the same in GR, but with a difference. "The remote, majestic symbol" in GR is William Slothrop, the first of the line, who challenged the Puritan Dream, was rejected and threatened, and who sailed east again, thereby repudiating the Saints' errand into the wilderness. For Adams, America was right in the beginning (or at least when the Republic was founded). For Pynchon even this view of a Golden Age in the beginning is an illusion: the historical enterprise of colonial conquest is the intolerant, demonic reality behind the vision of Eden.

In the twentieth century, the jeremiad has "spiraled past ambivalence to something like a state of conscious, self-denunciatory schizophrenia." Bercovitch closes his discussion of the jeremiad tradition with a discussion of Mailer's *The Armies of the Night* and finds that "Mailer explicitly revolts against the 'need of Mission' with its 'demand that the American Dream be realized' and 'the City of God . . . be constructed on this unhappy planet,' repudiates the aesthetic shelter of the 'quintessentially American' self for the real if crazy house of history." In other words, Mailer repudiates the chronometric dimension, while Pynchon's attempt to find a place for it in secular reality makes his GR the most important (as well as most self-conscious) reworking of the jeremiad tradition in twentieth-century American literature. While it repudiates utterly the Puritan venture into the New World, in its recasting of the chronometric-horological nexus it demonstrates the incredibly tenacious hold which Puritanism maintains on the American imagination.

DAVID SEED

Order in Thomas Pynchon's "Entropy"

Of all Thomas Pynchon's short fiction "Entropy" has attracted the most critical attention. Tony Tanner describes it roundly as "his first important short story" and other critics have paid tribute to its sophisticated structure. In view of Pynchon's subsequent novels one interest which the story possesses is its application of a modern scientific concept to fiction. Entropy, Anne Mangel has argued, is also an important concern in *The Crying of Lot 49*. But the story is not only important as an early treatment of subsequent themes in Pynchon's fiction; it stands in its own right as a dramatization of how the concept of entropy can be applied to human behavior.

The story is set in an apartment block in Washington, D.C. The date is February 1957. In one flat (the lower of the two which provide the setting) a party being given by one Meatball Mulligan is about to get its second wind. People are sprawled about in various stages of drunkenness and a quartet of jazz musicians are sitting in the living room, listening to records. Quite early in the story a man named Saul climbs into Mulligan's flat from the fire escape and explains that he has just had a fight with his wife Miriam. Subsequently other people enter—three coeds and five enlisted men from the U.S. Navy. As the drunkenness and noise increases, a fight breaks out and the party seems to be on the verge of chaos. After due consideration Mulligan decides to calm everyone down and restore order. This he does. The action of "Entropy" in fact alternates between Mulligan's party and the apartment above his where one Callisto and his companion Aubade are trying to heal a sick bird. The apartment is a kind of hothouse, a perfectly self-contained ecological system.

From *The Journal of Narrative Technique* 11, no. 2 (Spring 1981). © 1981 by *The Journal of Narrative Technique*.

Like Henry Adams, Callisto is obsessed with energy running down and—perhaps for posterity, but more likely as a solipsistic exercise—he is dictating his memoirs. The bird dies and, abandoning the ecological balance they have built up for the past seven years, Aubade goes to the window and smashes it. The story ends with the two waiting for the internal and external temperatures to equalize and for night to fall.

This bald summary of the action does not of course explain its relevance to the title and to understand this we must apply the various definitions of "entropy" offered by a standard modern dictionary. *Webster's Third New International Dictionary* defines the concept as follows:

> 1. [In thermodynamics] A quantity that is the measure of the amount of energy in a system not available for doing work . . .
> 2. [In statistical mechanics] A factor of quantity that is a function of the physical state of a mechanical system . . .
> 3. [In communication theory] A measure of the efficiency of a system (as a code or a language) in transmitting information . . .
> 4. The ultimate state reached in the degradation of the matter and energy of the universe: state of inert uniformity of component elements; absence of form, pattern, hierarchy, or differentiation.

Of these meanings the second is the least important for Pynchon's story, being only glanced at briefly in Callisto's dictation. If we consider the superimposed levels of action from Callisto's hothouse to Mulligan's party and finally to Saul's apartment below that, we can see that the apartments from a schematic analogue to the fourth, first and third definitions respectively. Callisto is preoccupied above all with the final run-down of energy, the "heat-death" of the universe. Mulligan's party-goers are all characterized by apathy and inertia and so ironically exemplify energy which is unavailable for work. And lastly Saul has had an argument with his wife over communication theory and discusses with Mulligan (very inconclusively) what a high proportion of sheer "noise" human speech contains. Outside the apartment block is the street and the weather which, by implication, are also outside this multilevel metaphor.

Tony Tanner has suggested another interpretation of the building as follows:

> The house . . . is some sort of paradigm for modern consciousness; the lower part immersed in the noise of modern distractions and sensing the failing of significant communication, while the upper

> part strives to remain at the level of music, yet feels the gathering
> strain as dream is encroached on by life. Life, in this context, is
> not only the party downstairs, but the weather.

Certainly this would explain the broad contrast between Callisto's "hothouse"
and Mulligan's party. The former is dreamlike and enclosed; the latter is
earthy and open to newcomers. But Tanner makes evaluations which the
story does not really invite. Callisto's world is like a dream but Pynchon
does not ironize it by contrast with outside "life." It, too, is part of life, the
life of the mind, and if it is inadequate to external pressures, Mulligan's party
seems equally so. Pynchon does not set up a distinction between "life" and
"non-life"; he dramatizes different meanings of the central concept and explores
their interconnection.

Already then it should be obvious that Pynchon is not using the term
"entropy" loosely. In the same study of modern American fiction quoted
above, Tanner found the concept so important that he devotes a whole chapter
to it and suggests that it has become a very fashionable term, one used
superficially to mean decline. While an undergraduate at Cornell Pynchon
took several courses on physics which certainly help to explain the precision
of the scientific references in this story. And yet, although the basic concept
is difficult to grasp, Pynchon's story requires little more technical knowledge
than that offered in the dictionary definitions.

Indeed the story's epigraph, taken from Henry Miller's *Tropic of Cancer*,
introduces us straight away to one area of metaphor. The passage prophesies
no change in the weather and assets, with gloomy fatalism, a chain gang image
for man's future: "We must get into step, a lockstep toward the prison of death."
Already we have one metaphor proposed to us—constant weather as an emblem
of the lack of hope. By juxtaposing the epigraph and title Pynchon now invites
us to broaden the metaphor, particularly in the direction of the fourth dictionary
definition of "entropy." The passage in fact omits two sentences immediately
preceding the one quoted above, namely: "Our heroes have killed themselves,
or are killing themselves. The hero, then, is not Time, but Timelessness." These
lines occur at the beginning of the novel and give an opening statement of
theme—the absence of change and the deliberate stress on negative or inverted
values. But it is important to recognize that Miller is summarizing Boris's
views. Miller's surrogate narrator does not give in to his friend's apocalyptic
gloom and even regards him as comically melodramatic. Indeed, only three
lines after the summary of Boris's "prophecies," the narrator comments "I am
the happiest man alive," a remarkably cheerful statement for a man preoccupied
with universal decline. In Miller's novel the interchange between the narrator

and Boris creates a considerable amount of humor, and by choosing such a
passage for an epigraph, Pynchon leads the unwary reader into a kind of trap.
On the one hand the weather metaphor makes the abstract concept of entropy
easy to grasp, on the other the prophecies lack authority even in Miller's novel.
And so we should not jump to the conclusion that Pynchon is endorsing the
metaphor. He is rather introducing one theme, one strand of meaning, which
will be taken up in the early stages of the story.

Outside the apartment block in Washington it is raining and the weather
has been very changeable. It is typical of Pynchon's scrupulous attention to
fact that there *was* freak weather in early February 1957, including widespread
snowfalls and flooding. Pynchon draws careful attention to the weather mainly
for its metaphorical resonances. The time of year is a kind of false spring
characterized by random weather changes and a general feeling of depression – at least for the members of Mulligan's party. They are, Pynchon states,
"inevitably and incorrigibly Romantic." He continues:

> And as every good Romantic knows, the soul (*spiritus, ruach,
> pneuma*) is nothing, substantially, but air; it is only natural that
> warpings in the atmosphere should be recapitulated in those who
> breathe it. So that over and above the public components – holidays,
> tourist attractions – there are private meanderings, linked to the
> climate as if this spell were a *stretto* passage in the year's fugue:
> haphazard weather, aimless loves, unpredicted commitments: months
> one can easily spend *in* fugue, because oddly enough, later on,
> winds, rains, passions of February and March are never remembered
> in that city, it is as if they had never been.

The opening clause, with its obvious implication that the narrator is not a
Romantic, pushes the reader back from the text far enough to recognize that
a method of ordering is being examined. The argument for a connection between
soul and weather proceeds by a false logic based on etymology and anyway
suggests a passivity on the part of those who believe in this connection. They
simply "recapitulate" the weather and submit to chance meanderings and
random change. As the last sentence draws out its own length Pynchon shifts
away from musical metaphor to a psychological meaning of "fugue" as a period
of apparently rational behavior followed by amnesia. At the beginning of the
passage it looks as if a principle is being offered us, but by creating detachment
in the reader, by shifting the main metaphor, and by implying passivity in
the people under discussion, Pynchon ironically reduces the importance even
of his own story. If the events are relative to weather change and amnesia,
then their representative and psychological status is brought into question.
They are simply local "warpings."

Against this notion of apparently random change Pynchon contrasts Callisto's view of the weather. He, too, has noted its changeability but is far more preoccupied with the eventual general run-down of energy, the final heat-death of the universe predicted by some cosmologists following Clausius's original proposition that entropy tends toward a maximum. Accordingly Callisto pays no attention to the prosaic details of the rain and snow; he is more disturbed by the fact that the temperature outside has stayed at a constant 37°F for three days. Like Miller's Boris he is "leery at omens of apocalypse," When dictating his memoirs the combination of terms like "vision" and "oracle" with scientific information suggests that Callisto is fitting his materials into a nonscientific, quasi-religious pattern. Indeed, for all the differences between his obsession with endings and the party-goers' version of the pathetic fallacy, both outlooks could loosely be described as "Romantic."

Three times in the course of the story Callisto asks Aubade to check the external temperature, thereby paralleling a similar action in an earlier modernistic work—Beckett's *Endgame* (1958). Early in the play Hamm sends Clov to the window:

> HAMM: (gesture towards window right). Have you looked?
> CLOV: Yes.
> HAMM: Well?
> CLOV: Zero.
> HAMM: It'd need to rain.
> CLOV: It won't rain.

The relation and clipped idiom between Hamm and Clov parallels that between Callisto and Aubade. Like Callisto, Hamm delivers lengthy monologues, the longest one trailing away into silence at the end of the play. It is an important difference between the two works that it is raining in Pynchon's story. Apart from the tenuous evidence of three days at a steady temperature, Callisto has only a theoretical justification for his gloom. In Beckett's play the gloom is relieved onstage by the dialogue whose humor literally fills the time before the final end. Both works have pre-apocalyptic elements, but Pynchon confines them mainly to Callisto. Once again he suggests a significance to the weather but does not commit himself one way or the other.

Pynchon's reservations about Callisto emerge very clearly in the description of the latter's apartment, particularly in the following lines:

> Mingled with the sounds of the rain came the first tentative, querulous morning voices of the other birds, hidden in philodendrons and small fan palms: patches of scarlet, yellow and blue laced through this Rousseau-like fantasy, this hothouse jungle it had taken him

seven years to weave together. Hermetically sealed, it was a tiny
enclave of regularity in the city's chaos, alien to the vagaries of the
weather, of national politics, of any civil disorder.

The comparison with a painting of Douanier Rousseau is hardly necessary to
suggest that the scene is a kind of artifact, a grotesquely displaced jungle which
may have its own internal balance, but which is also as stylized as Rousseau's
works. The emphasis on defensiveness, as if outside chaos was an aggressive
force, carries with it its own ironies. For Callisto's hothouse may be hermetically
sealed, but it also shuts in both himself and Aubade. It is, in other words,
an exotic prison. Secondly Callisto is determined to shut out chaotic elements,
but the one form of energy which he cannot control is sound. The noise of
the rain impinges from outside, of music from below. It seems, then, that
Pynchon is swift to indicate the futility of Callisto's enterprise as soon as we
see the apartment. If this is so, Aubade's final gesture of smashing the window
is implied from the very start.

    Pynchon makes the fragility of Callisto's hothouse explicit when presenting
Aubade's anxiety about external noise. It is a kind of "leakage" which poses
a clear threat to their sense of order:

> The architectonic purity of her world was constantly threatened
> by such hints of anarchy: gaps and excrescences and skew lines,
> and a shifting or tilting of planes to which she had continually to
> readjust lest the whole structure shiver into a disarray of discreet
> and meaningless signals.

The epithet "architectonic" is shrewdly chosen since it could refer either to
architects or architecture. In this way Pynchon manages to avoid separating
their "structure" from Aubade and, by implication, Callisto. Aubade even
personifies the order she is trying to maintain. Its maintenance is expressed
in terms of physical gesture and anxiety. She has to "readjust," but what—
herself or the structure? In fact Callisto and Aubade are melodramatists of form.
They think in terms of violently opposed extremes (anarchy versus order)
and, although Callisto is ostensibly waiting for a run-down of energy (which
would not be at all dramatic), he and Aubade are both arguably more anxious
about the point of fracture when their hothouse would collapse into chaos.
From their point of view this would be a virtual cataclysm.

    Once Callisto starts dictating his memoirs it becomes clear that he is a
parody of Henry Adams, specifically the author of *The Education*. Like Adams
at the time of composing the book, Callisto is living in Washington. Both
describe themselves in the third person; both are attempting to articulate the
cultural implications of modern scientific theory; both are particularly impressed

by Willard Gibbs who was, according to Adams, "the greatest of Americans, judged by his rank in science." Adams, for a variety of temperamental and biographical reasons, adopts a passive stance (hence his use of the third person) and continually mocks his own ineffectuality. The key chapters in *The Education* as far as Pynchon's story is concerned, is "The Virgin and the Dynamo," where two of Adams' central symbols come into confrontation. His aesthetic idealism, which Pynchon ironically hints at in Callisto's name (i.e. "most beautiful"), gives ground before the modern embodiment of force. In trying to balance the modern scientific notion of force against religion Adams feels himself groping in labyrinths. His answer is characteristically to turn the act of writing in on itself:

> In such labyrinths, the staff is a force almost more necessary than the legs; the pen becomes a sort of blind-man's dog, to keep him from falling into the gutters. The pen works for itself, and acts like a hand, modelling the plastic material over and over again to the form that suits it best. The form is never arbitrary, but it is a sort of growth like crystallization, as any artist knows too well . . .

Adams diverts the reader away from his main impulse towards final understanding and dramatizes the automatism of writing. The variety of analogies to writing conceal — but only partly — a tendency towards self-pity on Adams' part. In the last chapters of *The Education* he constantly refers to himself as aged or infirm, and there is a hint of the same melancholy when Callisto identifies his condition as "the sad dying fall of middle age." Adams calls himself "the new Teufelsdröckh" to clarify his feelings of perplexity. If uncertainty paralyzes Adams, it is fear of possible implications from the "random factor" introduced by Gibbs' and Boltzmann's equations. Randomness is the mathematical equivalent of the chaos which terrifies Callisto. One other important parallel with Adams needs to be noted here. Struggling to understand the kinetic theory of gases, he arrives at the stark conclusions that "Chaos was the law of nature; Order was the dream of man." Adams carried his pessimism with such urbanity that a statement such as this is never allowed to generate its full emotional impact. However, this contrast between order and chaos, dream and nature, parallels Callisto's polarities, especially that between his hothouse and the outside weather.

Perhaps Callisto's main statement in his dictation is to find in entropy a metaphor for certain social phenomena which he has observed. One example is in the increasing uniformity in American consumerism:

> He found himself . . . restating Gibbs' prediction in social terms, and envisioned a heat-death for his culture in which ideas, like heat-energy, would no longer be transferred, since each point in

it would ultimately have the same quantity of energy; and intellectual
motion would, accordingly, cease.

The irony bends away from Callisto on to American society briefly and it
is quite in keeping with the closely wrought texture of this story that prime
examples of the consumerism under attack should be found in Mulligan's party,
namely bottles of drink, hi-fi equipment and a refrigerator. Even in his fascina-
tion with entropy Callisto is following in Adams's footsteps. In "A Letter to
American Teachers of History" (1910), Adams develops implications in Clausius's
propositions and speculates that, although historians don't know physics

> they cannot help feeling curiosity to know whether Ostwald's line
> of reasoning would logically end in subjecting both psychical and
> physicochemical energies to the natural and obvious analogy of heat,
> and extending the Law of Entropy over all.

His argument is exactly like Callisto's in being based on an analogy and, in
an essay of one year earlier—"The Rule of Phase Applied to History," Adams
had similarly predicted an end point where the limits of human thought would
be reached.

In order to pinpoint what exactly is Pynchon's attitude towards Callisto
and Adams it would be helpful to turn at this point to an intermediary text—
Norbert Wiener's *The Human Use of Human Beings* (1950). Wiener is doing
more or less what Adams and Callisto are attempting: to relate diverse fields
of modern American culture to each other. But he has a great advantage over
them in being primarily a scientist and mathematician. Accordingly, when
discussing the notion of heat-death, he cautions: "it is necessary to keep these
cosmic values well separated from any human system of valuation." This is
exactly the mistake which Adams makes in *The Education* and essays of 1909–10,
and which Callisto repeats. Their use of metaphor and analogy leads them
to draw hasty inferences from badly digested scientific theory, and results in
a not completely unpleasant sense of pessimism and inertia.

In view of the scientific references in *The Crying of Lot 49* and the intellectual scope of *Gravity's Rainbow*, we can safely assume that Callisto's enterprise
would be congenial to Pynchon. However, the various ways in which he
limits his commitment to Callisto's viewpoint suggest that Pynchon has accepted
Wiener's caution. Firstly, Callisto's is only one viewpoint within the story.
Secondly, the story is too humorous in tone to underwrite his apocalyptic
gloom. Thirdly, Pynchon's use of musical references and form, which will be
examined later, suggests a detachment from Callisto. And there are enough
ironies to indicate that in some ways Callisto *embodies* entropy rather than

examines it. His dictation ends on the verb "cease," but it has stopped, not concluded. His dictation is a kind of monologue as if he were thinking aloud. Once the dictation has stopped we follow his line of thought in his search for "correspondences," and in ransacking literature for parallels he once again follows Adams. He variously notes De Sade (for libertinage, perhaps), the last scene from Faulkner's *Sanctuary*, where the exhausted and apathetic Temple Drake is listening to music with his father in the Jardin de Luxembourg, and Djuna Barnes' *Nightwood*, again perhaps for its presentation of moral and physical decline. Decline does seem to be the theme linking these works. Callisto also pays particular attention to Stravinsky's *L'Histoire d'un Soldat* (1918) whose tango section communicates the same interwar exhaustion:

> And how many musicians were left after Passchendaele, after the Marne? It came down in this case to seven: violin, double-bass. Clarinet, bassoon. Cornet, trombone. Tympani. Almost as if any tiny group of saltinbanques had set about conveying the same information as a full pit-orchestra.

The neatly organized sentences of his dictation have now begun to give way to questions and fragmentary phrases as if the more Callisto hunts for meaning, the more it eludes him. This uncertainty grows with his failed attempts to recapture the spirit of pre–World War II France and his words trail off completely when the bird he has been holding finally dies: " 'what has happened? Has the transfer of heat ceased to work? Is there no more . . .' He did not finish." Verbal communication could be regarded as a kind of transfer (cf. definition 3 of "entropy"), and as Callisto's uncertainty grows he in turn becomes more rambling and incoherent. As a means of self-examination or as a means of communicating with Aubade, his words become useless. With the death of the bird, like Beckett's Hamm, he lapses into silence.

Stravinsky's *L'Histoire* is a comparatively little-known piece to choose and it contains a number of elements which bear on the story but which are not brought out in Callisto's thoughts. The passage quoted above indicates that the First World War is seen as a cultural watershed by Callisto. Stravinsky's work for him exemplifies a general feeling of exhaustion, but this feeling is stimulated by works of art. Although he pats himself on the back for being "strong enough not to drift into the graceful decadence of an enervated fatalism," Callisto seems to be suffering from a hand-me-down pessimism, an ersatz gloom without any roots in his own experience. Despite its deep personal significance for Stravinsky, *L'Histoire* takes its place along with Callisto's other pessimistic works. *L'Histoire* was a revolutionary work in getting rid of the piano and in reducing the number of performers to a minimum. Add to that the influence of jazz and we shall see obvious parallels with the later discussion of Gerry Mulligan. In thematic terms these two musical references bring the party and Callisto's memoirs closer together.

The last important point about *L'Histoire* concerns Aubade. Callisto remembers the tango particularly as culturally significant and remembers the dance generally for its repeated automatic movements. There is a variety of dance tempi in *L'Histoire*, notably the tango, waltz and ragtime. When Aubade moves around the apartment her movements are stylized and balletic, as if she is taking part in some kind of dance. Further she describes her lovemaking in the following way:

> Even in the brief periods when Callisto made love to her, soaring
> above the bowing of taut nerves in haphazard double-stops would
> be the one singing string of her determination.

Of course the metaphor conveys tension. But double-stopping on the violin was one of the noticeable features in *L'Histoire*. And in one scene (II.5) the soldier enters a room where a princess lies sleeping. He wakes her and woos her with his violin playing. Unconsciously, then, Callisto and Aubade are partly miming out actions which repeat *L'Histoire* and which supply yet another reason why Callisto is "helpless in the past."

The choice of a piece of music which contains a number of then current dance rhythms suggests a preoccupation with the Lost Generation. Callisto, like Scott Fitzgerald, went to Princeton; and he tries to put the clock back by returning to France after the war, taking with him a Henry Miller novel as a substitute Baedeker. He fails, however, to recapture the past and here we meet yet another common element between himself and the other characters of "Entropy." The second paragraph of the story gives us the following description:

> This was in early February of '57 and back then there were a lot
> of American expatriates around Washington, D.C., who would talk,
> every time they met you, about how someday they were going
> to go over to Europe for real but right now it seemed they were
> working for the government. Everyone saw a fine irony in this.
> They would stage, for instance, polyglot parties where the newcomer
> was sort of ignored if he couldn't carry on simultaneous conversations
> in three or four languages. They would haunt Armenian delicatessens
> for weeks at a stretch and invite you over for bulghour and lamb
> in tiny kitchens whose walls were covered with bullfight posters.
> They would have affairs with sultry girls from Andalucia or the
> Midi who studied economics at Georgetown. Their Dôme was a

collegiate Rathskeller out on Wisconsin Avenue called the Old Heidelberg and they had to settle for cherry blossoms instead of lime trees when spring came, but in its lethargic way their life provided, as they said, kicks.

Here certain European elements are displaced, as incongruous in a Washington context as Callisto's hothouse. The references deliberately evoke memories of the Lost Generation but reduce the notion of "Europe" to a fashionably cosmopolitan style, a matter of exotic dishes and wall posters. The main irony grows out of a contradiction between stated intention (going to Europe for good) and actuality, especially as they are working for the government. The epigraph from Miller, who begins his narration in the Villa Vorghese, has already reminded the reader that at least the main members of the Lost Generation did go to Europe. Pynchon's scorn rises as the paragraph proceeds and ends on an open sneer at the fashionable pursuit of 'kicks.' Of this passage Peter Bischoff has commented:

> Durch die Parodierung einer bekannten literatischen Tradition deutet Pynchon an, dass die *Beat*-Bewegung in Gegensatz zur *Lost Generation* lediglich eine Modeerscheinung der *popular culture* ist.

He is certainly right that the contrast between the two periods is reductive as far as the present is concerned, but the description offers a pastiche not a parody, since it is the imitators of the Lost Generation who are being made the butt of the irony.

Bischoff is the only critic to date who has spotted the stereotyped nature of the story's characters. Mulligan's party-goers use the same fashionable jargon that Pynchon mocks in the description above. Callisto is a "romantic" in the Fitzgerald sense, and Saul and Miriam parody middle-class intellectuals who brandish slogans like "togetherness." Mulligan's guests, at the beginning of the story, are lying around in drunken stupors or simply sitting and listening to music. As more guests arrive, or as they wake up, lethargy gradually shifts into chaotic movement. The ironic implication of pointlessness runs throughout Pynchon's presentation of these scenes and looks forward to his satire of the Whole Sick Crew in *V.*

William M. Plater sees the party differently, as an attempted flight from death:

> The party is a community act in which people come together— one of the least complex manifestations of eros. However, the party is simultaneously a demonstration of the social equivalent

of entropy and a transformation toward death, as the party disintegrates and disorder increases.

Surprisingly, in view of this paradox, he later states that the party embodies
an "affirmation of life and union." He suggests in effect that it is almost a
sacramental act where all the willing performers come together. This sort of
moralistic reading is only possible if one ignores the ironies levelled against
the members of the party, which is exactly what Plater does. He misses the
sarcasm at their imitation of the Lost Generation and understates the chaos
and absence of communication in the party. "Death" is a portentous word to
use here, and rather too grand for the level Pynchon strikes. The party-goers
are not desperately staving off dread. They are simply bored, lethargic and
superficial; their main concern is filling their time but with the least effort
on their part.

   Apart from social ironies the party dramatizes one strand of meaning in
"entropy," namely that it measures the amount of energy unavailable for
conversion to work in a system. Tony Tanner has described the party as a
closed system, but surely this is not so since people are arriving continuously.
The real closed system, in intention if not in practice, must be Callisto's hothouse. As movement increases at Mulligan's party, so does its randomness.
Mulligan himself wakes up and goes to fix himself a drink which he can only
manage by cutting himself. Of course this was by accident, and so forms one
random detail. He tries to "arrange" the guests but ineffectually since he moves
a girl from the sink to the shower, where she almost drowns. Other guests
arrive and add to the bustle, the most chaotic being the five sailors who
imagine it is a brothel. The disorder and noise reaches a climax where we
could also say that the entropy within the party has approached its maximum.

   Mulligan's reaction to this situation is both important and surprising:

> Meatball stood and watched, scratching himself lazily. The way
> he figured, there were only about two ways he could cope: (a) lock
> himself in the closet and maybe eventually they would all go away,
> or (b) try to calm everybody down, one by one. (a) was certainly
> the more attractive alternative. But then he started thinking about
> that closet.

Faced with a comparable situation at the end of "Mortality and Mercy in
Vienna," Siegel just walks away, leaving the party to the tender mercies of
a berserk Ojibwa. Mulligan here is tempted to do something like that. He
watches the others; he, too, is lazy. But eventually he decides to restore order
which he then proceeds to do. Partly from the sheer amount of space devoted

to Mulligan's moment of decision, Pynchon is highlighting his choice. The closet offers an attractive alternative and in effect repeats a smaller scale Callisto's retreat into a hothouse. The very fact that Mulligan can choose to restore order and does so, contradicts a superficial fatalism which the notion of entropy might create. In an examination of the relation between entropy and general culture, Rudolf Arnheim has pinpointed this superficial application, specifically to the arts:

> Surely the popular use of the notion of entropy has changed. If during the last century it served to diagnose, explain, and deplore the degradation of culture, it now provides a positive rationale for "minimal" art and the pleasures of chaos.

The intricacies of Pynchon's story demonstrate conclusively that he has no interest in minimalist art and Mulligan's final actions reverse a trend toward chaos in his party. The party anyway is neither the universe nor a microcosm, and once again Pynchon is being true to a scientific theory. Wiener asserts that "in the non-isolated parts of an isolated system there will be regions in which the entropy . . . may well be seen to decrease." One such island is the party and its entropy apparently *does* decrease.

So far we have considered the representational significance of Mulligan's party and Callisto's hothouse. The third area of meaning in "entropy" is introduced when Saul climbs into Mulligan's apartment from the fire escape. John Simons has pointed out that Pynchon is here parodying the biblical narrative of Paul's visit to Ephesus. *Acts* 20. 9-11 recounts how a young man named Eutychos (i.e., "lucky") fell asleep while Paul was preaching and fell down from a loft. Paul embraced him and thereby restored him to life. He then continued his discussions until daybreak. Simons argues that

> Saul is an ironic parody of Paul in Pynchon's story, and . . . appears not as an apostle of the new Christian religion, but rather as a spokesman for the new science of decline and decay in the twentieth century.

Saul parodies Paul in having had a slanging match with his wife, not a proselytizing discussion; and he saves only the book which she threw at him, not a human being.

Before examining Saul further we need to consider the broader implications of the Pauline text. It centers on a quasi-miraculous act, Paul's lifegiving embrace. When we first see Mulligan and Callisto they are both asleep and embracing objects, the one an empty magnum of champagne, the other a sick bird. In other words they combine elements of Eutychos and a parody of Paul.

But the embraces are the opposite of life-giving. Obviously the champagne bottle offers no possibilities, but Callisto strokes the bird in an attempt to revive it. The gloomiest point in the story comes when the bird finally expires. Simons argues that Pynchon's recurring use of threes in the story is also biblical in the sense that it arouses expectations of resurrection but reverses them into death. Certainly the resurrection offers one kind of end point, the reverse side of the coin from catastrophe. But the whole point of Pynchon's examination of entropy is to undermine an apocalyptic gloom arising from it.

Saul himself is denied any of the stature of his biblical counterpart. He is like a "big rag doll" and combines professional arrogance with violence. He tells Mulligan with an air of pride "I slugged her," and obviously brings only words not *the* Word with him. Ironically, despite his claims to be a communications expert, he cannot understand why his wife flared into anger. His stumbling block appears to be love:

> "Tell a girl: 'I love you.' No trouble with two thirds of that, it's a closed circuit. Just you and she. But that nasty four-letter word in the middle, *that's* the one you have to look out for. Ambiguity. Redundance. Irrelevance, even. Leakage. All this noise. Noise screws up your signal, makes for disorganization in the circuit."

Here the biblical ironies shade into communication theory. Paul revived Eutychos by an act of love, but this word becomes a serious problem for Saul. It is so elusive, it disturbs his "signal" so much that it becomes a positive obscenity (a "four-letter word"). Like Callisto and Aubade, Saul is a believer in order. He is concerned to rule out any kind of interference to technical perfection. But once again we return to a crude analogy—that between an electronic signal and a speech act. Despite his theoretical expertise, Saul has lost his argument with Miriam (about cybernetics). He himself uses a disjointed language full of slang and technical jargon and, when Mulligan casts around for something to say, he, too, demonstrates a very high proportion of "noise" (i.e. hesitation-words, fillers, etc.).

Entropy grows in the conversation between the two men as their exclamations increase until finally Saul cuts off Mulligan with an abrupt "the hell with it." It is of course comical to witness a communication theorist break down into cliché and exclamation, and finally lapse into silence. But this episode carries ironic implications which spread through the whole story. Entropy in communications theory is a measure of the inefficiency of a signal. Accordingly the more noise, or the less coherence speech acts contain, the more their entropy will increase. In fact none of the characters in Pynchon's story demonstrate any sustained capacity to engage in dialogue. Callisto and Aubade speak in short, clipped phrases, as if they are cautiously husbanding their meaning. Mulligan's guests use short phrases containing in-jokes or jargon (like "tea time, man"). Krinkles' story to the girl about a pianist is absurd. The sailors' shouts are more noise and misapply even that, since the apartment is not, in the technical sense at least, a brothel. Apart from Mulligan's discussion with Saul, which breaks down into silence, there is only one other conversation in the story of any length. This occurs near the end where Duke puts forward a theory about modern jazz. On the face of it perfectly rational, the theory leads to absurd results when the musicians start playing silently. So, the ironies which Pynchon directs against Saul specifically, undermine yet another attempt to impose order, and suggest a broad scepticism about dialogue's capacity for meaningful communication.

In the course of his story Pynchon examines three levels of meaning in the central concept of entropy and uses a variety of ironic methods to criticize the implications or applicability of these levels. The first definition supplies a weapon for attacking the fashionable lethargy of the party guests. The third gives Pynchon an opportunity to satirize dialogue. The fourth allows him to examine Callisto's enervated intellectualism. He, too, is just as inert as the party guests and it is Aubade who makes the decisive gesture of smashing the window at the end. John Simons has described the story's theme as "the supplanting of universal order by universal chaos," but this makes "Entropy" sound like a work of cosmic proportions. Pynchon never allows an apocalyptic tone to be sustained and even at the end leaves a deliberate ambiguity. By Simon's account, Aubade's final action would be a gesture of despair, but only viewed from her perspective. It could equally well be seen as a liberating gesture which has the immediate result of freeing herself and Callisto from their hothouse.

The discussion of the story so far has concentrated on relatively traditional techniques such as allusion, contrast, parallelism and narrative irony. By devoting a story to a scientific concept, and by examining different meanings, Pynchon in effect alerts the reader to the fact that he must pay attention to different ways of ordering. Indeed order could be the ultimate theme of the story. Apart from any local satirical purposes, the narrative methods examined so far tend to carry a general expectation of intelligent detached scrutiny on the reader's part. Accordingly it is not surprising that Pynchon's most extensive narrative method should stand out, particularly as another artistic medium is being applied to literature. That medium is music.

"Entropy" contains a large number of references to musicians and musical technique. It begins with information about records and proceeds with allusions to Lili Marlene, Sarah Vaughan, *Don Giovanni* (Pynchon quotes the catalogue aria to satirize Sandor Rojas' lubricity), Krinkles' story is possibly

music

a sick joke at Dave Brubeck's expense, and Chet Baker and Mingus are named among others. Music, on a simple verbal level, fills the texture of the story. Two musical topics are examined in some depth. Stravinsky's *L'Histoire* has already been discussed. The second in Duke's theory arising out of Gerry Mulligan's "Love for Sale." In fact it is Mulligan's experimental technique which fascinates Duke. In 1952 Mulligan began using a pianoless quartet, comprising baritone saxophone, trumpet, drums and bass. It was startling for the absence of a piano, a feature which links this method strongly to Stravinsky's *L'Histoire*. Jazz is anyway common to both since Stravinsky's work contained a ragtime section. In Pynchon's story Duke argues that one has to think the root chords when improvising. So far his theory sounds plausible. But then he pushes it to an extreme by arguing that ultimately one must think everything. When the quartet try to put this into practice the result is an absurd spectacle of silent "performance" which anyway breaks down into chaos once because they get out of step, once because they are playing in different keys! Just as Callisto and Aubade unconsciously perform parts of *L'Histoire*, so the Duke di Angelis quartet follow absurdly in the steps of Gerry Mulligan's experimentalism. And once again an ideal of order (or form) has been proposed only to be found unworkable.

Apart from specific applications of musical topics, the structure of "Entropy" draws extensively on the techniques of the fugue, a term which actually occurs in the text several times. One of the distinguishing characteristics of fugue is the use of counterpoint which in fictional terms can emerge as a rhythmic contrast. The contrast is basically between the two apartments— Mulligan's and Callisto's—and the narrative moves to and fro in such a way that differences and similarities emerge clearly. For instance both Mulligan and Callisto awake from "rest" in the same posture, but the electronic noise downstairs contrasts strongly with the natural sounds in Callisto's hothouse. Even the physical positioning of the apartments, corresponds, as Redfield and Hays point out, to the printed arrangement of musical staves. Callisto, Mulligan and Saul offer us three possible voices and, after they have been introduced in turn, Pynchon is free to weave the voices together. Callisto, for instance, delivers a long monologue which contrasts sharply with the chaotic and fragmented speech of the party. But then "noise" creeps into his ruminations as they wander further and further from his single purpose, until, like Saul, he lapses into silence. Callisto's dictation, Saul's conversation and Duke's theory provide clear equivalents of exposition, so that the different dimensions of entropy are quite literally orchestrated together. Between the various themes occur other noises from the rain outside, from the arrival of other characters, and from the record being played at the party. These correspond to the invented passages in a fugue, as well as posing a threat to Pynchon's superimposed order.

If the basic theme of the story is the contrast order/disorder, then obviously Callisto's apartment represents the first. All the elements are synchronized into harmony, a harmony which Aubade personifies. Her very name refers to a musical form and her identity is defined in "terms of sound." When she is stroking a plant in the apartment, Pynchon similarly articulates it in musical terminology:

> In the hothouse Aubade stood absently caressing the branches of a young mimosa, hearing the *motif* of sap-rising, the rough and *unresolved* anticipatory *theme* of those fragile pink blossoms which, it is said, insure fertility. That *music* rose in a tangled tracery: arabesques of order competing *fugally* with the *improvised discords* of the party downstairs, which peaked sometimes in cusps and ogees of noise [my emphasis].

The third word takes its departure from a homophone in the preceding paragraph ("hoorhouse") which cuts across the broad contrast between harmony and discord. The two sentences actually mime out their lyrical subject through participial phrases, again contrasting with the fragments of speech in the preceding paragraph. It is as if disorder would literally stop Aubade's existence.

By contrast the noise in Mulligan's party approaches a crescendo, but the crescendo never comes since he reimposes a kind of order. This returns the revellers to their initial posture (prostration) and yet does not resolve the story. The party, we are told, "trembled on the threshold of its third day." The final resolution rests with Aubade. She breaks the window and, following this burst of sound, returns to Callisto to

> wait with him until the moment of equilibrium was reached, when 37 degrees Fahrenheit should prevail both outside and inside, and forever, and the hovering, curious dominant of their separate lives should resolve into a tonic of darkness and the final absence of all motion.

As the clauses fade away in diminuendo, the ending appeals to the reader's sense of form in resolving the story, although in fact the moment of resolution is in the future, and will only occur after the work has finished, as in Eliot's *Four Quartets*. The musical metaphor cuts across various interrelated fields of sensation—of balance, temperature and light which will disappear. Above all, however, the metaphor plays on the notion of rest. Formally speaking the story has begun from rest and comes back to it at the end. In that sense it seems satisfyingly symmetrical. But, because music is a nonconceptual medium, the use of music to create form in the story does not carry with it any epistemological implications. Plater and other critics notwithstanding, the story affirms nothing.

"Entropy" examines various notions of order and disorder in such a way as to make it very difficult to locate Pynchon's own viewpoint. Music is of course nonverbal and so an ideal means of binding his story together without committing himself to any one viewpoint. Pynchon ironizes all the theories which are proposed with a bewildering thoroughness, so that at times his method appears to be purely negative. A comment made by Saul, however, suggests a way out of this dilemma. Miriam is disturbed by the way computers act like people, but Saul simply reverses the analogy and suggests that people act like computers. In a story which focuses so much on analogy and implication, Pynchon in effect suggests a caution about drawing conclusions. Callisto's intellectual enterprise forms potentially the most solemn area of subject matter in the story and in this connection a proposition by Norbert Wiener is directly relevant. Answering the question whether the second law of thermodynamics leads to pessimism, he states that the solution

> depends on the importance we give to the universe at large, on
> the one hand, and to the islands of locally decreasing entropy which
> we find in it, on the other.

In other words, it is a matter of perspective. Similarly Pynchon's story forces a relativistic viewpoint on to the reader, which acts against a final resolving certainty, or one definite moral direction. The various aspects of form illuminate and examine different meanings of "entropy," while the different meanings of "entropy" illuminate the various aspects of form.

TONY TANNER

The Crying of Lot 49

The Crying of Lot 49 (1966) is one of the most deceptive—as well as one of the most brilliant—short novels to have appeared since the last war. It is a strange book in that the more we learn the more mysterious everything becomes. The more we *think* we know, the less we *know* we know. The model for the story would seem to be the Californian detective story—an established tradition including the works of writers such as Raymond Chandler, Ross MacDonald and Eric Stanley Gardner. But in fact it works in a reverse direction. With a detective story you start with a mystery and move towards a final clarification, all the apparently disparate, suggestive bits of evidence finally being bound together in one illuminating pattern; whereas in Pynchon's novel we move from a state of degree-zero mystery—just the quotidian mixture of an average Californian day—to a condition of increasing mystery and dubiety.

In the simplest terms, the novel concerns Oedipa Maas, who learns that she has been named as an executor ("or she supposed executrix") of the estate of a deceased Californian real-estate mogul named Pierce Inverarity. As she sets about exploring this "estate," she seems to discover more and more clues indicating the existence of an underground, anarchic organization called the Tristero, which possibly dating from thirteenth-century Europe, seems to oppose all the offical lines of communication and have its own secret system of communication. Seems. She can never be sure whether she is discovering a real organization, or is the victim of a gigantic hoax, or is wildly hallucinating. Her search or quest clearly has wider implications, for we are told that Pierce

---

From *Thomas Pynchon.* © 1982 by Tony Tanner. Methuen and Co., Ltd., 1982.

175

Inverarity was "a founding father," and near the end we read: "She had dedicated herself, weeks ago, to making sense of what Inverarity had left behind,
never suspecting that the legacy was America."

So on one level the driving question is simply: what does a contemporary
American "inherit" from the country's past? On the title page Pynchon included
this note: "A portion of this novel was first published in *Esquire* magazine
under the title 'The World (This one), the Flesh (Mrs Oedipa Maas), and the
Testament of Pierce Inverarity.' " Since he did not choose to give the title of
another extract that appeared in a magazine, we may infer that he wanted
this title definitely to appear under the main title of the book. Of course it
raises the question: is "the Testament of Pierce Inverarity" the Devil (following the World and the Flesh)? Like so much in the book it remains a question.
The name itself can suggest either un-truth or in-the-truth; I have seen it glossed
as "pierces or peers into variety" and "inverse" and "rarity." But then names
can be like that in Pynchon's work, and I shall return to this point in a moment.
The last phone call Oedipa receives from Pierce Inverarity is literally multi-
vocal: he speaks in "heavy Slavic tones," "comic-Negro," "hostile Pachuco
dialect," as "a Gestapo officer," and finally "his Lamont Cranston voice." He
does indeed speak in many "tongues"; the problem is which, if any of them,
is "true"? The phone call itself comes from "where she would never know,"
and the "phone line could have pointed any direction, any length." Origin,
intention, extension—all are insolubly ambiguous. What is Oedipa Maas
hearing? What should she listen to? Is it all cacophony? Or is she being somehow singled out for "revelations"?

I shall consider some details of Oedipa's quest for the meaning of the
Pierce Inverarity legacy—and our quest for the meaning of the book (the two
being intimately related)—but first I want to quote two crucial passages from
the novel. The first occurs shortly after Oedipa has engaged in a sexual game—
they call it "Strip Botticelli"—with the lawyer Metzger. They have been watching a film (in which he starred as a child) in a motel room, and in seeking
to anticipate the outcome of the plot (an anticipation of her larger concern
to come) she agrees to take off an item of clothing in exchange for every
answer he gives to her questions. But she prepares for this by loading herself
with endless garments, trinkets and adornments. In doing so she becomes a
grotesque image of an insanely eclectic culture which "over-dresses" itself with
bits and pieces of fabrics and fabrications taken from anywhere, and at the
same time she reveals a poignant vulnerability, for under the absurd multi-
layered "protection" she is oddly defenceless, naked and exposed. Metzger
does not fully undress her but he does seduce her. Later she starts to find clues

concerning the Tristero—in a bar, on a latrine wall—and we are given this summarizing paragraph:

> So began, for Oedipa, the languid, sinister blooming of the Tristero. Or rather, her attendance at some unique performance, prolonged as if it were the last of the night, something a little extra for who-ever'd stayed this late. As if the break-away gowns, net bras, jeweled garters and G-strings of historical figuration that would fall away were layered dense as Oedipa's own streetclothes in that game with Metzger in front of the Baby Igor movie; as if a plunge toward dawn indefinite black hours long would indeed be necessary before The Tristero could be revealed in its terrible nakedness. Would its smile, then, be coy, and would it flirt away harmlessly back-stage, say good night with a Bourbon Street bow and leave her in peace? Or would it instead, the dance ended, come back down the runway, its luminous stare locked to Oedipa's, smile gone malign and pitiless; bend to her alone among the desolate row of seats and begin to speak words she never wanted to hear?

It is an amazing passage, shifting in tone from vaudeville frivolity to a melo-dramatic note which is in fact quite chilling. But one important point to note is the conflation of "performance" with "historical figuration." History and theatre become almost interchangeable terms, and Oedipa will never know when she is, or is not, present at some kind of "performance"—a "play" which might end in harmless concluding knockabout, or with her hearing "words she never wanted to hear." Just what kind of a "performance" is America put-ting on anyway? All fun and jollity—or something "malign and pitiless" coming down the aisles? When—if—history is "undressed," what will it look like?

Later in the book Oedipa attends an actual theatre to see a performance of a Jacobean play called *The Courier's Tragedy*. Here is a description of a curious change in atmosphere which occurs during the "performance":

> It is at about this point in the play, in fact, that things really get peculiar, and a gentle chill, an ambiguity, begins to creep in among the words. Heretofore the naming of names has gone on either literally or as metaphor. But now, as the Duke gives his fatal command, a new mode of expression takes over. It can only be called a kind of ritual reluctance. Certain things, it is made clear, will not be spoken aloud; certain events will not be shown onstage; though it is difficult to imagine, given the excesses of the pre-

ceding acts, what these things could possibly be. The Duke does
not, perhaps may not, enlighten us. Screaming at Vittorio he is
explicit enough about who shall *not* pursue Niccolo: his own body-
guards he describes to their faces as vermin, zanies, poltroons. But
who then will the pursuers be? Vittorio knows: every flunky in
the court, idling around in their Squamuglia livery and exchanging
Significant Looks, knows. It is all a big in-joke. The audiences of
the time knew. Angelo knows, but does not say. As close as he
comes does not illuminate.

Those Who Know, know, But what is it they know? What does Oedipa
know? And what is the "big in-joke" anyway? No answers. But notice one
thing about this new atmosphere in the play. Before, we are told, "the naming
of names has gone on either literally or as metaphor. But now . . . a new mode
of expression takes over. It can only be called a kind of ritual reluctance."
Generally speaking, names can only be used either literally or metaphorically—
one of those either/or situations that Pynchon's work is not particularly fond
of. Here, then, is a moment, in the story and in the text, when a new mode
of expression is inserted between literality and metaphor: an ambiguity, a
hesitancy, a "ritual reluctance." We, like Oedipa, are teased and drawn into
a new and problematical area of semantic dubiety—between the literal and
the metaphorical. We—and she—can no longer be sure what "names" are
naming or not naming. Those who "know" (but what do they know?) do not
say. Words come "close": there are many suggestions—even too many. But
no final illumination.

Let us go back to the beginning, and the naming of names. "Mrs Oedipa
Maas"—now what kind of name is that? It is certainly right out of the line
of plausibility. Fanny Price, Dorothea Brooke, even Isabel Archer: all well
within the realm of possibility. But Oedipa Maas? Not so. So some critics have
taken the name as a signal or symbol. Oedipa is a female Oedipus, who was
of course the solver of the riddle in one of the first great detective stories in
Western literature. But given that the riddle Oedipus finally has to solve concerns his own parents, parricide and incest, and given that this in no way applies
to Oedipa, we may pause. Again "Maas" has been read as suggesting Newton's
second law of motion in which "mass" is the term denoting a quantity of inertia.
So the name suggests at once activity and passivity. But this will not do. In
Pynchon's texts names do not operate as they do in, for example, Fielding
in which Thwackum or Allworthy are—or do—exactly what their names indicate. One critic, Terry Caesar, is probably nearer the mark when he suggests
an audible joke in the name: "Oedipa my ass"; she is no Oedipus at all. As

Caesar suggests, noting how wild and improbable—or downright crude and silly—many of Pynchon's "names" are, he is probably undermining and mocking the very act of naming. We usually expect to find the person in his or her name. In a realist book as in life, the name comes to signify a real character with unique characteristics. This goes along with a very tenacious notion of the unique individual. Pynchon blows all this up. "Character" and identity are not stable in his fiction, and the wild names he gives his "characters," which seem either to signify too much (Oedipus and Newton indeed!) or too little (like comic-strip figures), are a gesture against the tyranny of naming itself. Lacan sees the fact that we are *named* before we can speak as a symptom of the degree to which we are at the mercy of language itself. Pynchon indicates that he can see how, in various ways, people are subject to the authority of naming: how a whole society can exercise its power through naming. As an author he also has to confer names on his figures, but he does so in such a way as to sabotage the conventional modes of naming. The relationship between individual and name is deliberately problematized—and caricatured—in Pynchon's texts. We find ourselves moving out of the literal or metaphorical and into—well, somewhere else.

We first encounter Oedipa Maas among the eclectic bric-à-brac of contemporary Californian culture, buying lasagne and *Scientific American* in shops that indifferently play Muzak or Vivaldi. When she hears the news about being named as Pierce Inverarity's executrix, she stands in her room "stared at by the greenish dead eye of the TV tube, spoke the name of God, tried to feel as drunk as possible." Amid the randomness of the thoughts and her surroundings she as it were instinctively turns to the three substitutes for true religion in the contemporary world: the TV (with no message), the name of God (now an empty word) and drink (which doesn't work). So she has to try to start "sorting it all out," "shuffling back through a fat deckful of days which seemed . . . more or less identical." She will have to go on sorting and shuffling to the end—and perhaps beyond.

Then Oedipa's husband "Mucho" Maas comes back. He had once worked in a used car "lot" (one of the many linking puns in the book), and Pynchon's elegiac evocation of the sheer pathos of the used car lot is characteristic of his uncanny sensitivity to the suggestive human traces and residues (a kind of information) to be found in the "used," the rejected, the abandoned refuse and waste of a culture. Mucho now works for a pop music station which sends out an endless stream of jabbering trash (i.e., no information). "He had believed too much in the lot, he believed not at all in the station." For him every day is a "defeat": the sadness of the car lot overwhelmed him; the pointlessness of the pop music station empties him out. He can be of no help to

Oedipa. Next she receives a middle-of-the-night telephone call from her hysterical psychiatrist (Dr. Hilarius), who wants her to join in an LSD experiment he is running. "But she would be damned if she'd take the capsules he'd given her. Literally damned." No help there. She goes to see her lawyer Roseman, who is mainly concerned with plans to mount a case against the TV lawyer Perry Mason and has no interest in Oedipa and her problem. He merely, vaguely, tries to make crude sexual advances to her. Again, no help. And this sets the pattern of what is to come. All the men who might (should?) help Oedipa recede from her in one way or another—into fantasy, madness, hallucination, some kind of private universe which has no room for any relationships.

The first chapter ends with a reference to her sense of herself as a Rapunzel who, although willing to let her hair down to someone, found that the one time she did so her hair fell out. The man could not reach her: she "had really never escaped the confinement of that tower." This is followed by her memory of a picture she had seen in Mexico City in which some girls who are imprisoned in a tower are "embroidering a kind of tapestry which spilled out the slit windows and into a void seeking hopelessly to fill the void." These "Embroiderers of the Terrestrial Blanket" made Oedipa "cry." She cried because she realized that there is "no escape" for a "captive maiden"; realized "that her tower, its height and architecture, are like her ego only incidental: that what really keeps her where she is is magic, anonymous and malignant, visited on her from outside and for no reason at all." As to this conviction concerning the existence of "anonymous and malignant" magic, the action of the book serves to open up the whole question. For, if it is true, then the only adequate rational reaction would be paranoia. But things are not so simple as that. Before leaving this consideration of what the first chapter opens up, I want to quote one rather strange passage, usually overlooked:

> As things developed, she was to have all manner of revelations. Hardly about Pierce Inverarity, or herself; but about what remained yet had somehow before this stayed away. There had hung the sense of buffering, insulation, she had noticed the absence of intensity, as if watching a movie, just perceptibly out of focus, that the projectionist refused to fix.

"Revelations" is suggestive enough—the word occurs often in the book—and opens up the possibility of a religious dimension to the novel (I'll come back to that). But that sense of something that had somehow remained and yet stayed away, and that absence of intensity which is like a movie slightly out of focus—this suggests strange states of mind, odd intimations of something between presence and absence, a sense of something, an image, a picture, a plot that is not quite visibly *there* but not quite visibly *not* there either. Such strange sensations, which seem to take place at the very interface between meaning and nonmeaning, will occur to Oedipa increasingly as she sets out on her quest, alone, to the suitably named city of San Narciso.

As she drives in and looks down at the city ("less an identifiable city than a grouping of concepts," she is reminded "of the first time she'd opened a transistor radio to replace a battery and seen her first printed circuit."

> Though she knew even less about radios than about Southern Cali-
> fornia, there were to both outward patterns a hieroglyphic sense
> of concealed meaning, of an intent to communicate. There'd seemed
> no limit to what the printed circuit could have told her (if she had
> tried to find out); so in her first minute of San Narciso, a revelation
> also trembled just past the threshold of her understanding.

She feels for a moment as though she and her car "seemed parked at the centre of an odd, religious instant"; but a cloud comes, or the smog thickens, and the " 'religious instant,' whatever it might've been," is broken up. Again she experiences a kind of brink moment—somewhere between smog and revelation, on the edge or verge of a possible "religious instant"—but the dubiety is, as always, there. There may be a "concealed meaning . . . an intent to communicate"; but there may not.

"Communicate" (cf. "communion" in *V.*) is the key word. The novel is concerned with all aspects of communication—voices, postal systems, postage stamps, newspapers, books, radio, TV, telephones, signs on walls, acronyms, drawings, doodlings, etc. Then there is the possibility of some kind of religious communication. Is something being "revealed" to Oedipa—whether on a sinister secular level, or on a more sacred plane—or is she simply sorting and shuffling clues of very uncertain status and validity? In any case, there are only "clues," "never the central truth itself," for if that should blaze out it "would destroy its own message irretrievably." Communication—if indeed there is any communication—can only be imperfect, incomplete. Oedipa is later to wonder if all the clues that come her way "were only some kind of compensation. To make up for her having lost the direct, epileptic Word, the cry that might abolish the night." The "Word" is singular; clues are uncontrollably plural. Having "lost"—or never having had—the "Word," Oedipa is doomed to be the recipient/percipient of an ever-increasing number of clues which point to other possible clues which point to other possible clues which . . . there is no end to it. The "cry" that might have ended the night is replaced by a "crying" that can only extend it.

To recount Oedipa's encounter with the many possible clues that seem to "bloom" for her as she pursues her inquires would be a pointless exercise. From the drawing of a muted horn on a latrine wall to the detailed academic reconstructions and speculations of an English professor (Emory Bortz), the clues and signs seem obvious enough and, regarded in a certain way, seem to cohere. Indeed that becomes part of Oedipa's problem: they are *too* obvious and seem to fit together only too neatly.

> If one object behind her discovery of what she was to label the Tristero System or often only the Tristero (as if it might be some-thing's secret title) were to bring an end to her encapsulation in her tower, then that night's infidelity with Metzger would logically be the starting point for it; logically. That's what would come to haunt her most, perhaps; the way it fitted, logically, together. As if (as she'd guessed that first minute in San Narciso) there were revelations in progress all around her.

As *if*. Oedipa does indeed become "sensitized" (starting with the motel seduc-tion) but can hardly be sure just what her new "sensitized" state is picking up. She may be "receiving," but who or what is "sending"?

The state of communication in the everyday world she comes from is zero. When she receives a letter from her husband, she has an intuition what "the letter would be newsless inside"—so she studies the outside for clues in-stead. When she and Metzger accidentally witness the secret mail distribution of the Peter Pinguid Society at the Scope Bar near the Yoyodyne aerospace plant, she discovers that it is indeed an illegal system ("Delivering the mail is a government monopoly,") which makes use of the Yoyodyne interoffice delivery. But, more to the point, the letters delivered have nothing to com-municate. The members of this secret society (there are a number of such eccentric societies in the book) simply have a rule that they have to send a letter a week: as Oedipa discovers, they are usually notes with no content. More newsless letters. Oedipa's problem is whether she has in fact discovered, stumbled across, been lured by, a *genuinely* alternative mode of communica-tion which does convey real messages in a way that subverts the "government monopoly"—namely, the Tristero (another name that invites being played with—a meeting with sadness and terror, for example). And, if so, will it release her from her isolation—or confirm it? Will it offer the possibility of real communication "and revelation"—or like the Peter Pinguid Society system merely reveal a pointless secrecy concealing meaningless, "newsless" repetitions? If, that is, it exists at all.

The play that Oedipa actually sees—the "performance" within that larger performance called history—is supposedly by one Richard Wharfinger, a

Jacobean dramatist. It is called *The Courier's Tragedy* and is indeed about competing "communications" systems. It is performed in a theatre located between "a traffic analysis firm and a wildcat transistor outfit"—that is, between circulation and communication, as Frank Kermode has noted. It concerns another postal monopoly, owned by the Thurn and Taxis family (this seems to be historically accurate); and a rebellious, insurgent counterforce which dedicates itself to subverting, muffling, "muting" the official system—the Tristero. Oedipa finds herself drawn into "the landscape of evil Richard Wharfinger had fashioned for his 17th-century audiences, so preapocalyptic, death-wishful, sensually fatigued, unprepared, a little poignantly, for that abyss of civil war that had been waiting, cold and deep, only a few years ahead of them." This, of course, refers to the civil war in England in the seventeenth century. But we should be alert to the fact that any novel about California which refers to "49" is bound to awaken echoes of the Gold Rush of 1849; and at this date too there was a civil war "waiting" for America "only a few years ahead" (twelve, in fact). The mining camps in the Gold Rush had their own kind of autonomous, somewhat anarchic organization—well outside any government control—and even, I gather, their own private mail systems. It is also suggested in the book that 1849–50 saw the arrival of the Tristero in America. The novel is making suggestive play with points and echoes in history, just as Wharfinger's macabre play involves the transformation of dead bones into ink, thus seeming to echo or anticipate an episode recounted in the novel in which the bones of dead GI soldiers in the Second World War were brought back from Italy (by the Mafia) and used in cigarette filters or wine. 1849 perhaps— perhaps—offered the possiblity of a new kind of America, run and arranged in an entirely different kind of way. But the civil war was just those few years ahead, and the possibility disappeared (or went underground). A century later, 1949, saw the start of the Cold War and the beginning of what was arguably one of America's most conformist periods.

This is all part of the "performance" of which Oedipa is a witness. In the course of this particular performance of Wharfinger's play there is a shock because it "names" the "name" that seemed to have been previously avoided:

> No hallowed skein of stars can ward, I trow,
> Who's once been set his tryst with Trystero.

"Trystero. The word hung in the air as the act ended... hung in the dark to puzzle Oedipa Maas, but not yet to exert the power over her it was to." This is Oedipa's crucial "tryst" with "Trystero"—the name, the word. It is indeed, chronologically, her first encounter with the actual word; she and the name literally "meet" just before the middle of the book. And after that she doesn't find clues—the clues find her, indeed, seem to besiege her in every form, while she tries to work out what, if anything, the Tristero really signifies.

The start of chapter 4 (the book has six chapters) makes the change explicit, referring to other revelations which now seemed to come crowding in exponentially, as if the more she collected the more would come to her, until everything she saw, smelled, dreamed, remembered, would somehow come to be woven into The Tristero." Her danger—or would it be her deliverance?—is that the "word" might come to have total "power over her." She might then become like Stencil, who "stencilized" all reality into "V."; or she might be moving into a significant discovery about history and the very reality of America itself. Obsession—or revelation. But she tries to go on sorting and shuffling, in the continuing absence of "the direct, epileptic Word."

While the word "Tristero" preoccupies Oedipa, another word equally bothers another of the "leads" she meets, John Nefastis, and that word—so important in Pynchon—is "entropy." As Nefastis explains, "there were two distinct kinds of this entropy. One having to do with heat-engines, the other to do with communication." Nefastis has a "machine" based on the Scotch scientist Clerk Maxwell's postulation of something known as Maxwell's demon. This machine (which Nefastis has tried to make literal) suggests a situation in which there is a box of molecules moving at different speeds and in which "the Demon" could simply sort out the slow ones from the fast one: this would create a region of high temperature which could be used to drive a heat engine. "Since the Demon only sat and sorted, you wouldn't have put any real work into the system. So you would be violating the Second Law of Thermodynamics, getting something for nothing, causing perpetual motion!" To which Oedipa sceptically replies: "Sorting isn't work?"

The problem here centres on the fact that there seems to be an opposition between thermodynamic entropy and entropy in information theory. As thermodynamic entropy increases in a system, variety and potential diminish, and the certainty of information about the system increases. However, in information theory, "entropy" refers to the measure of uncertainty in a system. Put very crudely, we can say this: in a thermodynamic system, as things tend towards stagnation, repetition, predictability, they approach a terminal state in which there is no more energy available for new work; in information theory, the higher the degree of disorganization, noise, uncertainty, the more possibility there is for new signals, new information. Nefastis tries to explain:

> She did gather that there were two distinct kinds of this entropy. One having to do with heat engines, the other to do with communication. The equation for one, back in the 30's, had looked

very like the equation for the other. It was a coincidence. The two fields were entirely unconnected, except at one point: Maxwell's Demon. As the Demon sat and sorted his molecules into hot and cold, the system was said to lose entropy. But somehow the loss was offset by the information the Demon gained about what molecules were where.

"Communication is the key," cries Nefastis. . . . "Entropy is a figure of speech, then, a Metaphor. It connects the world of thermo-dynamics to the world of information flow. The Machine uses both. The Demon makes the metaphor not only verbally graceful, but also objectively true."

His machine has a picture of Clerk Maxwell on it, and if the watcher is a true "sensitive" he or she will be able to receive and return information from the box, and then the eyes of the portrait will move. But Nefastis is, of course, a lunatic—a "believer," like so many other figures in the book. A "believer" not in any genuine faith but in a crazy fantasy of his own making. In the end it emerges that he only wants to have intercourse with Oedipa in front of the television. But it is true that in one form or another "communi-cation" *is* the key, and Oedipa—demonically or not—will have to go on "sort-ing" out the clues (molecules), trying to discover which information really works against entropy as opposed to the kind of noninformation ("newsless" letters) that effectively accelerates it. She has to try to decide what kind of revelation or revelations, exactly she is having.

Some critics regard the novel as unambiguously religious in its implica-tions. What happens to Oedipa, for instance, can be regarded as echoing epi-sodes in the life of Mary, mother of Christ. Then again, after a particularly gruesome scene in *The Courier's Tragedy*, a demented figure named Ercole who has just tortured someone to death (among other things, tearing out his tongue and leaving him to die amid "tongueless attempts to pray": the possi-bility of the gift—and the loss—of "tongues" runs through the book in various forms) says:

> The pitiless unmanning is most meet,
> Thinks Ercole the zany Paraclete
> Descended this malign, Unholy Ghost,
> Let us begin thy frightful Pentecost.

The context perverts the religious words, but perhaps this is a reflection of the perverse Pentecost towards which the book may be moving. As Edward Mendelson hass pointed out, 49 is the pentecostal number (the Sunday seven weeks after Easter), but Pentecost derives from the Greek for "fifty," so the moment at the end of the book when the auctioneer's spread arms are specifically likened to a "gesture that seemed to belong to the priesthood of some remote culture" is like the moment before a pentecostal revelation when we would all be able to speak in tongues—and understand "the Word" directly.

The word "God" is often used, and sometimes seriously. The Tristero system—in its ambiguous aspects—has been seen as representing the sacred dimension to existence, albeit often in a demonic form. Their sign of the muted posthorn may intimate not only a determination to disrupt conventional "profane" modes of communication but also a determination to block the trumpet of apocalypse. Certainly, although the Tristero may offer some kind of alternative to the apparently "normal" but utterly alienated irreligious and loveless, and "narcissistic," life of contemporary society (at least as depicted in the California of the book), their manifestations—if that is what they are—are nearly always sinister and connected with death. Their postage stamps, for instance, distort ordinary stamps by adding something menacing—poisonous flowers, for example, or a head at an impossible angle. On one stamp, which supposedly celebrated "Columbus Announcing His Discovery" (i.e. of America), "the faces of three courtiers, receiving the news at the right-hand side of the stamp, had been subtly altered to express uncontrollable fright." So, if we believe everything about the Tristero that seems to come our (or Oedipa's) way, we may conclude that the revelation of a "sacred" pattern underlying the profane patterns of the surface may be a revelation of ultimate terror and dread. Edward Mendelson has been quick enough to note that the word "hierophany" which appears in the book (a map Oedipa sees seems to offer "some promise of hierophany") is not a standard word but a coinage by Mircea Eliade, and he quotes Eliade's definition: "To designate the *act of* manifestation of the sacred, we have proposed the term hierophany . . . the manifestation of something of a wholly different order, a reality that does not belong to our world, in objects that are an integral part of our natural "profane" world." This might indeed cover the Tristero very well, though from such a "sacred" realm that it may well be a very "unholy ghost" indeed who descends. (Not for nothing are two of the acronyms associated with the Tristero—and with each other—W.A.S.T.E. and D.E.A.T.H.)

On the other hand, seen as a historical phenomenon—an underground movement composed of and standing for "the Disinherited," which now uses "silence, impersonation, opposition masquerading as allegiance," and which does have a secret method of communication which allows many "isolates" (Pynchon deliberately picking up Melville's word, from a context that suggests that all Americans are "isolates") to "keep in touch"—the Tristero system would not be the apocalyptic agents of death and doom and God knows what kind of Pentecost but rather the kind of protoanarchic group with which Pynchon's work shows sympathy. (The founder of the Tristero was "perhaps a madman, perhaps an honest rebel, according to some a con artist," so, if you want to take the historical account, then the movement was indeed rooted in total ambiguity and dubiety—or plurality of content and intent.)

"Anarchy" is perhaps a crucial clue. During the night when Oedipa lets herself drift through San Francisco she meets an old anarchist acquaintance, Jesus (*sic*) Arrabal. He says to her:

> You know what a miracle is. Not what Bakunin said. But another world's intrusion into this one. Most of the time we coexist peacefully, but when we do touch there's cataclysm. Like the church we hate, anarchists also believe in another world. Where revolutions break out spontaneous and leaderless, and the soul's talent for consensus allows the masses to work together without effort, automatic as the body itself. And yet, señá, if any of it should ever really happen that perfectly, I would also have to cry miracle. An anarchist miracle.

The "anarchist miracle" would not involve the intrusion of the "sacred" world into our profane one; rather it would be a kind of "revolution" leading to a whole new way of living together in this world. It would be "another world"— but still secular. A mundane miracle. Even here the possibility is undermined: Arrabal has an anarchist newspaper with him called *Regeneración*. But the date of the paper is 1904—a "communication" so delayed as perhaps to be, literally, out of date.

Oedipa's night of drifting in the Bay Area brings her problems to a head. The whole area is "saturated" with what seem like clues and references to the Tristero. She even comes across a group of children playing to a song that includes references to "Tristeroe" and "taxi"—by which time the clues are becoming worse than meaningless. Her "sorting" problem has reached its limit. "Later, possibly, she would have trouble sorting the night into real and dreamed." Possibly. Nothing is certain. As Driblette (the director of *The Courier's Tragedy*) had warned Oedipa: "You can put together clues, develop a thesis, or several. . . . You could waste your life that way and never touch the truth." It was after seeing that play that Oedipa wrote in her memo book "*Shall I project a world?*" And there is no way in which she can find out how much she is projecting, and how much she is perceiving or receiving. What might be accidental, random, chance, and what might be plotted, determined, purposive, she has no way of establishing; and she gives up trying to "check out" the possible clues. Her problem is beyond verification or falsification. She has emerged from "narcissism," but is it only to enter into "paranoia"? She runs over the possibilities:

> Either you have stumbled indeed . . . onto a secret richness and concealed density of dream; onto a network by which X number of Americans are truly communicating whilst reserving their lies, recitations of routine, arid betrayals of spiritual poverty, for the official government system; maybe even onto a real alternative to the exitlessness, to the absence of surprise to life, that harrows the head of everybody American you know, and you too, sweetie. Or you are hallucinating it. Or a plot has been mounted against you . . . so labyrinthine that it must have meaning beyond just a practical joke. Or you are fantasying some such plot, in which case you are a nut, out of your skull.

Looking at the possibilities, she does not like any of them and just hopes that she is "mentally ill." And this is where we feel the full poignancy of her position. "For this, oh God, was the void. There was nobody who could help her. Nobody in the world."

The problem is finally about America. There is the America of San Narciso, but is there perhaps another America? An America of the "disinherited" (but "What was left to inherit?" Oedipa wonders — transients, squatters, drifters, exiles within the system, people existing in the invisible interstices of official society, like those who live "among a web of telephone wires, living in the very copper rigging and secular miracle of communication, untroubled by the dumb voltages flickering their miles, the night long, in the thousands of unheard messages." The Tristero system might be a great hoax; but it might be "all true." And here is perhaps the most crucial and one of the most eloquent and powerful passages in the book:

> Who knew? Perhaps she'd be hounded someday as far as joining Tristero itself, if it existed, in its twilight, its aloofness, its waiting. The waiting above all; if not for another set of possibilities to replace those that had conditioned the land to accept any San Narciso among its most tender flesh without a reflex or a cry, then at least, at the very least, waiting for a symmetry of choices to break down, to go skew. She had heard all about excluded middles; they were bad shit, to be avoided; and how had it ever happened here, with the chances once so good for diversity? For it was now like walking among matrices of a great digital computer, the zeroes

and ones twinned above, hanging like balanced mobiles right and left, ahead, thick, maybe endless. Behind the hieroglyphic streets there would be either a transcendent meaning, or only the earth. . . . Ones and zeroes. So did the couples arrange themselves. . . . Another mode of meaning behind the obvious, or none. Either Oedipa in the orbiting ecstasy of a true paranoia, or a real Tristero. For there either was some Tristero beyond the appearance of the legacy America, or there was just America and if there was just America then it seemed the only way she could continue, and manage to be at all relevant to it, was as an alien, unfurrowed, assumed full circle into some paranoia.

The law of the "excluded middle" — as I understand it — is that a statement is either true or false. There cannot be anything in between. Either it is raining, or it is not. Yet there are those strange, atmospheric conditions, not easily classifiable, in which moistness and dryness seem strangely mixed, which might make us — illogically, unphilosophically — long to admit the "excluded middle," a middle term for something real but unascertainable. Oedipa is not at ease in a world of binary oppositions — ones and zeroes. Recall that apparently incomprehensible sentence in which it was stated that she would have revelations "about what remained yet had somehow, before this, stayed away." The law of the excluded middle would say that either it was there or it was not there. Quite apart from considerations of logic, such a rigidity forecloses on the possibility of unforeseen "diversity" and irresolvable dubiety. Yet it is into just such an area of possible diversity and dubiety that Oedipa has stumbled — and we, as readers, along with her. Oedipa is mentally in a world of "if" and "perhaps," walking through an accredited world of either/or. It is part of her pain, her dilemma and, perhaps, her emancipation. At the auction which concludes the book, leaving all in suspension, the auctioneer is indeed likened to a priest — but also to a "puppet-master." There is no way in which Oedipa can be sure just what kind of "performance" she has been — is — present at. And there is no way in which we can, either. And yet, at the end, as we both finish and wait to begin, something — and this is part of the deceptive magic of the book — seems to remain. Even while it stays away.

CRAIG HANSEN WERNER

Recognizing Reality,
Realizing Responsibility

Nothing since *Finnegans Wake* cries for commitment like the first sentence of *Gravity's Rainbow*: "A screaming comes across the sky. It has happened before, but there is nothing to compare it to now." Is the screaming human or the inanimate descent of the rocket? Is the coming messianic? Sexual? Is there actually "nothing" to compare it to; are we orphans in a void? Or has nothing else ever been as important as our agony? When we read Pynchon we decide, or They have already decided for us, how we live. Pynchon, shunning the robes of the aesthetic priest, preaches for the preterite, never dogmatic, but doomed (like one of his characters) to know "how phony it looks. Who will believe that in his heart he wants to belong to them out there, the vast Humility sleepless, dying, in pain tonight across the Zone? the preterite he loves, knowing he's always to be a stranger." However it looks, *Gravity's Rainbow* belongs to and with the wretched of the earth.

The screaming's human.

If we don't believe it's important now, we never will.

And our decisions are more important than any questions of literary influence or tradition. Our decisions can take us out of our conceptual systems into a life where the issues are worth talking about, where they have something to do with our humanity. Pynchon forces the resolution of modes off the page and into our lives, where it belongs. If we let him.

Joyce did influence *Gravity's Rainbow*, but he did not dominate it or direct it. Several critics have noted parallels between *Gravity's Rainbow* and *Ulysses*: both resolve questions of literary mode by rendering them irrelevant;

From *Paradoxical Resolutions: American Fiction since James Joyce.* © 1982 by the Board of Trustees of the University of Illinois. Originally entitled "Recognizing Reality, Realizing Responsibility: Joyce, Gaddis, Pynchon."

both extend symbolic and realistic modes until they seem meaningless impositions of abstract systems on a concrete reading experience. Joyce reinforces
his stylistic resolution by portraying his characters successfully resolving their
experiences. Pynchon, less sure both of his own aesthetic resolution and of
the ability of any individual to effect a resolution, demands that any resolution
take place in the minds and lives of his real readers—you and me—rather than
in an abstract "life" on the printed page. While literature is a part of "real life,"
it works on us individually; Pynchon challenges us to reach beyond our solipsism
and to contact our preterite brothers and sisters.

Inferring Pynchon's "position" on any issue is dangerous. We simply don't
know much about him. Still, *Gravity's Rainbow* provides sufficient evidence
to suggest that Pynchon reacts to Joyce ambivalently. It alludes to numerous
modern novelists, including Kerouac and Henry Miller, Beckett and Proust,
Ellison, [and] Gaddis. While Pynchon frequently catalogs the names of important scientists, he *names* few novelists, most notably Ishmael Reed and Joyce.
The direct reference to Joyce suggests Pynchon's belief that at times Joyce,
too, felt drawn to the preterite: "Lenin, Trotsky, James Joyce, Dr. Einstein
all sat out at these tables. Whatever it was *they* all had in common: whatever
they'd come to this vantage to score . . . perhaps it had to do with the people
somehow, with pedestrian mortality, restless crisscrossing of needs or despera-
tions in one fateful piece of street . . . dialectics, matrices, archetypes all need
to connect, once in a while, back to some of that proletarian blood, to body
odors and senseless screaming across a table, to cheating and last hopes, or
else all is dusty Dracularity, the West's ancient curse." The small "t" in "they"
which Pynchon emphasizes with italics hints that he sees Joyce in essential
conflict with the capital T They who have no sense of the screaming of the
preterite.

Several other allusions to Joyce in *Gravity's Rainbow*, however, emphasize
Joyce's participation in the destructive elitism of western culture. Identifying
1904, the year of *Ulysses'* action, as one of the "critical points" of history when
some major change might have been possible, Pynchon quickly asserts that,
in fact, nothing changed: "1904, Achtfaden. Ha, ha! *That's* a better joke on
you than any singed asshole, all right. Lotta good it does *you*. You can't swim
upstream, not under the present dispensation anyhow, all you can do is attach
the number to it and suffer." At times Pynchon openly rejects the entire
Joycean dedication to craft, the dedication which drew Joyce to the mythic
figure of Daedalus: "Weissmann's cruelty was no less resourceful than Pökler's
own engineering skill, the gift of Daedalus that allowed him to put as much
labyrinth as required between himself and the inconvenience of caring." If
Pynchon feels an affinity with Joyce, he qualifies it so as to preclude any tempta-

tion to compress *Gravity's Rainbow* into a narrowly Joycean mold. One of the ironies of the reception of *Gravity's Rainbow* has been the development of an image of the book as a new *Finnegans Wake*, inaccessible to all but a highly educated elite. The *Wake* indeed presents the reader with numerous puzzles, some demanding special knowledge for solution. Doomed by his vision of complexity, Pynchon uses a vocabulary no more complex than his content absolutely demands and employs numerous popular cultural references in a way which emphasizes his desire to communicate with the very people who are least likely to read his book. Joyce wanted to be studied as well as read; Pynchon would clearly accept the reading.

Pynchon's "attacks" on Joyce reflect his distrust of attempts to include reality within systems: scientific, literary, religious, whatever. To Pynchon, attempts to impose systematic constraints on experience are murderous: Pointsman (following Pavlov) struggles to explain all life in behaviorist terms because he feels threatened by the idea that another shares his own complexity. Pointsman's meditation on Pavlov reveals that he values his system more highly than human life:

> Pavlov thought that all the diseases of the mind could be explained, eventually, by the ultraparadoxical phase, the pathologically inert points on the cortex, the confusion of the ideas of the opposite. He died at the very threshold of putting these things on an experimental basis. But I live. I have the funding, and the time, and the will. Slothrop is a strong imperturbable. It won't be easy to send him into any of the three phases. We may finally have to starve, terrorize.

Weissmann's analogous vision of humanity as simple raw material for propagating his own obsessions inspires some of Pynchon's most bitter prose.

> What more do they want? She asks this seriously, as if there's a real conversation factor between information and lives. Well, strange to say, there is. Written down in the Manual, on file at the War Department. Don't forget the real business of the War is buying and selling. The murdering and the violence are self-policing, and can be entrusted to non-professionals. The mass nature of wartime death is useful in many ways. It serves as a spectacle, as diversion from the real movements of the War. It provides raw material to be recorded into History, so that children may be taught History as sequences of violence, battle after battle, and be more prepared for the adult world. Best of all, mass death's

> a stimulus to just ordinary folks, little fellows, to try 'n' grab a
> piece of that Pie while they're still here to gobble it up. The true
> war is a celebration of markets.

The Daedalus figure (the film director Gerhardt von Göll—der Springer) provides the artistic analog to the scientific and economic systemizer. Von Göll
believes that the people he meets are literally his creations: "His film has somehow brought them into being. 'It is my mission,' he announces to Squalidozzi,
with the profound humility that only a German movie director can summon,
'to sow in the Zone seeds of reality.' " Von Göll sees them simply as pieces
in a chess game he controls. Each of these systems is futile; each lacks the control of reality it claims, and each deceives its creator.

Pynchon may believe, as several critics suggest, in an entropic vision of
a world doomed to an eventual lack of order and energy. But he recognizes
the presence of very important ordering systems at work in the world as we
have it, systems which, even if ultimately doomed, pose a much more serious
threat than those of individuals such as the Pointsman, von Göll, or even
Weissmann. Unlike these systems, the "controlling" system rests not on individual
delusion, but on massive social forces which no single person directs. The system
which Pynchon images as "They" involves a large number of individuals, most
of whom do not consciously endorse the destruction they contribute to. Pirate
Prentice, a well-meaning paratrooper capable of acting kindly, listens to Father
Rapier's sermon on the nature of "They" and realizes that "with everything
else, these are, after all, people who kill each other: and Pirate has always been
one of them." The system, whether or not it reflects individual volition and/
or an inherent order of reality, destroys human lives and reduces the survivors
to unresisting accomplices.

Pynchon suggests one relatively simple technique for resisting Their pressure: reject Their categories, live on the interface between the terms of Their
dichotomies. Roger Mexico, who contrasts directly with Pointsman, commits
himself to life and love even when the commitment contradicts the statistical
system with which he works: "If ever the Antipointsman existed, Roger Mexico
is the man. Not so much, the doctor admits, for the psychical research. The
young statistician is devoted to number and method, not table-rapping or
wishful thinking. But in the domain of zero to one, not-something to something. Pointsman can only possess the zero and the one. He cannot, like Mexico,
survive anyplace in between . . . to Mexico belongs the domain *between* zero
and one—the middle Pointsman has excluded from his persuasion—the probabilities." The domain between one and zero, the interface between dream and
reality, between self and society, the internal and the external, recurs fre-

quently in *Gravity's Rainbow*. Denying the absolute validity of dichotomies—
including that of realism and romance—results in a sense of common humanity
as a weapon against the solipsism which insists on perceiving situations simply
in either/or terms: "Kevin Spectro did not differentiate as much as he between
Outside and Inside. He saw the cortex as an interface organ, mediating between the two, but *part of them both*. 'When you've looked at how it really
is,' he asked one, 'how can any of us be separate?' "

Weakening the sense of separateness, existing on the interface, challenges
our basic modes of perception. Pointsman observes that while we accept positions of certainty, yeses and nos, the process of transition frequently frightens
us, as it does him, back into solipsistic isolation. "In each case, the change from
point to no-point carries a luminosity and enigma at which something in us
must leap and sing, or withdraw in fright." Nonetheless, as Mondaugen believes,
the deepest life transpires precisely in that flow, that process of change:

> Think of the ego, the self that suffers a personal history bound to
> time, as the grid. The deeper and true Self is the flow between
> cathode and plate. The constant, pure flow. Signals—sense-data,
> feelings, memories relocating—are put onto the grid, and modu-
> late the flow. We live lives that are waveforms constantly changing
> with time, now positive, now negative. Only at moments of great
> serenity is it possible to find the pure, the informationless state of
> signal zero.

To overcome our fear of the interface, we must break out of our solipsism. This struggle demands both Slothrop's recognition "that the Zone can
sustain many other plots besides those polarized upon himself" and his later
perception that the multiplicity of individual struggles is not taking place in
a vacuum: "For the first time now it becomes apparent that the 4 and the
Father-conspiracy do not entirely fill their world. Their struggle is not the
only, or even the ultimate one. Indeed, no only are there many *other* struggles,
but there are also *spectators*, watching, as spectators will do, hundreds of
thousands of them." In essence, Slothrop learns to read the text of his *Gravity's
Rainbow* in human rather than nihilistic terms. Most important, however, is
the possibility of human contact which develops when two people find their
way beyond the dichotomies and onto the interface at the same time and place:
"Well. What happens when paranoid meets paranoid? A crossing of solipsisms.
Clearly. The two patterns create a third: a moire, a new world of flowing
shadows, interferences." Slothrop possesses something of this sense of possibility
all along. Following his comic nightmare descent through the toilet, Slothrop

finds himself on what he believes is the deepest level of his psyche. Expecting isolation, he discovers what appear to be archetypes: "only one fight, one victory, one loss. And only one president, and one assassin, and one election. True. One of each of everything. You had thought of solipsism, and imagined the structure to be populated—on your level—by only, terribly, one. No count on any other levels. But it proves to be not quite that lonely. Sparse, yes, but a good deal better than solitary. One of each of everything's not so bad." Soon Pynchon reveals even this degree of solipsistic isolation as an illusion:

> the plaza is seething with life, and Slothrop is puzzled. Isn't there supposed to be only one of each?
> A. Yes.
> Q. Then one Indian girl . . .
> A. One *pure* Indian. One *Mestiza*. One *criolla*. Then: one Yaqui. One Navaho. One Apache—.

Obviously, if we pursue this path far enough, each of us is unique, each of us exists even on Slothrop's deepest solipsistic level of awareness. The secret lies in perceiving and accepting the similarity of our own isolation and that of others.

Gravity's Rainbow devotes a great deal of attention to those who fail to overcome their fear and perceive this bond, those who fall off the interface and commit themselves to solipsism. Such a commitment, Pynchon implies, inevitably contributes to Their system and results in physical and psychic death. While the end result may be the same, there are several different ways of retreating into solipsism. General Pudding, whose sexual life centers on eating and drinking Katje's excrement, provides the most striking example of the horrors of solipsism. His behavior, as Paul Fussell demonstrates, stems from his inability to confront the horror of World War I. He allows himself to degenerate into a perfect symbol of Their success in destroying human brotherhood in the twentieth century.

While Pudding provides the most extreme example, Major Duane Marvy, Franz Pökler, and Tchitcherine pursue lives leading to a similar dehumanization. Pökler believes he can remain personally removed from the immorality of the rocket-cartel system. However, "Pökler found that by refusing to take sides, he'd become Weissmann's best ally." Weissmann successfully manipulates Pökler, even while condemning Pökler's daughter to life in a concentration camp adjacent to the laboratory where her father words. Pökler's "neutrality," based on a naïve belief that integrity can survive without reference to external context, results in the very destruction he fears most.

Marvey and Tchitcherine share a fear of blackness which leads them to personal hells similar to Pökler's. The simpleminded Marvy sees blacks as bestial threats to American purity, while the more complex Tchitcherine reacts to his black half-brother Enzian as a threat to his personal sense of purity. Neither can accept any suggestion of a human bond with blackness, internal or external. Pynchon connects the inability of most whites in *Gravity's Rainbow*, and in Euro-American culture as a whole, to accept blackness with their (Their?) insistence on ignoring death:

> Shit, now, is the color white folks are afraid of. Shit is the presence of death, not some abstract-arty character with a scythe but the stiff and rotting corpse itself inside the whiteman's warm and private own *asshole*, which is getting pretty intimate. That's what that white toilet's for. You see many brown toilets? Nope, toilet's the color of gravestones, classical columns of mausoleums, that white porcelain's the very emblem of Odorless and Official death. Shinola shoeshine polish happens to be the color of Shit. Shoeshine boy Malcolm's in the toilet slappin' on the *Shinola*, working off whiteman's penance on his sin of being born the color of Shit 'n' Shinola.

Malcolm X's pursuit of Slothrop down the toilet, which ends with Slothrop in the solipsistic cesspool of his psychic sewer system, emphasizes the white tendency to dehumanize the self rather than accept the ambiguities of any relationship with blackness. While Slothrop recovers a sense of contact, at least in part, most whites in *Gravity's Rainbow* fail. Whether their solipsistic retreat stems from realistic social pressures (Marvy and Pudding) or individual symbolic reactions (Pökler and Tchitcherine), it aggravates both realistic and symbolic problems. By demonstrating the identical outcomes of apparently diverse situations, Pynchon effectively rejects the dichotomy between characters confronting experience on a realistic level and those confronting it on a symbolic level. The mode matters little. The human outcome demands attention.

In addition to the characters who surrender, Pynchon portrays several who struggle to escape their isolation and establish human contact. Significantly, the extent of their success has little to do with their theoretical beliefs. Roger Mexico, the statistician involved in a love affair with Jessica Swanlake, is unable to fit the experience into any of his "normal" categories of perception: "The time Roger and Jessica have spent together, totaled up, still only comes to hours. All their spoken words to less than one average SHAEF memorandum. And there is no way, first time in his career, that the statistician can make these figures mean anything. Together they are a long skin surface, flowing sweat, close as muscles and bones can press, hardly a word beyond her name, or his." But he accepts the interface, the unquantifiable love he feels. Conversely, von Göll articulates the theory of human contact well: "Be compassionate. But don't make up fantasies about them. Despise me, exalt them, but remember, we define each other. Elite and preterite, we move through a cosmic design of darkness and light, and in all humility, I am one of the very few who can comprehend it *in toto*." But his Daedalian arrogance leads him to force his aesthetic system onto life, leaving him with a perception of himself as one of the elite and negating any realistic application of his compassion.

Small acts of kindness glimmer through *Gravity's Rainbow*. In addition to Mexico's love for Jessica, Tantivy's loyalty to Slothrop, Bodine's gift of Dillinger's preterite blood and Katje's willingness to submit herself to the desperate needs of several lovers hint that some escape from solipsism into compassion is possible. The small gestures, however, dissolve frequently in frustration and at times generate new retreats into solipsism. Unable to separate herself from her fiance, Jeremy, Jessica abandons Roger after the immediate threat of the external war passes. Neither Tantivy nor Bodine saves Slothrop; Katje's shit kills Pudding.

The fate of the Hereros emphasizes the difficulties of realizing love and points out its tendency to collapse eventually into solipsism. The plot involving the Southwest African blacks who set up an independent rocket-oriented society within the Zone originates in the visit of Enzian's and Tchitcherine's Russian father to Africa in 1904. Old Tchitcherine, AWOL from a Russian ship, attains fleeting contact with a Herero girl: "It was nearly Christmas, and he gave her a medal he had won in some gunnery exercise long ago on the Baltic. By the time he left, they had learned each other's names and a few words in the respective languages—afraid, happy, sleep, love, . . . the beginnings of a new tongue, a pidgin which they were perhaps the only two speakers of in the world." Communication demands just this shared experience, a reaching beyond the self and a recognition that another shares both fears and joys. But their communication dissolves when Tchitcherine returns to Russia, leaving his lover and their child, Enzian, to the genocidal German policy. Enzian survives, eventually leading the *Schwarzkommando*, who seemingly promise a creative force counterbalancing the death-oriented Euro-American culture. But Enzian's visions of a redeemed rocket, a rocket of escape rather than of destruction, gradually generate a counterforce among the Hereros: the Empty Ones, devoted to tribal suicide. Preaching "a day when the last Zone-Herero will die, a final zero to a collective history fully lived," the Empty Ones are in fact defined by the very intensity of their opposition to European pressure. While symbolically their plan "has appeal," realistically it accomplishes exactly what Europeans from the Germans on most desire: the final repression of the black other. The original contact between old Tchitcherine and Enzian's mother simply extends the influence of the death-obsession to those blacks caught up in the political and psychological dichotomy of black and white.

Similarly, Slothrop's attempts to escape his solipsism ultimately fail. Despite his recognition of the bonds of humanity, despite his willingness to accept as full a range of reality as confronts him on whatever terms that confrontation generates, Slothrop simply dissolves. Neither his symbolic awareness nor acceptance of reality saves him. He falls victim to a sense of emptiness similar to that which affected Wyatt in *The Recognitions*: "If there is something comforting—religious, if you want—about paranoia, there is still also anti-paranoia, where nothing is connected to anything, a condition not many of us can bear for long. Well right now Slothrop feels himself sliding onto the anti-paranoid part of his cycle, feels the whole city around him going back roofless, vulnerable, uncentered as he is, and only pasteboard images now of the Listening Enemy left between him and the wet sky." Unlike Wyatt, however, Slothrop does not recover:

> Slothrop, as noted, at least as early as the *Anubis* era, has begun to thin, to scatter. "Personal density," Kurt Mondaugen in his Peenemünde office not too many steps away from here, enunciating the Law which will one day bear his name, "is directly proportional to temporal bandwidth." "Temporal bandwidth" is the width of your present, you *now*. It is the familiar "Δt" considered as a dependent variable. The more you dwell in the past and in the future, the thicker your bandwidth, the more solid your persona. But the narrower your sense of Now, the more tenuous you are. It may get to where you're having trouble remembering what you were doing five minutes ago, or even—as Slothrop now—what you're doing *here*.

Soon he will be unnameable. Slothrop's disintegration reflects Pynchon's insistence that his characters cannot resolve the experiences of *Gravity's Rainbow*. Pynchon states the limitations of the characters directly:

> Who would have thought so many would be here? They keep appearing, all through this disquieting structure, gathered in groups, pacing alone in meditation, or studying the paintings, the books, the exhibits. It seems to be some very extensive museum, a place of many levels, and new wings that generate like living tissue— though if it all does grow toward some end shape, those who are here inside can't see it. Some of the halls are to be entered at one's peril, and monitors are standing at all the approaches to make this clear.

Rather than following the modernist approach by resolving *Gravity's Rainbow* through his own aesthetic structures (imposing his own perceptual system),

Pynchon insists that, once we enter the halls, we find the exit for ourselves. He can offer us points of advice, guideposts, but they won't matter if we can't step outside our solipsism, first to confront the reality of *Gravity's Rainbow* and then to take it into our own lives.

When it matters most, Pynchon speaks to us directly. Using the second-person pronoun, Pynchon draws us into *Gravity's Rainbow*; our response depends on both our own experiences and our ability to empathize with others. Frequently, Pynchon attempts to make us particpate in his vision through the use of traditional devices such as minutely detailed realistic settings or slap-stick parody sequences written in third person. Having drawn us into his fictional world, Pynchon abruptly shifts to a direct form of address, reminding us that his world is also ours, demanding that we surrender our own solipsism and interact with the book. What Pynchon wants us to share, what he employs the second person to communicate, is his vision of a world of the preterite, a world in agony, a world in desperate need of love. The "you" passages occur throughout the book—there are some twenty in all—and when juxtaposed they challenge us to recognize the similarity of our own isolation and that of others, our share of responsibility for Their dominance, the serious consequences of giving in to isolation, and the necessity of extending ourselves to our brothers and sisters among the preterite in order to forge a new sense of moral community.

Slothrop's ancestor William wrote of the preterite as the source of moral value every bit as important as the elect: " 'That's what Jesus meant,' whispers the ghost of Slothrop's first American ancestor William, 'venturing out on the Sea of Galilee. He saw it from the lemming point of view. Without the millions who had plunged and drowned, there could have been no miracle. The successful loner was only the other part of it: the last piece to the jigsaw puzzle, whose shape had already been created by the Preterite, like the last bland space on the table.' " Tyrone clings to the vision, extending it to our own world:

> Could he have been the fork in the road America never took, the singular point she jumped the wrong way from? Suppose the Sloth-ropite heresy had had the time to consolidate and prosper? Might there have been fewer crimes in the name of Jesus, and more mercy in the name of Judas Iscariot? It seems to Tyrone Slothrop that there might be a route back—maybe that anarchist he met in Zurich was right, maybe for a little while all the fences were down, one road as good as another, the whole space of the Zone cleared, depolarized, and somewhere inside the waste of it a single set of

coordinates from which to proceed, without elect, without preterite, without even nationality to fuck it up.

Straining to break even the dichotomy of elect and preterite, Tyrone refuses simply to invert the terms and condemn the elect; preterition becomes a metaphor for the condition of all of us caught in systems based on arbitrary dichotomies.

Pynchon hymns the preterite, reminding us of our own preterition, of

> men you have seen on foot and smileless in the cities but forget, men who don't remember you either, knowing they ought to be grabbing a little sleep, not out here performing for strangers, give you this evensong, climaxing now with its rising fragment of some ancient scale, voices overlapping three—and fourfold, up, echoing, filling the entire hollow of the church—no counterfeit baby, no announcement of the Kingdom, not even a try at warming or lighting this terrible night, only, damn us, our scruffy obligatory little cry, our maximum reach outward—*praise be to God!*—for you to take back to your war-address, your war-identity, across the snow's footprints and tire tracks finally to the path you must create by yourself, alone in the dark. Whether you want it or not, whatever seas you have crossed, the way home.

He writes of "Your own form immobile, mouth-breaking, alone face-up on the narrow cot next to the wall so pictureless, chartless, mapless; so *habitually blank.*" He places us on the target as the rocket descends, staring up with Pökler to confront the physical symbol of the destructive effect of our own attempts to remain uninvolved:

> Now what sea is this you have crossed, exactly, and what sea is it you have plunged more than once to the bottom of, alerted, full of adrenalin, but caught really, buffaloed under the epistemologies of these threats that paranoid you so down and out, caught in this steel pot, softening to devitaminized mush inside the soup-stock of your own words, your waste submarine breath? It took the Dreyfus Affair to get the Zionists out and doing, finally: what will drive you out of your soup-kettle? Has it already happened? Was it tonight's attack and deliverance? Will you go to the Heath, and begin your settlement, and wait there for your Director to come?

He forces us either to retreat to solipsism or to share the agony, and the responsibility for the agony. If we refuse to see ourselves in the "you" Pynchon addresses, we aren't going to get much out of *Gravity's Rainbow*.

All we have, finally, is love. It may be too much to expect, but nothing's more important than trying to find, to love:

> You have waited in these places into the early mornings, synced in to the on-whitening of the interior, you know the Arrivals schedule by heart, by hollow heart. And where these children have run away from, and that, in this city, there is no one to meet them. You impress them with your gentleness. You've never quite decided if they can see through to your vacuum. They won't yet look in your eyes. . . . Tonight's child has had a long trip here, hasn't slept. Her eyes are red, her frock wrinkled. Her coat has been a pillow. You feel her exhaustion, feel the impossible vastness of all the sleeping countryside at her back, and for the moment you rally are selfless, sexless . . . considering only how to shelter her, you are the Traveler's Aid.

If nothing else, we can shelter strangers. Occasionally we can love like Mexico loves Jessica. Pynchon pulls us deeper than direct address at the end of section one of *Gravity's Rainbow*. He has spoken to us. Here we speak to Jessica. There are no quotation marks, no Joycean distancing techniques. Living under attack, we merge with Mexico: "You go from dream to dream inside me. You have passage to my last shabby corner, and there, among the debris, you've found life. I'm no longer sure which of all the words, images, dreams or ghosts are 'yours' and which are 'mind.' It's past sorting out. We're both being someone new now, someone incredible." Pynchon offers us a "we" which can include Roger, Jessica, Pynchon, you and me. Recognizing the fragility, we share our cry with Mexico: "You're catching the War. It's infecting you and I don't know how to keep it away. Oh, Jess. Jessica. Don't leave me . . ."

She leaves.

Just as Pynchon refuses to offer us a traditional resolution through Slothrop, he refuses to offer us a vicarious resolution through Mexico. If we love, we love in reality, not on a printed page. We love with our dreams and our bodies, but we love together, not alone with our books. The last words are Pynchon's: "All together now, all you masochists out there, specially those of you don't have a partner tonight, alone with those fantasies that don't look like they'll ever come true—want you just to join in here with your brothers and sisters, let each other know you're alive and sincere, try to break through the silences, try to reach through and connect."

Now Everybody.

CHARLES BERGER

Merrill and Pynchon:
Our Apocalyptic Scribes

"WE SPEAK FROM WITHIN THE ATOM," Mirabell and his cohorts declare, thereby placing Merrill's trilogy at the center of our deepest anxieties since the end of World War II. *Mirabell's* final sections eloquently and movingly detail the reasons why JM and DJ were chosen to receive the vision of things as they are — *de natura rerum*. But early on in the second poem of the trilogy, Mirabell reveals an even more urgent fact, the reason why the otherworldly messengers have chosen this time and place to stage their epic descent: "THE MUSHROOM CLOUD APPALD YR PRINCIPAL SOUL DENSITY," The dropping of the atomic bomb on Hiroshima threatened the whole structure of lab work (or V work) by obliterating the gene pool and thus introducing the specter of annihilation rather than mere death. "All trace was lost/Of souls that perished in that holocaust," DJ remembers, referring to a hint left by Ephraim many years earlier. The message that Mirabell and his superiors are intent on conveying through the medium of the Scribe is a simple one: "THE ATOM CANNOT BE MAN'S FRIEND." The epigraph to *Mirabell* reinforces the idea that the trilogy's center of anxious concern, its deep origin, however clouded by mythic analogue or autobiographical excursus, is the development of the atomic bomb:

> The three men decided they would prepare a letter to President
> Roosevelt, and that Einstein would sign it. . . . Einstein's eyes slowly
> moved along the two full, typewritten pages. . . . "For the first time
> in history men will use energy that does not come from the sun,"
> he commented and signed. The scientists operated their pile for

From *James Merrill: Essays in Criticism.* © 1983 by Cornell University Press.

the first time on December 2, 1942. They were the first men to
see matter yield its inner energy, steadily, at their will. My husband
was their leader.

— LAURA FERMI

Merrill's trilogy is an epic of survival. It is also the longest and most self-
consciously successful elegy in the language. Some readers are put off by Merrill's
apparent lack of eschatological anxiety, his unfaltering graveyard wit. They
may be falling into a trap here: by taking the verbal antics of JM, DJ, and
WHA as the poet's "authorized" reaction to the news of revelation, they forget
that just as we recognize the difference between Dante the Pilgrim and Dante
the Poet, so Merrill's role as an actor in the poem needs to be distinguished
from the shaping spirit who put the whole structure together. *Mirabell*, in
particular, offers sharp contrasts between the anxiety of the spirit world over-
looking human history and the players themselves. If we brood upon the whole
trilogy, we can see that Merrill's foray into the region of the dead, or their
foray into his sphere, is not a parlor game, despite its trappings, but a reaction
to the poet's sense of an ending: in other words, an apocalyptic poem.

In the book whose title has now become part of the critical lingua franca,
Frank Kermode has a seminal chapter on "The Modern Apocalypse," in which
he attempts to discriminate between early and late modernism on the basis
of how each responds to apocalyptic pressure. He takes for granted a lasting
sense of eschatological anxiety throughout the century, so that what we have
is not a moment but an age of crisis. According to Kermode, certain features
remain constant in the works of artists acutely conscious of the End, especially
when the End is conceived of as a New Beginning. These features include:
the certainty that universal bloodshed must accompany the final days, an
emphasis upon a phase of transition, periods of decadence and renovation,
paradigms of justice or judgment imposed upon historical reality, recognition
of an elect who will survive and a demonic host who will perish, and the attempt
in the last days to provide a language of renovation. What Kermode finds to
be the distinguishing factor between early and late modernism is the emphasis
in the former upon our link to the past. Apocalypse, for Yeats, Eliot, or Pound,
means restoration of an earlier (superior) order. The newer, or what Kermode
calls the schismatic modernism, does not mythologize earlier orders in its quest
for a lost stability or hierarchy. The heroes of *The Sense of an Ending*, those
who resist the dangerous confusion of ideology and myth, are those who resist
the dangerous confusion of ideology and myth, are those supreme artificers
Joyce and Stevens. (Thus the temporal distinction gives way to a truer, syn-
chronic struggle between orthodox and schismatic modernism.) They create

literary forms that are open to transition and flux; they worship no strange gods, but language; they convey the pathos of endings without any rancor.

Merrill's poetic pantheon might at first incline one to place him with Yeats, and the trilogy is often compared to *A Vision*. But there is nothing hieratic about Merrill's scheme—conversation, even between the upper and lower cases, tends to equalize—though there is much hierarchy. Yeats and even Pound are greater celebrants than Merrill, more attuned to the sacred. Despite everything, Merrill remains a secular epiphanist. He took seriously the injunction to write Poems of Science (which does not mean that he bothered to gather any scientific knowledge.) What the Poem or Epic of Science does is to liberate mythology from its grounding in a particular culture. The result is a pure ideology of myth assigned, as we might expect, to a prehistorical era—indeed, to an era preceding the formation of our world. Much of *Paradise Lost*, as well, takes place prior to the creation of Earth, and Milton's emphasis on universal Christian culture was a corrective to the pagan—and Christian Renaissance—focus on the native epic. By mythologizing history, Yeats and Pound open the way to dangerous, even Fascist, notions of past wholeness, lost origins, true cultural centers. V work is Merrill's equivalent of the privileged cultural enterprise, which Yeats assigns to "Byzantium" and Pound to "Provence." The sacred spot becomes an invisible laboratory. (The visual arts matter little to Merrill; in *Mirabell*, Book 3, painters and sculptors are said to be too dependent on the body, as opposed to poets and musicians. Merrill's only icon is the board itself.) And while the ahistorical and impalpable nature of Merrill's central myth reduces its sacramental value, it does grant the prestige of anteriority.

Of course, the nature of V work does require an elect, certain also to be shadowed by what Kermode, following tradition, terms the demonic host. Whether we identify Merrill's corps as the Five, or the Twelve Percent, depending on which account we find more coherent, it is clear that he is at ease with the idea of an elect, despite DJ's democratic protestations. Mirabell's density ratios and his talk of cloning favorable spirits might be excused, if one thinks they need to be, by the urgency of the moment, the need to save the Greenhouse of Earth. Terms such as "Jew-density"—though intended, of course, as the highest compliment—come as a shock in this most civilized of recent literary productions; the shock is healthy, however, if it is taken as a sign or index of the poem's extreme nature, which is ours as well. All sorts of orthodoxies go by the board—no pun?—in crisis, and the apocalyptic text often brims with the energy of the forbidden, especially forbidden knowledge. In the case of Merrill, such knowledge obviously centers on the Ouija board and what it represents as a counter to "legitimate" modes of acquiring information. Merrill's science is a pre-science, but not less legitimate for that. Just as the trilogy labors to ground culture in science, so it authenticates science by stressing its continuity with magic. That "E. German physicist," who is declared an avatar of Montezuma, is not thereby exposed as a fraud. But scientific arrogance does need to be chastened. Laura Fermi's boast in the epigraph—"They were the first men to see matter yield its inner energy, steadily, at their will"—must be corrected, and Mirabell himself does so. Those may have been the first *men*, but they were not the *first*. Mirabell and the fallen spirits can claim priority for that. And since they have gone before, they can legitimately warn us.

The apocalyptic text attempts to counter or ward off total destruction. One of its strategies is to establish a grand heterocosm—a world elsewhere, a rival plenitude designed both to imitate and to preserve the totality of our world, now threatened by extinction. It is no accident that *Ulysses*, for instance, was written during World War I; its encyclopedic scope attempts to protect the world by enclosing it. And yet, although the desired end of such effort might be innocence—the Yes of affirmation—Joyce's heterocosm is hardly innocent. His capacious order is always on the verge of dissolving into disorder, and the strenuous effort to hold things together creates a formal violence of its own. Joyce's rage against the limits of narrative and language is itself a war. Apocalyptic texts, even more than others, must internalize violence. For this reason, as in the case of Blake and Joyce, such texts often veer into savage intellectual satire. This is not Merrill's way. There is nothing Rabelaisian about him. Following Dante, he maintains civility in even the darkest regions, assigning violence to the other, the interlocutor. The message, however, remains clear: save the Greenhouse!

This central anxiety is also shared by the only American work of the last decade that can rival Merrill's trilogy in scope, design, and density: *Gravity's Rainbow*. Neither Pynchon nor Merrill fit into any contemporary movement; it goes without saying that they work worlds apart from each other. Yet each is, or has become, something of an apocalyptic scribe, returning by such different routes to the origin of our impending end.

Mirabell locates that origin in the Fall brought on by the technological *hubris* of Mirabell's own species. They overthrew the Centaurs and seized the secrets of the atom:

> WE SAW THE POWER & WITH IT BUILT A GREAT GREAT GLORY
> A WORLD YOU COULD NOT IMAGINE.

Then they pushed too far, this race of Master Builders, ruining their own handiwork:

AND THEN   ONE ATOM TOO MANY   WE WANTED MORE   THE BLACK
LIGHT ON OUR EYELIDS   OUR BLINDNESS   OUR ARROGANCE   WE CHOSE
TO MOVE ON INTO SPACE   ABANDONING THE WORLD WE ROSE
THE CRUST LIKE A VEIL SHREDDED FAR BEHIND US EXPOSING
THE ALREADY ARID EARTH   WE DESPISD IT & FLUNG BACK
A LAST BOLT & THE UNIVERSE FELL IN ON US   WE FELL.

There is more than a touch of the Mad Scientist in this hyperbole, so that it is crucial to keep "the dark undertone of Hiroshima" (Helen Vendler's phrase) firmly in mind. Mirabell's attractiveness as epic instructor is also likely to disarm us if we do not remember how wide and imponderable is the gulf between character and deed. The full consequences of an act cannot be gauged by the intentions of the actor; sometimes they can barely be glimpsed. The growing bond between Mirabell and JM cannot blind us to the disasters brought on by the atomic tinkering of Mirabell and his race.

Pynchon shrewdly situates his epic narrative just *before* the beginning of the atomic age proper. The German V-2 rocket, whose presence hovers over *Gravity's Rainbow*, is only a precursor of the greater destructiveness to come. Pynchon's true subject must be the ICBM, but he cannot write directly about it. Instead, he gives us the more "rational" or comprehensible phenomenon of the V-2. The latter becomes a microcosm in which we can study the effects, infinitely reduced, of technological madness. The Zone, the name Pynchon gives to the ruined German sector at war's end, also serves as a laboratory for all the forces that we, as readers located in the 1970s, know will come to dominate the postwar scene. We know that the V-2 rockets will metamorphose into nuclear bombs—indeed, it happens at the very end of the novel—but by taking us back to that moment in history just prior to the transformation, Pynchon makes us experience the Fall all over again. We gather the news of Hiroshima through the eyes of Slothrop, the novel's picaresque protagonist, who glances at a front-page photograph of the phallic cloud and this bit of headline:

MB DRO
ROSHI.

Slothrop is of course baffled by this Ouija-like communiqué. When the puzzle is put together, a new world order will have emerged.

For Pynchon, the villains of this new dispensation are not so much the scientists as the technicians who follow and parody them. To import Blakean terms, the technological end of "sweet science" should be epitomized in the

effort to build the New Jerusalem, antithesis to the blind buildings of the
tyrannical pharaohs. I think Merrill, also, tends to center on the demonic
distortion of science. Mirabell and his cohorts are the opposites of Blake's Los.
Worse yet, they are bureaucrats, for what is the technician but a scientific
bureaucrat? One of the more startling aspects of Merrill's otherworldly nexus
is the role played there by bureaucratic censorship and control—Dante's hierarchy
brought up to date. Pynchon, for whom all forms of bureaucracy partake of
sinister beauty, coins a phrase that Merrill might readily subscribe to. Speaking
of dreams, Pynchon writes:

> So that the right material may find its way to the right dreamer,
> everyone, everything involved must be exactly in place in the pattern.
> It was nice of Jung to give us the idea of an ancestral pool in which
> everybody shares the same dream material. But how is it we are
> each visited as individuals, each by exactly and only what he needs?
> Doesn't that imply a switching-path of some kind? a bureaucracy?
> Why shouldn't the IG [Farben, that is] go to séances? They ought
> to be quite at home with *the bureaucracies of the other side.*
>
> [*GR*; italics added]

The idea that the unconscious is a vast bureaucracy is not far removed
from Merrill's notions of an interlocking system of patrons, representatives,
and sorting agents who administer the composition of earthly souls. Nor are
we far from Spenser's Garden of Adonis, for that matter. Literary syncretists
like Merrill and Pynchon, though they develop highly distinctive styles, tend
to efface the role of personality in literary composition; tradition, however
disfigured by the avant-gardist, becomes another version of bureaucracy. Some
of the more notorious episodes in the trilogy concern revelations of ghost-
written masterpieces. We discover that Dante was dictated to, and that the
peculiar physiological combination we refer to as Rimbaud actually wrote "The
Waste Land." Pynchon has little use for the literary artist as such, replacing
him with the scientist. But the ground rules for scientific creation obviously
have much to say about the way writers work. The recipient of the dream
material quoted above was Friedrich August Kekulé von Stradonitz, a great
German chemist who discovered the structure of the benzene molecule. Kekulé
began his studies as an architect and "brought the mind's eye of an architect
over into chemistry." He found that the six atoms of carbon and six atoms
of hydrogen in benzene are arranged in a closed, ringlike structure resembling
a hexagon. Kekulé claimed that the shape of benzene came to him in a dream.
Pynchon interprets this episode of inspiration not as a triumph for Kekulé

but an example of how the System uses the scientist for its own ends. Kekulé becomes the Scribe of the bureaucracy:

> Kekulé dreams the Great Serpent holding its own tail in its mouth, the dreaming Serpent which surrounds the World. But the meanness, the cynicism with which this dream is to be used. The Serpent that announces, "The World is a closed thing, cyclical, resonant, eternally-returning," is to be delivered into a system whose only aim is to *violate* the Cycle. . . . No return, no salvation, no Cycle—that's not what They, nor Their brilliant employee Kekulé have taken the Serpent to mean. . . . we had been given certain molecules, certain combinations and not others. . . . we used what we found in Nature, unquestioning, shamefully perhaps—but the Serpent whispered, "*They can be changed*, and new molecules assembled from the debris of the given."
>
> [GR]

In such a universe, when even a scientist of Kekulé's stature is only an employee, what place is there for the assertion of will, for the individuating choice? Merrill often puzzles over the role of will in the midst of executing his grand arabesques. When we learn what has gone into the programming of even the saving Twelve Percent, we are not likely to regard their achievements as willed. Both Merrill and Pynchon array enormous forces over and against the individual: even the idea of assertion almost begins to seem comical or outmoded, like the dream of narrative continuity. We scan Merrill and Pynchon for those moments in which the will is present, and we take what we can. So we read *Ulysses*, for example, looking for something, anything, that Leopold Bloom might be said to *do*, actually or effectually. His sparing of Molly's suitors, a refusal to "act," becomes Bloom's prime assertion in the course of the novel. Joyce's internalization of the will becomes the norm in the encyclopedic mock-epic. The strength of JM and DJ comes to reside in their being able to provide a space in which things happen: they are loving mediums. They bring about Mirabell's transformation precisely by doing nothing at all. The same negative prescription for the will that we find in Joyce and Merrill doing nothing—is perhaps the only formula for genuine activity in *Gravity's Rainbow*, a book filled with frenetic semblances of action. Pynchon delights in narrowing the room for action to the point where only refusal fits. And yet this refusal can take on a nobility denied to anything else. as when the Nazi rocket technician Pökler refuses to have intercourse with a young woman whom the SS has provided for him, a young woman who pretends to be his daughter in order to further his delight. "No. What Pökler did was choose to believe she wanted comfort that night, wanted not to be alone. Despite Their game, Their palpable evil, though he had no more reason to trust "Ilse" than he trusted Them, by an act not of faith, not of courage but of conservation, he chose to believe that" (*GR*). Nowhere else in *Gravity's Rainbow* is the act of choice so accentuated. Pökler will go on to quit the game and, by doing so, join the Counter-Force.

Stymying the will, yet also committed to the precepts of quest romance, Merrill and Pynchon end up courting the moment of mazy error, to invoke a Miltonism, the moment in which it is recognized that finding the true way means losing oneself to the world, because of either conceptual bewilderment or overcertainty. One can wonder in search of the truth through an ever-increasing forest of signals, or one can become blinded by the brightness of a terribly clear message. The first way is typical of Pynchon's characters, the second, of Merrill himself. By saying this I do not mean to imply that the content of Merrill's vision is always clear. Far from it. But the *value* or the *import* of the clues he puts together is never seriously questioned beyond the bound of "The Book of Ephraim." We observe JM in the process of being educated and tested, as a good romance hero should be; much renunciation is demanded of him, politely enough, for the privilege of being chosen. But even though he converses with the avatars of Beelzebub and Co., the sources of JM's revelations remain surprisingly trustworthy. If Mirabell misleads, he does so only because of his lower place in the hierarchy. Merrill's trilogy is, after all, a much more straightforwardly didactic work than *Gravity's Rainbow*. Wandering and error are seen to have their corrections and rewards. Merrill's confessions of his growing isolation avoid the note of terror that would certainly be present were the vision doubted.

> About us, these bright afternoons, we come
> To draw shades of an auditorium
> In darkness. An imagined dark . . .
> . . . .
> Lighthouse and clock tower, Village Green and neat
> Roseblush factory which makes, upstreet,
> Exactly what, one once knew but forgets—
> Something of plastic found in luncheonettes;
> The Sound's quick sapphire that each day recurs
> Aflock with pouter-pigeon spinnakers
> —This outside world, our fictive darkness more
> And more belittles to a safety door

Left open onto light. Too small, too far
To help. The blind bright spot of where we are.

[M]

Merrill's instructors have personalities and they expect their students to possess the same, even if the end of prophecy, as they predict, will be the extinction of self. We hear much throughout the trilogy about this presumed annihilation of self, yet within the poem itself the voices and the selves they embody never really cease:

JM THE STRIPPING IS THE POINT YR POEM WILL PERHAPS TAKE UP FROM
ITS WINTRY END & MOVE STEP BY STEP INTO SEASONLESS & CHARAC-
TERLESS STAGES TO ITS FINAL GREAT COLD RINGING OF THE CHIMES
SHAPED AS O O O O O

[M]

They of course come through
—It's what, in any Quest, the heroes do—
But at the cost of being set apart,
Emptied, diminished. Tolkien knew this. Art—
The tale that all but shapes itself—survives
By feeding on its personages' lives.
The stripping process, sort of. What to say?
Our lives led *to* this. It's the price we pay.

[M]

In *Gravity's Rainbow*, on the other hand, we do witness the end of instruc-tion, quite literally, as the hero of the epic romance is finally bombarded into quiescence. In *The Crying of Lot 49*, Oedipa Maas may or may not fade into the mass of others at novel's end, but in *GR* there is no question that Slothrop disappears. The puzzle is what he disappears into. Maxwell's demon, the sort-ing agent of *Lot 49*, became the guiding spirit of that novel, enabling Oedipa at least to attempt to sort out her fate, her *sort*. Slothrop, however, equally assaulted by instruction, comes to a true soldier's end—he just fades away:

instructing him, dunce and drifter, in ways deeper than he can explain, have been faces of children out the train windows, two bars of dance music somewhere, in some other street at night, needles and branches of a pine tree shaken clear and luminous against night clouds, one circuit diagram out of hundreds in a smudged yellowing sheaf, laughter out of a cornfield in the early morning as he was walking to school, the idling of a motorcycle

at one dusk-heavy hour of the summer . . . and now, in the Zone,
later in the day he became a crossroad, after a heavy rain he doesn't
recall, Slothrop sees a very thick rainbow here, a stout rainbow
cock driven down out of public clouds into Earth, green wet valleyed
Earth, and his chest fills and he stands crying, not a thing in his
head, just feeling natural. . . .

                                                                    [GR]

    I think we can read in Slothrop's demise the danger of taking in all that
instruction, all those portents, unaided; and in this danger might be the motive
for Merrill's invention or discovery of the Instructor. All the classic romance
fictions provide a guide for the hero, and Merrill's trilogy continues this tradition
with a vengeance. He is as guided as any quester since Dante. Even Oedipa
Maas had her precursors along the way to aid her. But much of the darkness
permeating *Gravity's Rainbow* comes from the absence of any such sponsoring
guides. The novel abounds in messages that must be deciphered in the absence
of any guiding ideology, much less any figure of instruction. Slothrop realizes
this at long last in a passage just preceding the one quoted above. Wandering
through the Zone he gathers a sense of design to it all, a possible legibility
to the chaos. "Omens grow clearer, more specific. He watches flights of birds
and patterns in the ashes of his fire, he reads the guts of trouts he's caught
and cleaned, scraps of lost paper, graffiti on the broken walls where facing
has been shot away to reveal the brick underneath—broken in specific shapes
that may also be read" (*GR*). Slothrop stumbles into a public latrine abounding
in graffiti. Might he now encounter some definitive revelation as to which
"Kilroy" had been there, preceding him? But instead of finding the name of
his precursor scrawled on the wall, Slothrop finds only the traces of himself:
"ROCKETMAN WAS HERE." (Slothrop's nickname is Rocketman.) The
uppercase provides no deliverance from the albatross of self.
    It is too easy to point out how the reader is tested, constantly. in his abil-
ity to decipher the difficult, swirling surfaces of these two epic romances.
Merrill and Pynchon have a certain stake in making the very page itself harder
to read. The typographic peculiarities of Merrill's trilogy are likely to occupy
new readers fully as much as the various realms of being they serve to distinguish.
The different type cases and schemes of indentation followed by Merrill may
help or hinder his readers, but it should be pointed out that what they literalize—
the narrative's frequent and elliptical shifts between *kinds* of speech—goes on
constantly in modern texts, both of poetry and fiction. Merrill's poem is of
course difficult to read sequentially, but it is hardly alone in stymying that
expectation. Although Merrill has little in common with someone like Pound,
one would do well to study the technique each poet adopts to create boundaries

of discourse, to mark off intrusive voices. Merrill codifies where Pound often mystifies, but his voices would retain their individuality even if typography did not prepare us to know who was speaking. The trilogy is always a conversational poem. Merrill is able to sustain a modernist revival of that poetic mode by crossing conversation with ellipsis, polite dialogue with sharp interruption. Speakers are always cutting each other off without ever undercutting what the other says.

Merrill's transitions between speakers never demand that skeptical distrust of preceding discourse that is the prime function of ellipsis in modernist texts. In other words, Merrill is never structurally ironic. His repartee is sprinkled with gentler, passing ironies that the reader welcomes as a release from the severity of instruction, but they do not compel us to suspect what has gone before. This is a crucial point: while it is certainly true that JM and company add piece by piece to their structure of messages, with each new bit revising earlier beliefs, this process of revision is grounded in a growing certainty about the truth. Vergil is superseded by Beatrice, but this does not mean that Dante intends Vergil's doctrine to be undercut by the greater instructor. What he knows is amplified by her knowledge; so Mirabell will yield to the angels. Higher authorities supersede lower, while the notion of authority remains intact. The connection between blocks of speech in the trilogy appear more ragged than they really are, primarily for typographical reasons. The cut-and-paste look of the page inclines one to think of the poem as a disjunctive collage. But its true spirit resides in its formal resolutions, such as the pavane composed in praise of V work (*Mirabell*, Book 3), which perfectly blends disparate voices.

Pynchon represents a more savage school of irony. Authority is always put into question in his fiction, error is endless. *Gravity's Rainbow* abounds with false centers of authority, moments that lure the reader into anchoring the quest for certainty, only to slide away like the false bedrock of Leviathan. (Every reader of Pynchon, myself included, nonetheless believes that there *is* an unassailable passage or two in which the authorial hand betrays itself.)

In its lighter moments, Pynchon's legerdemain resembles Merrill's flaunting of poetic conceit. Improvisational wit keeps readers offguard; they know something is up but do not know where it will lead. As a poet, Merrill confines himself more to the local effects of wordplay and, as a mortal, to the lowercase commentary embroidering his blocks of literal truth. (Mirabell's frequent resort to (M), the parenthetical metaphor notwithstanding.) Pynchon's more raucous wit is less susceptible to closure. His improvisations spin off on widening arcs of unpredictability, and his readers are hardly able to tell when or where they have landed. The outrageous pop lyrics that dot the pages of

Gravity's Rainbow can usually be found at the center of these improvisations. As bits of low culture they might presumably add a touch of stability to the narrative, bringing evidence of a lighthearted world outside the Zone. But Pynchon makes this comfort impossible to derive by skewing the lyrics both to illustrate how malleable they are to any given situation and how unstable or potentially made they are in their own right.

Take this swatch of narrative from the novel's final section, "The Counter-Force" (*GR*). Roger Mexico comes storming into the office of Dr. Pointsman, the sinister Pavlovian, looking for revenge; instead, he finds Pointsman's assistant, Geza Rozsavolgyi. Mexico's anger degenerates into a slapstick session with the latter. But then something strange happens. Rozsavolgyi, retreating from his tormentor, backs into a shadowy corner of the room from whose vantage point "the rest of the room seems to be at more of a distance, as through the view-finder on a camera. And the walls—they don't appear to be . . . well, *solid*, actually. They flow: a coarse, viscous passage, rippling like a piece of silk or nylon, the color watery gray but now and then with a surprise island in the flow." (Compare Merrill's fantasia on the wallpaper in the parlor at Stonington, which opens *Mirabell*.) It is a short step from this "surprise island" to a fantasy about two fighter pilots who crash-land on the island: "We—we're *safe*? We are! Mangoes, I see mangoes on that tree over there! a—and there's a girl—there's a *lotta* girls! Lookit, they're all gorgeous . . . and they're all swingin' those grass skirts, playin' ukuleles and singing (though why are their voices so loud and tough, so nasally like the voices of an American chorus line?): 'White man, welcome to Puke-a-hook-a-look-i I-i-i-island!' Rozsavolgyi's dream vision ends only when one of the pilots raises his goggles and smiles mockingly, familiarly, at the dreamer, thus stepping out of the frame: "I know you, don't you know me? Don't you *really* know me?"

What a Rozsavolgyi sees may only add up to an amusing divertimento, but it is Pynchon's habit throughout *Gravity's Rainbow* to assign even the most seemingly profound visions to peripheral characters. This almost seems a defensive gesture on his part, a reflexive appeal to an irony easily available to the writer of fiction: the untrustworthy narrator, or character, as in this case. But I think a more radical motive is at work. The assignment of these core moments to ephemeral characters seems rather to abolish the perspectives by means of which the reader has been deciding just who is central and who peripheral.

Pynchon's "revelations" often take the form of undoing the mimetic or naturalistic frame of his narratives, calling into question the whole concept of discrete characters of persons. As I have mentioned, the logical denouement of Merrill's schema does the same thing, although his poem cannot bear to eradicate the trace of human personality. Vocal inflections ring true for Merrill even then speech emanates from "WITHIN THE ATOM." Pynchon's character probes of the molecular underworld bring back news of a structuralist's heaven, a realm of law that abolishes the mere subjectivity or intentionality of its subjects. One Blobadjian, a bureaucrat and minor linguist, is abruptly removed from the action (centering on a commission set up to bring the New Turkic Alphabet to an oral tribe in Central Asia) and is brought into touch with the bureaucracy of the other side.

> How alphabetic is the nature of molecules. One grows aware of it down here: one finds Committees on molecular structure which are very similar to those back at the NTA plenary session: "See: how they are taken out from the coarse flow — shaped, cleaned, rectified, just as you once redeemed your letters from the lawless, the mortal streaming of human speech. . . . These are our letters, our words: they too can be modulated, broken, recoupled, redefined, co-polymerized one to the other in worldwide chains that will surface now and then over long molecular silences, like the seen parts of a tapestry."
>
> [GR]

"One grows aware of it down here": this conversion of the natural locus of all waste, all loss — the underworld — into a scene of instruction is finally what Pynchon and Merrill have most in common. "NOTHING IS EVER EVER LOST THE WATERFALL WILL HOLD / YR 2 BRIGHT DROPS & YOU WILL SPLASH INTO THE GREAT CLEAR POOL" (M), are perhaps the most poignant lines in all of Merrill. This faith justifies the extraordinary feats of conservation, retrieval, assemblage, that make up the body of Gravity's Rainbow or Merrill's trilogy. Pynchon looks upon gravity itself as the preserving force in nature: "To find that Gravity, taken so for granted, is really something eerie, Messianic, extrasensory in Earth's mindbody . . . having hugged to its holy center the wastes of dead species, gathered, packed, transmuted, realigned, and rewoven molecules to be taken up again by the coal-tar Kabbalists of the other side" (GR). Something of us will survive, if only as "bright drops" in gravity's rainbow.

Chronology

1937   Thomas Pynchon born May 8, in Glen Cove, Long Island.

1958   Graduates from Cornell University. Editorial writer at Boeing Company, Seattle.

1963   *V.* published. Pynchon receives Faulkner Prize for best first novel.

1966   *The Crying of Lot 49.*

1973   *Gravity's Rainbow.*

1984   *Slow Learner* (a collection of short stories).

Contributors

HAROLD BLOOM, Sterling Professor of the Humanities at Yale University, is the author of *The Anxiety of Influence*, *Poetry and Repression*, and many other volumes of literary criticism. His forthcoming study, *Freud: Transference and Authority*, attempts a full-scale reading of all of Freud's major writings. A MacArthur Prize Fellow, he is general editor of five series of literary criticism published by Chelsea House.

FRANK KERMODE is Professor of English at Columbia University. He is the author of *D. H. Lawrence*, *The Sense of an Ending*, and *Forms of Attention*.

EDWARD MENDELSON is Professor of English at Columbia University. He is the author of several studies of W. H. Auden, and is the literary executor of Auden's estate.

ALAN J. FRIEDMAN is a Professor in the Department of Science and Math Education at the University of California at Berkeley.

MANFRED PUETZ has published several essays on the works of Thomas Pynchon.

JOSEPHINE HENDIN is Assistant Professor of English at New York University. She is the author of *The World of Flannery O'Connor* and *Vulnerable People: A View of American Fiction Since 1945*.

RICHARD POIRIER is one of the editors of *Raritan* and of the Library of America. He is Professor of English at Rutgers University, and his books include studies of Mailer and Robert Frost, as well as *A World Elsewhere* and *The Performing Self*.

GEORGE LEVINE is Professor of English at Rutgers University. He is the author of *The Boundaries of Fiction* and *The Realistic Imagination: English Fiction from Frankenstein to Lady Chatterley*.

CATHARINE R. STIMPSON, Professor of English at Rutgers University and Director of its Institute for Research on Women, has written both criticism and fiction, including *Class Notes*.

MELVYN NEW is Professor of English at the University of Florida. He has written on eighteenth-century English literature, and is coediting the Florida edition of the works of Sterne.

MAUREEN QUILLIGAN is Associate Professor of English at the University of Pennsylvania. She is the author of *The Language of Allegory* and *Milton's Spenser: The Politics of Reading*.

MARCUS SMITH is Professor of English at Loyola University, New Orleans.

KHACHIG TOLOLYAN is Professor of English at Wesleyan University. He is the founding editor of *Pynchon Notes*.

DAVID SEED teaches English at Liverpool University in England.

TONY TANNER is Reader in English at Cambridge University. His books include *The Reign of Wonder, City of Words*, and *Adultery in the Novel*.

CRAIG HANSEN WERNER teaches in the English Department at the University of Mississippi. He is the author of *Paradoxical Resolutions: American Fiction since James Joyce*.

CHARLES BERGER is Associate Professor of English at Yale University. He is the author of a study of Wallace Stevens and of many essays on contemporary literature.

Bibliography

Abernathy, Peter L. "Entropy in Pynchon's *The Crying of Lot 49*." *Critique* 14, no. 2 (1972): 18–33.

Bloom, Harold, ed. *Modern Critical Interpretations: Thomas Pynchon's* Gravity's Rainbow. New Haven: Chelsea House, 1986.

Cowart, David. *Thomas Pynchon: The Art of Allusion*. Carbondale, Ill.: Southern Illinois University Press, 1980.

Davis, Robert Murray. "Parody, Paranoia, and the Dead End of Language." *Genre* 5 (1972). 367–77.

Fowler, Douglas. "Pynchon's Magic World." *South Atlantic Quarterly* 79, no. 1 (1980). 51 60.

Golden, Robert E. "Mass Man and Modernism: Violence in Pynchon's *V*." *Critique* 14, no. 2 (1972): 5–17.

Hausdorff, Don. "Thomas Pynchon's Multiple Absurdities." *Wisconsin Studies in Contemporary Literature* 7 (1966): 158–69.

Henderson, Harry B., III. *Versions of the Past*. New York: Oxford University Press, 1974.

Kirby, David K. "Two Modern Versions of the Quest." *Southern Humanities Review* 5 (1971): 387–95.

Kolodny, Annette, and Daniel J. Peters. "Pynchon's *The Crying of Lot 49*: The Novel as Subversive Experience." *Modern Fiction Studies* 19 (1973): 79–87.

Leland, John P. "Pynchon's Linguistic Demon: *The Crying of Lot 49*." *Critique* 16, no. 2 (1974): 45–53.

Levine, George, and David Leverenz, eds. *Mindful Pleasures: Essays on Thomas Pynchon*. Boston: Little, Brown, 1976.

Lewis, R. W. B. *Trials of the Word*. New Haven: Yale University Press, 1965.

McConnell, Frank D. "Thomas Pynchon." In *Contemporary Novelists*, edited by James Vinson, 1033–36. London: St. James Press, 1972.

Marquez, Antonio C. "Everything is Connected: Paranoia in *Gravity's Rainbow*." *Perspectives on Contemporary Literature* 9 (1983): 92–104.

Mendelson, Edward, ed. *Pynchon: A Collection of Critical Essays*. Englewood Cliffs, N.J.: Prentice-Hall, 1978.

Olderman, Raymond S. *Beyond The Waste Land: A Study of the American Novel in the Nineteen Sixties*. New Haven: Yale University Press, 1972.

Ozier, Lance W. "Antipointsman/Antimexico: Some Mathematical Imagery in *Gravity's*

Rainbow." *Critique* 16, no 2 (1974): 73–90.

Pearce, Richard, ed. *Critical Essays on Thomas Pynchon*. Boston: G. K. Hall, 1981.

Plater, William. *The Grim Phoenix*. Bloomington: Indiana University Press, 1978.

Puetz, Manfred. "Thomas Pynchon's *The Crying of Lot 49*: The World Is a Trystero System." *Mosaic* 7, no. 4 (1974): 125–37.

Redfield, Robert, and Peter Hays. "Fugue as Structure in Pynchon's 'Entropy.' " *Pacific Coast Philology* 12 (1977): 50–55.

Richardson, Robert O. "The Absurd Animate in Thomas Pynchon's *V.: A Novel.*" *Studies in the Twentieth Century* 9 (1972): 35–58.

Richter, David. *Fable's End*. Chicago: The University of Chicago Press, 1974.

Schmitz, Neil. "Describing the Demon: The Appeal of Thomas Pynchon." *Partisan Review* 42 (1975): 112–25.

Schwartz, Richard Alan. "Thomas Pynchon and the Evolution of Fiction." *Science Fiction Studies* 8, no. 2 (1981): 165–72.

Siegel, Mark. *Creative Paranoia in* Gravity's Rainbow. Port Washington, N.Y.: Kennikat Press, 1978.

Simmon, Scott. "A Character Index: *Gravity's Rainbow.*" *Critique* 16, no. 2 (1974): 68–72.

———. "*Gravity's Rainbow* Described." *Critique* 16, no 2 (1974): 54–67.

Slade, Joseph. *Thomas Pynchon*. New York: Warner Paperbacks, 1974.

Solberg, Sara M. "On Comparing Apples and Oranges: James Joyce and Thomas Pynchon." *Comparative Literature Studies* 16, no. 1 (1979): 33–40.

Tanner, Tony. *City of Words*. New York: Harper and Row, 1971.

———. *Thomas Pynchon*. London: Methuen and Co., 1982.

Thiher, Alan. "Kafka's Legacy." *Modern Fiction Studies* 26 (1981): 543–62.

Trachtenberg, Stanley. "Counterhumor: Comedy in Contemporary American Fiction." *Georgia Review* 27, no. 1 (1973): 33–48.

Twentieth-Century Literature 21, no. 2 (1975). Special Thomas Pynchon issue.

Vidal, Gore. "American Plastic: The Matter of Fiction." In *Matters of Fact and Fiction: Essays 1973–1976*. New York: Random House, 1977.

Wagner, Linda, W. "A Note on Oedipa the Roadrunner." *Journal of Narrative Technique* 4 (1974): 155–61.

Weixlmann, Joseph. "Thomas Pynchon: A Bibliography." *Critique* 14, no. 2 (1972): 34–43.

Wood, Michael, "Joyce's Influenza." *The New York Review of Books*, October 13, 1977.

Young, James Dean. "The Enigma Variations of Thomas Pynchon." *Critique* 10 (1968): 69–77.

Acknowledgments

"The Use of Codes in *The Crying of Lot 49*" (originally entitled "The Use of the Codes") by Frank Kermode from *Approaches to Poetics* edited by Seymour Chatman, © 1973 by Columbia University Press. Reprinted by permission.

"Pynchon's Gravity" by Edward Mendelson from *Yale Review* 62, no. 4 (Summer 1973), © 1973 by Yale University. Reprinted by permission of The Yale Review.

"*Gravity's Rainbow*: Science as Metaphor" (originally entitled "Science as Metaphor: Thomas Pynchon and *Gravity's Rainbow*") by Alan J. Friedman and Manfred Puetz from *Contemporary Literature* 15, no 3 (1974), © 1974 by the Board of Regents of the University of Wisconsin System. Reprinted by permission of the University of Wisconsin Press.

"What Is Thomas Pynchon Telling Us?" by Josephine Hendin from *Harper's* 250, no. 1498 (March 1975), © 1975 by The Minneapolis Star & Tribune Co., Inc. Reprinted by permission.

"The Importance of Thomas Pynchon" by Richard Poirier from *Mindful Pleasures: Essays on Thomas Pynchon* edited by George Levine and David Leverenz, © 1975 by Richard Poirier. Reprinted by permission of the author.

"Risking the Moment" (originally entitled "Risking the Moment: Anarchy and Possibility in Pynchon's Fiction") by George Levine from *Mindful Pleasures: Essays on Thomas Pynchon* edited by George Levine and David Leverenz, © 1976 by George Levine and David Leverenz. Reprinted by permission of Little, Brown, & Co.

"Pre-Apocalyptic Atavism: Thomas Pynchon's Early Fiction" by Catharine R. Stimpson from *Mindful Pleasures: Essays on Thomas Pynchon* edited by George Levine and David Leverenz, © 1976 by George Levine and David Leverenz. Reprinted by permission of Little, Brown, & Co.

"Profaned and Stenciled Texts: In Search of Pynchon's *V.*" by Melvyn New from *Georgia Review* 33, no. 2 (Summer 1979), © 1979 by the University of Georgia. Reprinted by permission of *The Georgia Review* and the author.

"Thomas Pynchon and the Language of Allegory" by Maureen Quilligan from *Critical Essays on Thomas Pynchon* edited by Richard Pearce, © 1981 by Richard Pearce. Reprinted by permission of Twayne Publishers, a division of G. K. Hall & Co.

Originally reprinted, with slight adaptation, from *The Language of Allegory: Defining the Genre,* © 1979 by Cornell University Press. Reprinted by permission of Cornell University Press.

"The New Jeremiad: *Gravity's Rainbow*" by Marcus Smith and Khachig Tololyan from *Critical Essays on Thomas Pynchon* edited by Richard Pearce, © 1981 by Richard Pearce. Reprinted by permission Twayne Publishers, a division of G. K. Hall & Co.

"Order in Thomas Pynchon's 'Entropy' " by David Seed from *The Journal of Narrative Technique* 11, no. 2 (Spring 1981), © 1981 by *The Journal of Narrative Technique.* Reprinted by permission.

"*The Crying of Lot 49*" by Tony Tanner from *Thomas Pynchon* by Tony Tanner, © 1982 by Tony Tanner. Reprinted by permission of the author.

"Recognizing Reality, Realizing Responsibility" (originally entitled "Recognizing Reality, Realizing Responsibility: Joyce, Gaddis, Pynchon") by Craig Hansen Werner from *Paradoxical Resolutions: American Fiction since James Joyce* by Craig Hansen Werner, © 1982 by the Board of Trustees of the University of Illinois. Reprinted by permission of the University of Illinois Press.

"Merrill and Pynchon: Our Apocalyptic Scribes" by Charles Berger from *James Merrill: Essays in Criticism* edited by David Lehman and Charles Berger, © 1983 by Cornell University Press. Reprinted by permission of the publisher.

Index

Acts of kindness, 75, 198
Adams, Henry, 81, 154, 158, 165; Callisto
    as parody of, 162–63, 164
Aggregat 4, 30. *See also* Rocket
Aieul (*V*), 66–67
Allegory, 111–37; in cultural context, 114,
    objective meaning of, 136; techniques
    of, 127
Alphabetic nature of molecules, 215
American culture as plastic shit, 42
American Dream, 155
American society, 128–29, 154, 163
Anarchist miracle, 71–72, 187
Anarchy, 73–74, 76, 187; vs. order,
    162–63
Antiparanoia, 35
Apocalyptic dread in modern world, 139,
    142
Apocalyptic scribes, 203–15
Apocalyptic text, 206
Armies of the Night, The (Mailer), 155
Arnheim, Rudolph, 169
Arrabel, Jesús (*The Crying of Lot 49*),
    72–73, 187
Ashbery, John, 1, 6
Astarte, 85
Atomic bomb, 203. *See also* Rocket
Aubade ("Entropy"), 85, 157–58, 161–62,
    166, 170–71, 173
Augustine, Saint, 152

Barnes, Djuna, 165
Barth, John, 53
Barthes, Roland, 14
Beatrice (*V.*), 86
Beckett, Samuel, 161, 165

Benzene ring, 42, 57–58, 208
Bercovitch, Sacvan, 139, 143–46, 151,
    152, 153, 154–55
Berger, Peter, 12
Betrayal, 58, 62, 91
Bianca (*Gravity's Rainbow*), 62, 75, 76,
    134, 149
Bible, *Acts*, parody of, 169
Bischoff, Peter, 167
Blacks in Pynchon's work, 88
Bland, Lyle (*Gravity's Rainbow*), 118
Blicero, Captain (*Gravity's Rainbow*), 20,
    33, 121; Gottfried and, 26, 31, 42,
    44–45; rocket and, 21, 25, 26, 31,
    44–45, 129, 141. *See also* Weissmann
Blobadjian (*Gravity's Rainbow*), 215
Bloom, Leopold (*Ulysses*), 209
Bodine, Seaman Pig (*Gravity's Rainbow*),
    80, 88, 119, 132, 134, 198
Bongo-Shaftesbury (*V.*), 83
"Book of Ephraim, The" (Merrill), 210
Borges, Jorge Luis, 16, 53, 125
Borgesius, Katje (*Gravity's Rainbow*), 28,
    33–34, 41, 130–31, 196, 198
Boris (*Tropic of Cancer*), 159–60, 161
Bortz, Emory (*The Crying of Lot 49*), 182
Brillouin, Leon, 56
Brown, Norman O., 38, 51
Bureaucracies, 17, 208
Burgess, Anthony, 52
Byron the Bulb (*Gravity's Rainbow*), 1, 3–9,
    30, 43, 129
Byron, Lord, 4, 6

Caesar, Terry, 178–79
Calculus, 20, 24, 28, 69

Callisto ("Entropy"), 81, 85, 161–67, 168, 169, 170–71; Adams and, 81; entropy and, 157–59, 172

Calvinism, preterite and elect of, 63. *See also* Elect; Preterite

Caring: helplessness and, 68, 74–75; inconvenience of, 192

Catholicism, 84

Cause and effect, 28, 74, 128, 129, 136; Pointsman's philosophy and, 19, 27; thinking and, 31, 33, 71, 72

Cesare (*V.*), 103

Chance as god, 30

Changing Light at Sandover, The (Merrill), 1

Chaos: of experience, 51; of meaning, 50; order and, 35, 72, 162–63, 173; pleasure of, 168–69; randomness of, 163

Charisma, 17–19, 63

Child–parent relationships, 104, 106

Children as possibility of grace, 83, 90, 133, 202

Choice, 12, 70, 73, 95, 168–69; binary, 69, 79, 126, 127, 188–89, 194; of fates, 147–49; multiple, 69, 79, 127–28, 135; national, 183; personal, 134–35, 148–49, 150, 209–10; of reader, 136–37

Chomsky, Noam, 123

Chronometric time, 143–47, 151–52

Cinematography: as American mythic consciousness, 132; Pynchon's use of, 20, 31, 55, 63, 122

City of Words (Tanner), 97

Clausius, Rudolph, 161, 164

Clov (*Endgame*), 161

Codes, 11–14, 89, 120, 126

Colonization, sins of, 101, 145–46

Commerce, 128–29; and war, 193–94

Commitment, 191

Communication, 114, 171, 181, 185, 198; entropy and, 14, 165, 170, 171; systems of, 13, 14, 116, 123, 126, 181

Compost-garden image, 26

Confessions (Augustine), 152

Connectedness of world, 15, 21, 34, 75

Consumerism, 42, 163

Continuity of reality, 128

Cotton, Charles, 93

Counterforce, 2, 19, 127, 131, 183, 198, 210; of freedom, 34

Courier's Tragedy, The (*The Crying of Lot 49*), 13–14, 126, 177, 183

Crying of Lot 49, The, 49, 53, 164, 175–89, 211–12; allegory and, 111–14, 125–27; awareness in, 21; choice in, 21, 79, 134, 151; codes in, 11–14; communication in, 181–83; as detective story, 175–76, 181–82; dichotomy in, 15; entropy image in, 23, 55–56, 88, 157, 183–84; historical context of, 32; images of, 17, 23; language of, 16; naming in, 112, 178–79; order in, 23; puns in, 115, 122; as quest narrative, 89–91, 175–76; religious dimension of, 180–81, 185–87; structure of, 88, 95, 118

Daedalus, 192, 194, 198

Daedalus, Stephen (*Ulysses*), 51

Dante, 136–37, 213

Death described, 74–75

Dehumanization, 196. *See also* Isolation

Derrida, Jacques, 117

Determinism, 28, 29

Dichotomy, 41, 93–96, 198, 214; and interface, 94, 195; as system base, 201; types of, 69, 71, 105–8; validity of, 95, 194–95

Dickens, Charles, 51

Dictionary of Literary Terms (Shaw), 139

Dillinger, John, 132

Discontinuity, effect of, 128

Disorder, accelerating, 51

DJ (*Mirabell*), 203, 204, 205, 209

Drake, Temple (*Sanctuary*), 165

Dreams, 102, 103, 105, 106, 108, 208

Driblette, Ralph (*The Crying of Lot 49*), 14, 91, 187

Dryden, John, 98

Duino Elegies (Rilke), 25

Duke di Angelis ("Entropy"), 172

Education of Henry Adams, The (Adams), 17, 81, 154, 162–63, 164

Edwards, Jonathan, 154

Eigenvalue (*V.*), 60

Elect, 69, 79, 198, 200. *See also* Preterite

Electro-mysticism, 29. *See also* Mondaugen's Law

Eliade, Mircea, 17, 186

Eliot, T. S., 50, 51, 150

Emerson, Ralph Waldo, 9
Endgame (Beckett), 161
Entropic reductionism, 61, 63
"Entropy," 23, 81, 85–86, 99, 157–74;
    dialogue satrized in, 171, musical
    references in, 164–66; orchestration of
    voices in, 171, 172–73; weather
    metaphor in, 159–60
Entropy, 37, 41, 45, 88, 99, 154; in
    communication, 14, 165, 170, 171;
    defined, 158; management of, 24–25;
    maximum, 26, 30; as metaphor, 31,
    56, 69; order in, 157–74, 194;
    thermodynamic vs. information theory
    in, 23, 25–27, 184–85; of world, 12,
    79, 88
Enzian (*Gravity's Rainbow*), 29, 30,
    120–21, 129–31, 150, 197
Ercole (*The Crying of Lot 49*), 185
Erdmann, Greta (*Gravity's Rainbow*), 11–12
Eschatological anxiety, 204
European colonialism, 101, 145–46

Faerie Queene, The (Spenser), 127
Fairing, Father (*V.*), 104
Fall, the, 206, 207
Farben (*Gravity's Rainbow*), 208
Faulkner, William, 47, 165
Fermi, Laura, 203–4, 206
Fetishism, 84–85
Fiction: factual, 52–53; naturalistic, 63–64
Fielding, Henry, 178
Fina (*V.*), 62
Finnegans Wake (Joyce), 191, 193
Fitzgerald, F. Scott, 166, 167
Forty-nine, significance of, 90, 112, 126,
    127, 183, 185
Foucault, Jean-Bernard-Léon, 120, 123–25
Four Quartets (Eliot), 150
Fragmentation, 43, 62, 136; and order,
    93–94, 95, 97, 103, 107; patterning
    of, 98; into whole, 96
Franklin, Benjamin, 128
Frazer, J. G., 80–81
Freud, Sigmund, 122
Frost, Robert, 120
Frye, Northrop, 97–98
Fugue, 172–73

Gaddis, William, 54
Gaucho (*V.*), 73

Gaussian formula for normal distribution,
    123
Gibbs, Willard, 163–64
Giles Goat-Boy (Barth), 53
Glozing, Ray (*Crying of Lot 49*), 113
Gnosticism, 2, 3, 6, 17
Godel's theorem, 41, 61
Godolphin, Evan (*Gravity's Rainbow*), 99,
    104–6
Godolphin, Hugh (*Gravity's Rainbow*), 38,
    73, 99–102, 105, 106; child–parent
    relationship and, 103–4
Golden Bough, The (Frazer), 81
Goodfellow (*V.*), 66
Gottfried (*Gravity's Rainbow*), 26, 31, 42,
    44–45
Graves, Robert, 80
Gravity: defined, 45; as preserving force in
    nature, 215
Gravity's Rainbow, 1–9, 17, 63, 164,
    allegory in, 114–24, 127–36;
    apocalyptic vision in, 206, 207, 209,
    211–12, 213–14; attitudes toward
    blacks in, 196–98, basic metaphor of,
    113; connectedness in, 15–21, 61;
    dichotomy in, 191–96; history and,
    16–21, 53, 55, 56–58; as jeremiad,
    139–55; preterite in, 67; reader
    response to, 198–202; science as
    metaphor in, 23–35; sex and death in,
    39–44

Hamm (*Endgame*), 161, 165
Harvitz, Esther (*V.*), 63–65, 86, 101,
    147–48
Heat-death, 69, 85, 158, 161, 163, 164.
    See also Entropy
Heisenberg Uncertainty Principle, 29, 30
Hereros (*Gravity's Rainbow*), 30, 61, 65,
    198
Heterocosm, 206
Hierophany, 17, 186
High magic to low puns, 16, 73, 74,
    113–14, 115
Hilarius, Dr. (*The Crying of Lot 49*), 180
Hod, Pappy (*V.*), 87
Homosexuality, 80
Hope, 147, 159
Horological time, 143–47, 148, 151–52
*Horologicals to Chronometricals: The Rhetoric
    of the Jeremiad* (Bercovitch), 143–44

Human Use of Human Beings, The
    (Wiener), 164

IG. *See* Imipolex G
Illuminati, 28
Imipolex G (IG), 42, 44, 62, 208
Inanimate passivity, 15
Information theory, 123
Interface of dichotomy, 94, 195
Interpretation of Dreams (Freud), 122
Interpretations, multiple, 135
Inverarity, Pierce (*The Crying of Lot 49*),
    11, 13, 180; symbolism of, 53, 88;
    will, significance of, 56, 112, 125–26,
    175–76
Isis, 82
Isolation, 14, 89, 182, 196, 200, 210;
    solipsistic, 195

Jamf, Laszlo (*Gravity's Rainbow*), 28, 33
Jazz, 166
Jeremiad, 139–55
Jessica (*Gravity's Rainbow*), 198, 202
Jesus, 200
Jews, 87
JM (*Mirabell*), 203, 204, 207, 209, 210,
    213
Johnson, Dr. Samuel, 2
Joyce, James, 31–32, 50, 51, 52, 191–93,
    202, 206, 209
Judas Iscariot, 200
Jung, Carl, 208

Kabbalism, 2, 17, 120, 215
Kali, 83
Kekulé von Stradonitz, Friedrich August
    (*Gravity's Rainbow*), 42, 56–58, 208–9
Kepler, Johannes, 45
Krinkles ("Entropy"), 171

Language, 73, 215; and action, 121–22; as
    bureaucratic system, 116; as circular
    process, 136; as magic, 114, 115–19,
    121–22; as noise, 170; power of, 115,
    116–17, 179; of quest, 135; theory
    of, 115; and the Word, 89–90;
    worship of, 205
Lehrbuch der Ballistic (Cranz), 32
Leibniz, Gottfried Wilhelm, 20, 55
Lemming point of view, 200. *See also*
    Preterite
"Letter to American Teachers of History,
    A" (Adams), 164

Leverenz, David, 134, 135
l'Heuremaudit, Mélanie (*V.*), 84–85, 99
L'Histoire d'un Soldat (Stravinsky), 165–66
Liebig, Justus von Freiherr, 56–57
Life: diversity of, 159; as machine, 37, 39;
    transitoriness and transformation of,
    25
Light as hope, 7
Linguistics: in context of twentieth century,
    124–25; French, 116–17, 123;
    revolution in, 122–23
Literary allusions, 80
Literary analysis, 93–96; criticism, 102;
    open and closed texts, 95–99;
    structuralists, 94, 95
Literary parody, 51
Loneliness, 44–45
Lord, A. B. (*Singer of Tales*), 116
Lost and dispossessed. *See* Preterite
Lost Generation (Entropy), 166–67, 168
Love: ability to, 44; and death, 85;
    fragility of, 202; parental, 42–43, 44;
    as "real present," 103; and suffering,
    37–39, 42–43, 74; world and, 200
"Love for Sale" (Mulligan), 172
Luckmann, Thomas, 12
Lyrical Ballads (Wordsworth), 54

Maas, "Mucho" (*The Crying of Lot 49*),
    11–12, 62, 114, 179
Mass, Oedipa (*The Crying of Lot 49*), 71,
    87, 95, 111–14, 175–89; choice and,
    62, 134, 151; fiction and, 53; and
    "high magic to low puns" 115; as
    literary critic, 59; quest of, 59–60,
    88–91; as reader, 125–27; reality and,
    53, 67–68; as sorting demon, 11–14,
    55–56, 211–12
McConnell, Frank D., 141, 153
Machiavelli, Niccolò, 83–84
Machine as ideal woman, 17, 82, 83
Magic, 30, 180, 205–6
Magnalia Christi Americana (Mather), 153
Maijstral, Fausto (*V.*), 44, 67, 82, 104,
    109
Mailer, Norman, 2, 155
Mangel, Anne, 157
Mantissa, Rafael (*V.*), 84, 101, 103, 106
Man vs. machine, 17
Mara (*V.*), 86
Marcel (*Gravity's Rainbow*), 43
Marina (*V.*), 87

Marvy, Major Duane (*Gravity's Rainbow*), 33, 196–97
Maryam (*V.*), 66–67
Maternal tenderness, 89
Mathematics, 40–41, 63, as communication system, 123; randomness in, 29, 40, 75, 163
Mather, Cotton, 153
Maximilian (*Gravity's Rainbow*), 43
Maxwell, James Clerk, 23–24, 55, 56, 57, 184, 185
Maxwell's demon, 14, 23, 24, 211; theory of, 53, 55, 184–85
Meaninglessness, 38–39, 41, 102
Mechanical causality, 28. *See also* Cause and effect
Mechanistic determinism, 29
Mehemet (*V.*), 84, 86, 108
Merrill, James, 1, 203–15; laboratory as sacred spot, 205; Pynchon compared to, 213–15; and transitions between speakers, 213; typographic peculiarities of, 212
Metaphor, 23–35, 63, 109; central, 35; filmic, 122; linkage of past and present in, 140; of salvation, 120; of science, 123; sexual, 80, 90; of the Text, 121; of weather, 160
Metzger (*The Crying of Lot 49*), 13, 176
Mexico, Roger (*Gravity's Rainbow*), 27, 119, 214; as anti-Pointsman, 40–41, 194; love interest of, 41, 197–98, 202; as statistician, 29–31, 123, 128
Mildred (*V.*), 83
Miller, Henry, 159–60, 161, 166, 167
Miller, Perry, 139, 141–42, 143
Mirabell (Merrill), 205, 206–7, 208, 209, 210, 213, 214
Mirabell, 203, 204, 206
Miriam ("Entropy"), 157, 167, 174
"Modern Apocalypse, The" (Kermode), 204
Modernism, 204
Moments, 61–62, 63, 69–70, 75, 181; of choice, 147, 150–51, 209–10; as freedom, 146
Mondaugen, Kurt (*Gravity's Rainbow*), 71, 87–88, 195; sferics, 98, 101
Mondaugen's Law, 29, 134, 199
Montaigne, Michel de, 93–94, 98
Moon-goddess trinity, 80, 81, 82, 85
"Mortality and Mercy in Vienna," 168
Motley, Lothrop, 32
Mulligan, Gerry, 166, 172

Mulligan, Meatball ("Entropy"), 157–58, 167, 168–69, 171, 172
Music, 164–66, 171–72, 173
Myrtle the Miraculous (*Gravity's Rainbow*), 43
Myth, 60, 82–85, 91

Nabokov, Vladimir, 53, 125
Naming, 53, 112, 178–79
Nature, random state of, 29. *See also* Randomness
Nefastis, John (*The Crying of Lot 49*), 184–85
New England Mind: From Colony to Province, The (Miller), 141
Nightmare Abbey (Peacock), 2, 33
Nightwood (Barnes), 165
"Ninth Elegy" (Rilke), 25
Novel, 107; as fiction, 94, 96–97, 98–99

Of Grammatology (Derrida), 117
"Of the Inconstancy of our Actions" (Montaigne), 93
Ojibwa ("Morality and Mercy in Vienna"), 168
Ombindi, Josef (*Gravity's Rainbow*), 150
Oral tradition, power of, 115–17
Orchestration, 171, 172–73
Order, 11, 12, 69, 94–95, 157–74; belief in, 170; chaos and, 35, 72, 162–63, 173; dream of, 102, 105, 106, 108; fictional devices and, 144; fragments and, 93–94, 95, 97, 103, 107; human need for, 101, 107; mystery and, 102, 107; systems of, 194; varieties of, 171–72
Orthodoxies, 205
Owlglass, Rachel (*V.*), 86–87, 88, 147–48

Paola (*V.*), 87, 104
Paranoia, 1, 14, 15, 113, 180, 201; anarchic structure and, 63, 69; death and, 40, 126; fantasies and, 12, 58; necessity of, 34–35, 61, 119–20, 124; patterns of, 195; proverbs and, 34–35; as system, 94; writing and, 97
Passivity, inanimate, 15
Patterns, 195; of international cartel, 8; vs. random events, 105
Pavlov, Ivan, 193
Peacock, Thomas Love, 2, 33
Penetration and possession, 103
Pentecost, 112, 126–27, 185

Personal responsibility, 148
Personification, 111–37
Peter Pinguid Society, 182
Pinguid, Peter (*The Crying of Lot 49*), 13
PISCES (*Gravity's Rainbow*), 33, 39–40
Plastic culture, 62, 69
Plastic man, 42
Plastics, 1, 42, 44, 62, 208
Plater, William M., 167–68
Poems of Science, 205
Poetry, oral, 116–17
Pointlessness, 167
Pointsman, Dr. Edward the Pavlovian
    (*Gravity's Rainbow*), 18, 27–28, 30,
    33, 40, 193, 195, 214; cause and
    effect, philosophy of, 27, 33, 75, 128;
    predictability and determinism, 27–28
Pointsmanesque conditioning, 61
Pointsman faction, 28, 29
Poisson distribution of rocket strikes, 29,
    30
Pökler, Franz, (*Gravity's Rainbow*), 20, 33,
    69–71, 74, 192, 196, 201, 209–10
Pökler, Ilse (*Gravity's Rainbow*), 20, 74
Pökler, Leni (*Gravity's Rainbow*), 69–71,
    72, 74, 77
Polysemy, 118
Pope, Alexander, 97
Porpentine (*V.*), 66
Possibilities, 63, 68, 73, 76, 146, 149, 188
Predictability, 28. *See also* Cause and effect
Prentice, Pirate (*Gravity's Rainbow*), 194
Present, as past and future, 99, 106
Preterite, 20, 65, 124, 152, 192, 200–201;
    Pynchon's love for, 67, 69, 191, 192;
    as salvation metaphor, 120, 141;
    Slothrop as, 75
Probability, 29, 40–41. *See also* Choice,
    multiple
Profane, Benny (*V.*), 62, 75, 86–87, 91,
    99, 101; myth and meaninglessness
    and, 38, 104, 108; technology and,
    65, 82; woman and, 39, 82, 86
Pudding, Brigadier General (*Gravity's
    Rainbow*), 118, 119, 196, 198
Puns, 118–19
Puritanism, 141, 149; American, 139; and
    denial of here-and-now, 144–45;
    dream of, 154–55; heritage of, 153;
    imagination of, 143; religion of, 146;
    vision of, 150
Pynchon, Thomas: academic readers of,
    48, 50; allegory used by, 111–37;
    amateur readers and, 49–50;
    ambiguity of, 65. 192; on American
    binary choice, 188–89; on the
    American dream, 143; anarchic style
    and structure of, 62–63; as apocalyptic
    writer, 108–9, 141; authority and,
    213; on blacks, 88; characters as
    readers, 125–26; on colonialism,
    85–86, 101; cultural allusions and,
    51–52; death, convenant with,
    39–40, 45; death, poet of, 76; as
    devil, 39, 46; and distrust of the
    street, 84; on "everything is
    connected," 15, 34, 53, 67; film
    techniques used by, 20; historical
    accuracy of, 32–33, 63, 117–18; on
    humanity, 114, 200–201; isolation of,
    153; Jews, image of, 87; language of,
    60, 73, 112–14, 177–78; modern
    American culture and, 48, 167;
    musical references and, 164–66,
    171–72, 173; myth used by, 60;
    names used by, 53, 178–79; past and
    future, use of, 99; popularity of,
    47–48; present tense used by, 151;
    preterite and, 67, 69, 91, 192; prose
    of, 63–69; puns used by 112–13; and
    reader involvement, 129–31, 132,
    200–202; relativistic viewpoint of,
    174; revelations, 214; riddle of
    paradise, 100–103; salvation, search
    for, 121; sensitivity of, to modern
    dream, 45; sexual conservatism of,
    80–81; tourism as theme of, 67; use
    of character by, 67–68; vision of hope
    of, 147; on Western culture, 79–80;
    on women's place, 79–91; wordplay
    and, 111–37. *See also The Crying of
    Lot 49*; "Entropy"; *Gravity's Rainbow*; *V.*

Queen Victoria, 83
Quest, 114, 131, 211; for code, 135;
    narrative, 89; romantic, 38, 210
Qulan, Dzaqyp (*Gravity's Rainbow*), 115–16

Radnichy (*Gravity's Rainbow*), 115
Rainbow curve of existence, 35
Rainbow defined, 45
Randomness, 160–61, 168, 179;
    mathematics and, 29, 40, 75, 163;
    patterns and. 105; struggle against,
    66–67, 107; uncertainty principle and,
    30; of world systems, 11, 12, 79

Rapier, Father (*Gravity's Rainbow*), 194
Rathenau, Walter (*Gravity's Rainbow*), 69, 72
Reader, 129–31, 132, 135, 200–202, 212
Reality, continuity of, 128
Redcrosse Knight (*The Faerie Queene*), 127
Reductionism: literary critical and human, 63; of systems, 61. *See also* Entropy
Re Joyce (Burgess), 52
Religion, 179
Revelations, 180, 185
Rilke, Rainer Maria, 25, 39, 41, 42, 46, 152
Rise of the Dutch Republic (Motley), 32
Risk-taking, 63, 69–70, 74–75, 77
Rocket(s), 31, 73, 75, 129–30, 146, 147; A4, 57; compared with church steeples, 120, 123; ICBM, 207; symbiosis and fusion of, with man, 26–27, 30; Western obsession with, 144–45. *See also* V-2 rocket
Rocket cartel, 114
Romance, 107; as fiction, 94, 95–97, 98–99; hero in, 210; outlook of, 160–61
Roseman (*The Crying of Lot 49*), 180
Rousseau, Douanier, 162
Rózsavölgyi, Dr. Geza (*Gravity's Rainbow*), 33, 214
Ruby (*V.*), 87
"Rule of Phase Applied to History, The" (Adams), 164

Sacrament of the Eucharist, 131–32
Salvation, 37
Sanctuary (Faulkner), 165
Sanders, Scott (*Gravity's Rainbow*), 134, 139
Saul ("Entropy"), 157, 158, 167, 169–70, 171, 174
Schaub, Thomas, 149, 150
Schoenmaker (*V.*), 64, 86, 147
Science: alphabetic nature of molecules, 215; applied to fiction, 63, 157, 169; calculus, 20, 24, 28; cultural implications of, 53–55, 162–63; demonic distortion of, 208; as magic, 205–6; as metaphor, 23–35; as religion, 205–6. *See also* Mathematics; Technology
Scythrop (*Nightmare Abbey*), 33
Secular scripture, 97
Secular Scripture, The (Frye), 98

Self, 211
Sense of an Ending, The (Kermode), 139, 144, 204
Sexuality, 80–81, 86–87; death and, 38, 40–41, 80; images of, 34; legitimate, 86; in procreative relationships, 99; sadistic, 101
Shaw, George Bernard, 139
Siegel ("Mortality and Mercy in Vienna"), 168
Silence, 6, 9, 98
Silvernail, Webley (*Gravity's Rainbow*), 28, 76
Simons, John, 169–70, 171
Singer, Isaac Bashevis, 48
Singer of Tales (Lord), 116
Slothrop, Constant (*Gravity's Rainbow*), 140
Slothropian Episodic Zone, Weekly Historical Observations (SEZ WHO), 33
Slothrop, Lieutenant Tyrone (*Gravity's Rainbow*), 2–3, 75–76, 193, 200–201, 202, 207; bookishness of, 119–20, 122; childhood of, 17–18; disintegration of, 19, 62, 127, 130, 131, 133–34, 199, 211–12; failure and solipsism of, 121, 149, 195–96, 199; history and, 19, 148–49, 154; Puritan heritage of, 114–15; quest and, 135–36; sex and death theme, 40–43
Slothrop, Mother (*Gravity's Rainbow*), 140
Slothrop, William (*Gravity's Rainbow*), 31, 120, 140, 145, 154, 200; and V-2 rocket, 27, 33–34, 140
Social Construction of Reality, The (Berger and Luckmann), 12
Solipsism, 195–98. *See also* Isolation
Sonnets to Orpheus (Rilke), 152
Spectro, Kevin (*Gravity's Rainbow*), 195
Spenser, Edmund, 112
Sphere, McClintic (*V.*), 82, 88, 103
Squalidozzi (*Gravity's Rainbow*), 73–74, 76
Statisticians, 29
Stencil, Herbert (*V.*), 15, 59, 65–66, 80–81, 87–88, 103, 184; in search of order, 23, 82–83, 97, 99–100, 106
Stencil, Sidney (*V.*), 84, 85, 99, 104, 106, 108
Stravinsky, Igor, 165–66
Structuralist critics, 94, 95
Swanlake, Jessica (*Gravity's Rainbow*), 197
Systems, 194, 201; communication, 13,

14, 116, 123, 126, 181; conceptual, 191; of control, 17; crystals in, 26; destructive power of, 52; empty, 11–14; as order, 26, 94–95; paranoia and, 34, 94; psychological, 17–18; Pynchon's distrust of, 193; symbol in, 94–95; technocratic, 142–43; They, 194, 196, 200

Tanner, Tony, 97, 157, 158–59, 168, 178–89
Tantivy (Gravity's Rainbow), 198
Tchitcherine (Gravity's Rainbow), 30, 33, 115–16, 119, 196–97
Technocratic systems, 142–43
Technology, 28–29, 60, 121, 146; as anti-life, 42; cultural implications, 53–55, 207–8; as false freedom, 74, 148; as religion, 37–38. See also Science
Temporal bandwidth, 62, 199
Terror, 73, 149, 210
Thanatz (Gravity's Rainbow), 128–29
Thermodynamics, 23, 26–27, 63, 123; of life, 24–25, 53
They, 33, 132, 192, 209–10; audience and, 48; communication and, 116; decisions of, 191; paranoia and, 119; system, 194, 196, 200
Thoreau, Henry David, 154
Thoth, Mr. (The Crying of Lot 49), 88
Throsp, Corydon (Gravity's Rainbow), 26
Thurn and Taxis, 183
Time: differentiation of, 112–13; and reverse-time, 147; two levels of, 143–47
Todorov, Tzvetan, 135
Trench (V.), 64
Tripping, Geli (Gravity's Rainbow), 119
Tristero (The Crying of Lot 49), 13, 14, 186; Oedipa's search for, 91, 126, 177, 182; as underground mail delivery system, 89, 90, 175, 183
Tropic of Cancer (Miller), 159

Uncertainty principle, 29, 30
Unconscious as bureaucracy, 208

V. (V.), 39, 82, 85
V., 15, 17, 49, 65–67, 93–109, 154, 167; as archetype, 82–85; Catholicism in, 84; entropy theme in, 15; experience and, 37; love and, 44; machines and, 38, 40; mythological allusions in,

82–85, 91, 184; sexual conservatism of, 80–81, 84, 86, 89; symbolism in, 23, 82, 147–48
V2 rocket, 16–17, 24–25, 44; ethical decisions about, 21, 147; parabolic path of, 16–17, 24, 26, 141; and Slothrop, 18, 33, 43
Vendler, Helen, 207
Verbal communication as transfer, 165
Victoria (V.), 83, 99, 100–101, 105
Violence, 39, 193; by the letter, 116
"Virgin and the Dynamo, The" (Adams), 163
Vocabulary, religious, 126
Vogelsang, Hedwig (V.), 83
von Braun, Wernher (Gravity's Rainbow), 25
von Göll, Gerhardt (Gravity's Rainbow), 194, 198
Vulnerability, 176; conquered, 37, 39, 45; of love and understanding, 149

War and commerce, 193–94
Waste, 13, 71, 75, 121, 179; catalogues of, 67, 76
Weber, Max, 17
Weissmann (Gravity's Rainbow; V.), 31, 98, 192, 193, 196. See also Blicero, Captain
Wharfinger, Richard (The Crying of Lot 49), 182–83
Wharfinger's play (The Crying of Lot 49). See Courier's Tragedy, The
White Goddess, The (Graves), 80–81
Whitman, Walt, 154
Whole Sick Crew, The (V.), 60, 99, 167
Wiener, Norbert, 164, 169, 174
Winsome, Mafia (V.), 86
Women's roles: Catholic view of, 84; in The Crying of Lot 49, 88–91; in "Entropy," 85–86; as machine, 38, 39; in V., 79–88
Word, the, 123
Wordsworth, William, 54
World, connectedness of, 15, 21, 34
Wren, Mildred (V.), 65
Wren, Victoria (V.), 60, 83, 99, 100–101, 105

Yeats, William Butler, 205

Zone, the, 18, 21, 120, 133, 148–49, 194, 195, 198, 207, 212, 214